AS
LEVEL

Psychology

the student's textbook

Nigel Holt and Rob Lewis

First published by
Crown House Publishing Ltd
Crown Buildings, Bancyfelin, Carmarthen, Wales, SA33 5ND, UK
www.crownhouse.co.uk

and

Crown House Publishing Company LLC
6 Trowbridge Drive, Suite 5, Bethel, CT 06801, USA
www.crownhousepublishing.com

First printed 2008. Reprinted 2008, 2010

British Library of Cataloguing-in-Publication Data
A catalogue entry for this book is available
from the British Library.

ISBN 978-184590093-9

LCCN 2008923497

Printed and boundin the UK by
Stephens & George Ltd, Merthyr Tydfil

contents

INTRODUCTION

AS Psychology: The Student's Textbook

Authors: Nigel Holt and Rob Lewis

Nigel Holt works at Bath Spa University and is an active researcher in perception and cognition, and also e-learning. He has substantial experience as a senior examiner for A level psychology and regularly talks to teachers and students around the UK. Nigel is the co-author of a leading university-level introductory textbook, as well as co-editor with Rob Lewis of the Insights in Psychology series.

Rob Lewis is an extremely experienced teacher and examiner. He has over twenty years experience of teaching A level psychology, and for most of that time has also been an A level examiner. He is regularly involved in INSET and CPD events for teachers and currently holds a senior examining post at a major examination board. Rob can currently be found working in the Cardiff School of Education at UWIC.

ACKNOWLEDGEMENTS

Nigel and Rob would like to thank Kate and Nicola for their support during this project. At times it has seemed interminable, but their confidence was never ending. We'd also like to take the opportunity to thank MC in his role as friend and mentor over the years.

WHAT IS PSYCHOLOGY?

You'll hear this question all the time. One answer is that it is one of the most popular subjects to study in colleges and universities in Britain. If you are reading this book because you are thinking about whether to study psychology then we strongly recommend it. Whether it is something that just interests you or you regard it as a rung on a ladder to a career, psychology is a fine choice at AS level. The information within the subject is varied and there will most certainly be something in it that you will find interesting. Some people will tell you that psychology is just 'common sense'. There is certainly a little truth in that, but it is so much more. When you have an opinion of something, or whenever you experience an emotion, psychology is the subject that helps you understand why you think or feel as you do. To give you an idea of how broad the topic is, psychology's range covers such things as the relationship between heart disease and stress, to possible explanations of why perfectly normal people can commit terrible crimes.

WHO IS THIS BOOK FOR?

Whilst we expect that teachers and psychologists will find this book useful, it is written for STUDENTS. That's why we've called it 'The Student's Textbook'. It provides a balance of classic and contemporary research whilst engaging the reader with an accessible style.

WHY HAVE WE WRITTEN THIS BOOK?

The inspiration for this book is drawn from our shared passion for psychology and our dedication to teaching. Our combined experience of school, college and university education provides us with vital perspectives on how the subject can be explained to those with little or no experience of it.

Years of working as examiners has shown us how good students answer questions using the right amount of information expressed in the right kind of way, and how sometimes even good students have difficulty because they don't do what the examination question requires.

We have also learned that really doing well involves more than the accumulation of facts and figures – it involves developing a knowledge and understanding of psychology. We hope that we can help develop your interest in psychology and that you continue with your studies of this fascinating subject beyond AS level. Experience tells us that you will benefit later on by taking this knowledge and understanding with you and building on it with further learning.

Because of this, we have not written a 'bare bones' book which only gives you a series of organised facts and does not attempt to nurture your interests. Neither have we scattered lots of information across the page from which you have to select the relevant bits. We have set out to give you the right information in the right kind of way, avoiding cross-referencing to other parts of the book, avoiding leaving ideas 'hanging' and unexplained, and avoiding using unnecessary jargon. Everything in this book is relevant to someone learning the subject to pass an examination. Everything you need to know for the AQA/A AS level Psychology specification is here.

PSYCHOLOGY AND RESEARCH

One common element that underpins all of psychology is that evidence to support psychological ideas is gathered through research. It is this foundation of research that psychology shares with the other sciences. Indeed, psychology is regarded as the science of behaviour. Studying behaviour can be relatively straightforward, but it can also be a very complex undertaking. It can sometimes seem as though the findings of research raise more questions than they answer. We live around and observe other people every day, yet people are still hard to understand. This is because human beings are very complicated and their behaviour is subject to many influences, from the actions of tiny brain cells to the impact of being in a large crowd. It is only through scientific research, where there are carefully controlled observations and tests, that we can determine why people behave the way they do.

Knowledge of how psychologists gather information through research is vital to your own success at AS level. By placing this section first we are making a statement to you about the importance of research methods. We cannot stress enough how important it is to have a sound understanding of research methods at both AS and A2 level Psychology. The specification requires that you not only develop knowledge of psychological research methods but that you are able to apply your knowledge. This is especially the case at AS level where in Unit 1 (Cognitive Psychology, Developmental Psychology and Research Methods) a third of the marks are allocated to assessing your ability to demonstrate this skill. You will notice as you progress through the book that frequent reference is made to the methods used by psychologists in their research. In order to deepen your understanding we would recommend that you refer back to more detailed descriptions in the Research Methods section.

FURTHER HELP

This book contains all the information you need to achieve the highest grades at AS level. We understand however that some students appreciate further assistance with their learning and exam technique. Because of this we have written a companion Study Guide which you might find very useful.

It contains easy to follow summaries and lots more Ask An Examiner tips and guidance

about how to achieve top grades in the AS exams. There are self-assessment features, glossaries of key terms and an example exam paper (complete with model answers!). There is also additional material designed to promote 'stretch and challenge'.

IMPORTANT FEATURES

STUDY IN FOCUS

Throughout this book some studies are described in more detail than others. We have called these 'Study in Focus' because they have been carefully selected to illustrate good examples of psychological research using a particular method.

STUDY IN FOCUS

The Strange Situation
Ainsworth and Bell (1970)

What were they doing and why? The researchers wanted to see how a child behaved towards strangers and their caregiver under controlled conditions of stress, in which the infant might seek comfort, and also conditions of 'novelty' where the infant might be encouraged to explore their surroundings. The researchers would then use 'exploration behaviour' and 'comfort-seeking behaviour' as indicators of type of attachment.

How did they do it? 100 middle class American mothers and their children took part. The researchers employed a *controlled observational* technique, which means that the researchers controlled the activities in which the mother and child took part.

The following procedure was used, and is made up of eight episodes. Each episode, apart from the first one, lasts about three minutes, the whole procedure lasting not more than half an hour.

1. Mother and child enter the room.
2. Mother responds to child if baby seeks attention.
3. Stranger enters the room, speaks to mother and slowly approaches baby, mother leaves room
4. Stranger lets child play, encouraging play with toys if child shows inattention. If child becomes distressed the procedure ends.
5. Mother enters room. Stranger leaves. Child settles again. Mother leaves infant alone in room.
6. If infant is distressed, procedure ends.
7. Stranger enters, and repeats procedure outlined in step 3.
8. Mother returns. Stranger leaves.

During the procedure, the researchers noted down how much the following behaviours were exhibited.

- The infant's unease when the mother left the room – '**separation anxiety**'
- The infant's willingness to explore
- The way the infant greeted the mother on her return – '**reunion behaviour**'
- The infant's response to a stranger – '**stranger anxiety**'

What did they find? The results led the researchers to conclude that there were three main attachment types that they described as Type B (secure) and Types A (insecure-avoidant) and Type C (insecure-resistant). These are outlined in Table 3. In this study the researchers concluded that the type of attachment formed by the child depends upon the responsiveness and sensitivity of the caregiver.

Take a closer look: ● The standardised procedure is a really strong point of the Strange Situation. It means that others can replicate it easily and accurately.

● It might be that the behaviour of the child in the Strange Situation is unnatural because the situation is extremely unusual and unfamiliar to the child. This means that the Strange Situation may not be a very realistic measure of attachment.

STUDY OUTLINES

These are not as detailed as the key studies, but provide additional evidence to support a point and increase background knowledge.

> ### STUDY OUTLINE
>
> ### Sound matters in short-term memory Conrad (1964)
>
> Conrad used strings of **letters** to investigate short-term memory. A typical string might be 'AKJBSL'. These were presented extremely quickly on a screen for approximately three quarters of a second. The errors in recall were very interesting. B and V were muddled with P but the letter S was only very rarely muddled with P. Conrad said that it was the sound of the letters that mattered in encoding in the STM. Even though presented on a screen, the visual information must have been changed into sound (on the way to the subjects' memory) for the errors to have occurred.

ASK AN EXAMINER

The phrase 'Ask an Examiner' is used because we know that an expert perspective is invaluable. These short sections appear throughout the book and give advice and tips based upon our considerable experience as examiners. Again, they are directed at you, the learner, and are often responses to questions that we have been asked in the past by others in exactly the same boat as you.

"There are only so many questions we can ask you in the exam and we can only ask you what the specification allows us to. Here's a tip. The specification tells you that you MUST know about the multi-store model AND the working memory model. Remember, you need to know about BOTH."

IMPORTANT RESOURCES

www.askanexaminer.com

From the Ask an Examier page you'll discover useful information and links that we update on a regular basis. We also include a facility here where you can get additional support, tailored to your needs, directly from experienced examiners.

www.aqa.org.uk

The Assessment and Qualifications Alliance (AQA) organise the examination. They write the specification and the exam papers, and they employ examiners and award your marks. You'll find the specification on this site (remember, we are Specification A!), as well as past examination papers and reports when they become available. You will also find information on how your examination is marked and graded.

www.bps.org.uk

The British Psychological Society (BPS) is the professional body for psychology and psychologists in the UK. You'll see from their website that they have a national responsibility for developing and also promoting and applying psychology for the public good. There are loads of links to other sites containing useful information.

A full Bibliography and a list of all sources used in writing this book are identified in the Reference Section that will appear online at www.askanexaminer.com/holtandlewis.php

Section 1

Research
Methods

WHAT YOU WILL LEARN ABOUT

Psychology is a science and for its accumulated knowledge depends on research. To fully appreciate the findings of psychological research it is necessary to understand the methods used by psychologists in their research. This includes knowledge of their strengths and weaknesses of the various research methods used in psychology, as well as an appreciation of their design and conduct. Psychologists communicate the findings of their research, so therefore a familiarity with data analysis and presentation is also essential.

WHAT YOU NEED TO KNOW

Research Methods is in Unit 1 of the specification. As you learn you are expected to develop your knowledge and understanding of Research Methods. You also need to develop the skills of analysis, evaluation and application. Rather than just recall and reproduce information, you are expected to be able to apply a knowledge and understanding of Research Methods to all areas of the specification. The subject content is split into three parts:

Methods and techniques

- Research methods in psychology, including experimental methods, and non-experimental methods such as observation, self-report, correlation and case study
- Advantages and weaknesses associated with these various research methods

Investigation design

- Designing and conducting psychological research

Data analysis and presentation

- Analysis, presentation and interpretation of psychological research findings

Research Methods

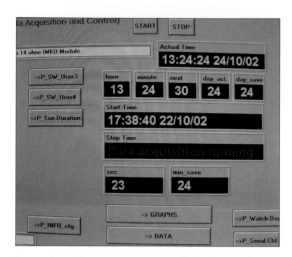

Researchers often use computers to help them with their research.

Psychologists use research to evaluate their theories. The kind of research they do depends partly on the type of theory they are investigating. We use different methods and techniques for different reasons, and we'll talk about that in this section.

DOING PSYCHOLOGICAL RESEARCH

© Mike Baldwin / Cornered

How do we know whether one idea is better than another? How do we really know why those with dyslexia have the problems they do? Psychologists test their ideas using careful research methods, and what better place to begin than by looking at how best to find things out.

"The research proves tall rats are more confident than short rats. At least I think it does. I've never been good at this."

PSYCHOLOGY IS A SCIENCE!

This may come as a bit of a surprise to some of you, but psychology is not all about lying on couches and telling people all about your problems. It is a much bigger subject than that and it progresses very carefully for those who practise it professionally. The goal of psychology is to describe and understand behaviour. This understanding will allow us to predict, control or change the way people behave.

Psychology is a science. This means that psychologists rely on scientific methods of acquiring knowledge in order to achieve their goals, and it is these methods that we will be describing in the following sections. These methods highlight the importance of evidence about human behaviour gathered by careful observation and measurement. This is called *empirical* evidence. An empirical approach assumes that observations are not influenced by emotions or personal opinions; they are *objective*. It is very difficult in psychology to be entirely objective about events – we all have ideas and expectations, about people and why they behave the way they do, which are

formed before we begin to look carefully and objectively. Because of this, psychologists have to be extremely careful about how they conduct their research.

When beginning a research project, it is a good idea to go through certain steps, to ensure that we really are investigating what we intend. Similarly, the way we describe what we are researching allows others, who are following our research, to be in no doubt about what is going on. This is very important. In the future, someone may want to check our findings and add to our work, so well thought out and clearly described research is essential. All of this leads us to a discussion of *experimental methods* which is how research in psychology progresses. First of all though, we'll look at the first steps in carrying out research.

AIMS

Psychologists get their ideas for research from either direct observation of behaviour or indirectly through background knowledge and theory. The best attribute you can have as a psychologist is a real desire to seek out the origins and motives of human behaviour.

Have you ever wondered why a teacher or a friend gets cross or reacts the way they do to something? Why some people have the 'right' attitude and some just do not? What makes the difference between a good athlete and a gold medallist? What role does luck play in our success? What's the best way to remember things for an exam? All of these things really interest us as psychologists.

Once you've decided on an idea for your research the next step is to generate research *aims*. An aim is a reasonably precise idea about the area of the study and what the study is going to try to achieve. It is important that the aim clearly describes the purpose of the proposed research. This will help us make it clear very early on whether or not the proposed research is realistic. An 'aim' doesn't need to be very detailed, it just needs to say very clearly what the focus of your research is all about.

An example of an aim might be 'To describe the effects of stress on our memory', Another might be 'To look at whether listening to music while revising helps us remember things'.

'You shouldn't work in front of the television with members of your family bothering you'. How would you find out whether this really is true?

THE HYPOTHESIS

Once you've got your research aim you need to change it into a statement that psychologists refer to as an *hypothesis*. The idea is to try and find evidence in your research that will 'support your hypothesis'. A hypothesis *predicts* what we expect to find. An example will help here. Take the research aim we used earlier:

Aim: To describe the effects of stress on memory.

Hypothesis: The more stressed we are, the worse our memory will be.

The hypothesis takes the 'aim' and makes a statement of it. Our hypothesis predicts that we will find that people who are stressed will have a worse memory than people who are not stressed. What we now need to do, as researchers, is design a study that lets us investigate this problem. The results of the study will either support our hypothesis or not. If the results do not support the hypothesis we have to reject it, and think again!

How do we use our hypothesis?

The way we use our hypothesis depends on the type of research we are doing. In the type of research we have been describing, we may choose a predictive hypothesis – one that 'predicts' what will happen in our study. We call this an *experimental hypothesis*, because we are doing an experiment. This is often written as 'H_1'. In other types of research, where we are not really doing an experiment but making observations of behaviour or collecting opinions perhaps, the hypothesis is called an *alternative hypothesis* and we use the symbol 'HA' to represent it.

To make the hypothesis complete we also write something called the *null hypothesis*. A null hypothesis (written as 'H_O') predicts that what we find in our research just happened by chance. It looks like the opposite of the main hypothesis. Take the hypothesis we described earlier. This is how we form the null hypothesis.

Null hypothesis: Our memory will not become worse as stress increases, any change is due to chance.

The null hypothesis must be included in our research because psychologists can never rule out the possibility that the results gained in any investigation are due to chance. What this really means is that if the hypothesis is not supported by the research findings then the null hypothesis is probably true. Put another way, if you have to reject the hypothesis then you have to:

Accept the null hypothesis,

and if you accept the hypothesis because your research supports it then you then you must:

Reject the null hypothesis.

"This is one of those points that is sometimes difficult to get your head around. Forming the NULL hypothesis is important, but really easy. It's not a trick question when you are asked to do it in an exam for instance. Sometimes it's as easy as sticking the words 'DOES NOT' in the sentence. For instance, if our hypothesis was 'Being good at maths means that you will also be good at chess' the null hypothesis is simply 'Being good at maths DOES NOT mean that you will also be good at chess.' Sometimes examiners are not asking sneaky questions! If it looks simple, sometimes it is!"

The hypothesis and operationalising 'variables'

A hypothesis will also express the things of interest to the researcher in the piece of research. These are *variables*. They are called variables because they change or *vary* during the research. Some variables are changed by the researcher, and some change *because* the

researcher has changed something. This is much easier to explain with an example: for instance, the time it takes to get to the shops.

You decide to see whether taking different routes to the shops makes your journey time faster or slower. The *variable* under your control is '*the route you take*'. The '*time taken to get to the shops*' varies because of the route you have taken. You (the 'researcher') have changed the route. The time taken to get to your destination changed *because* you have changed the route.

In research, a variable is a something which is observed (looked at and watched), measured (length, temperature or time perhaps), controlled or manipulated. The hypothesis should tell us how these variables will relate to each other in your research. We want to know how the variables will be 'brought into being' or how they will be *operationalised*.

Operationalising variables means putting them in a situation where you can measure them. This is extremely important because we need to be clear about what it is we are studying and measuring in our research. If we are successful, and we are clear enough, it makes it easier for people to understand our findings and compare them to findings from other research.

For example, intelligence is a notoriously tricky area of research because few psychologists agree on what intelligence actually is! A psychologist might be interested in the relationship between 'social class' and intelligence, in which case the terms will need to be made very clear by operationalising them. This involves stating very clearly, in our work, what is meant by the terms 'social class' and 'intelligence', to avoid any misunderstandings, and ensure that people who look at the findings of our research are not confused in any way. We can operationalise social class as 'annual family income'. Intelligence could be operationalised as 'performance on a standard IQ test'. So, now we have the main variables and we have decided how to operationalise them, we can state our aim very clearly.

The aim is to investigate the relationship between social class as defined by annual family income and intelligence as measured by performance on a standard IQ test.

is a much clearer statement than:

The aim is to investigate the relationship between social class and intelligence.

It is very important to understand research variables and we will be returning to them later in our coverage of research methods but, for now, just concentrate on the idea that a variable is a factor in research and we have to indicate to those reading our work how these factors are going to be measured or manipulated.

Directional and non-directional hypotheses

Look at the two hypotheses. The type of research to which they relate is very similar indeed. In fact, the tasks you might decide on to investigate these two hypotheses could be identical, but the predictions here are very slightly different.

Hypothesis 1: Eating potatoes for dinner makes you sleep more.
Hypothesis 2: Eating potatoes for dinner alters the amount you sleep.

ASK AN EXAMINER

"Sometimes there are a bunch of different ways to operationalise a variable. You can try to test 'how good your memory is' by getting someone to remember lists of words, or showing them a tray of items, covering it, removing an item and showing them the tray again to identify what is missing. You could operationalise 'intelligence level' as a score on an IQ test, or on a measure of how fast it takes you to do ten maths problems. You could operationalise 'fitness level' by seeing how fast it takes someone to run 300 metres, or you could see how far they could run in one minute. One is often as good as another."

Hypothesis 1 predicts a 'direction' for the results. Potato eating will INCREASE the amount of sleep we have. This type of hypothesis is called *directional*. You may also see it described as a *one-tailed* hypothesis. Hypothesis 2 does *not* predict a direction. It simply states that potato eating will change the amount we sleep. It does not predict an increase or a decrease. Either may happen. For this reason, hypotheses of this type are known as *non-directional* and may also be described as *two-tailed*.

Which is best? Directional or non-directional?

It depends. A non-directional hypothesis might be chosen if the researcher is not terribly clear what will happen. Eating chocolate may keep people awake or it may help them go to sleep, for instance. If you

don't know the answer to a problem, but think something might happen, then choose a non-directional hypothesis. That way, if *anything* happens to your variables (in this case, the amount of chocolate consumed and the amount we sleep) then you are bound to find it. In your next piece of research, once you have an idea of what might happen, your hypothesis may change to a directional prediction.

A directional hypothesis is generally used when a researcher is confident enough to make a clear prediction. Previous research may suggest that something quite specific will be found, or a quick study the researcher may have tried out (often called a *pilot* study) may have suggested a direction for the findings. However, because the hypothesis makes a specific prediction the results of the research have to be reliable in that particular direction for the hypothesis to be supported. If we choose a directional hypothesis our results have to be even more convincing for it to be supported; in other words, a directional hypothesis is easier to reject than a non-directional one. The benefit of choosing a directional hypothesis is, however, that because they are harder to support, research that *does* support a directional hypothesis is regarded highly.

SAMPLING

The people who take part in research are termed *participants*. Researchers get their participants from a *population*. A population is defined as all the members of a particular group from which participants are selected. For example, if you were interested in investigating attitudes to bullying in 14 to 16 year olds, your target *population* would be 14 to 16 year olds. You might want to make the population more specific, for example 14 to 16 year olds in a geographical area, or even 14 to 16 year olds from a particular school within that area. You might want to see whether there is a bullying problem amongst 14 to 16

year olds in South London, amongst people of a particular ethnic group. Your *population* in this case would be 14 to 16 year olds, from a particular ethnic group who live in South London. These kinds of decision are all part of the design process.

Because it is usually impractical for everyone to take part in a study, researchers need to *select* from the population. This selection of participants is called the *sample*. The main aim of *sampling* is to select a number of people who are typical, or representative, of the rest of the population from which they were chosen. Because the sample is a typical cross section of people, the findings can be safely *generalised* to everyone else in the target population. If the sample is not *representative* then it is *biased*, and *sample bias* is something to avoid if we want to be able to generalise the findings.

A good deal of psychological research takes place at universities around the world. The most available participants at these institutions are students. Psychology has often been criticised for its over-reliance on students as participants. Have a think about this. Why might it be a bad thing to test ideas with students in this way? Is it always a bad decision to do this? You'll find examples of research throughout this book that have used students as participants. A knowledge of the concept of sample bias can be a really useful way of evaluating these studies.

How large should the sample be?

The choice of the number of participants used in the study will be influenced by a number of factors. The larger the population then the larger the sample size should be; for a smaller population, you might choose a smaller sample. For instance, if you are interested in investigating a possible difference in intelligence between men and women, then you might choose a quite large sample to be representative, since the number of individuals in each population investigated (males and females) is very large indeed. However, if you were investigating whether actors suffer with an unusually large incidence of depression then the sample might be smaller, actors making up only a relatively small part of the community.

The rule is that the sample must represent, i.e. be typical members of the target population. Remember though that the larger the sample, the greater the difficulty in handling your results, the longer the research takes and the more expensive it becomes. Like many other areas of research design, the size of the sample is often down to good judgement and common sense.

Where do I get my participants from?

When psychologists collect data they choose participants in a number of different ways, and the method they use to do this depends on a number of things. It might be that their research targets such a tiny population that they are left with very little choice! For instance, if you were studying 'attitudes of males over the age of 105' it is unlikely that you'd find too many of them to test, but investigating 'attitudes to TV violence in the general population' would provide you with a much larger target group of people, so choosing an appropriate sample would take more thought!

Selecting participants 1: Random sampling

In a *random sample*, every member of the target population has exactly the same chance of being included in your sample. There are several ways of doing this. The most straightforward is the 'names-from-a-hat' method, whereby all members of the target population are identified on slips of paper. These are then shuffled in a container and the desired number are selected. Whilst this appears simple, names-from-a-hat is not practical with anything other than a small population, such as the members of an A-Level class. Fortunately, there are computer programs which can select a random sample from even very large populations, so that there is no need to spend hours writing names on hundreds of bits of paper! The simplest program requires each member of a population to be given a unique number. The program randomly generates a series of numbers within the limits set for it. All we need to do then is match the numbers produced by the computer to the names on the list.

There are some problems with random sampling though. One problem is that it relies on all the target population being available to take part if chosen. If you select someone using your clever random number generating program and one of those people cannot take part you will need to replace them, and your random sample is no longer as random as you might have liked it to be. Another is the possibility that, by chance, the randomly selected sample might end up

Randomly sampling different coloured lottery-balls.

being biased anyway! If you shuffle a pack of cards, and drop them all into a hat, you may just pull out ten red cards one after the other, weighting your sample in favour of red cards. In a psychology study you might be interested in investigating the effects of alcohol on reaction time. By chance alone you might end up with a group of participants with unusually high or low tolerances to alcohol or very fast or very slow reaction times or reflexes. The results these people may provide may not give you a true picture of what is happening and your investigation may be flawed.

Selecting participants 2: Opportunity sampling

A very common method of sampling is to use anyone you can get hold of. This is very straightforward. Little planning is needed since the sample selection is based on whoever is willing and available to take part at the time. Some students of psychology think that just picking people to take part, without any obvious selection criteria, makes it a random sample, but this is not the case at all. Remember, a random sample gives *everyone* in a population an equal chance of being chosen, which will clearly not happen here. If you decide that your target population is a sixth form department and then you set about waiting at a doorway for someone to pass, although you are selecting from your population, you are not doing it randomly. Not only is most of the population excluded because they are unlikely to all come marching past you, but all sorts of unconscious biases are going to be at work guiding who it is you approach. For example, is the participant the same or different sex from you? Are you attracted to this person? Do they owe you a favour? Some people rather like helping people, so these people are more likely to help you collect your data. There are all sorts of things that can influence an opportunity sample.

Whilst this method can lead to sample bias, the extent to which this matters varies according to the topic of the research you are doing. For example, it is likely to be much less important in studies of physiological responses to stress than it is in social psychological studies of friendship patterns and helping behaviour!

Selecting participants 3: Volunteer sampling

It is not uncommon to find, pinned on university notice boards, appeals for people to take part in a piece of psychological research. Here, either through goodwill, curiosity or financial encouragement (some researchers may pay a small fee to those taking part!), participants are asked to volunteer themselves. Whilst it is a quick and easy way of gathering participants, this method does have its problems.

Choose me!

It is possible that people who volunteer are not typical of members of a population. In fact, it has been suggested that people who volunteer in this way have particular personality types which makes them different from the rest of the population – just as in an opportunity sample, some people are more likely than others to help out. Similarly, the placing of the poster for volunteers to sign up might influence the type of people volunteering. If the poster is situated in a psychology department, then you'll get mainly psychology students signing up. The problem here is that psychology students may have a good idea of what you are looking for and their responses might be biased. Similarly, placing a poster in the sports department may provide you with volunteers of higher fitness than those provided by a poster placed elsewhere. If your research is concerned with the relationship between attention and tiredness, a higher level of fitness in the participants may influence your results, so the sample collected from this poster may not be ideal.

ETHICAL ISSUES IN PSYCHOLOGICAL RESEARCH

The breadth of the subject matter studied within psychology makes it unique amongst the sciences. Psychology might be described as the study of the experiences of living, feeling organisms and, as such, special care must be taken. There is the potential for participants to be affected by their experiences of taking part in psychological research. For instance, investigating the relationship between emotion and memory may require the researcher to bring about certain emotional states in the participant. This is often achieved by showing the participant a short film which makes them feel happy or perhaps a little sad. Generating an emotional state such as 'happiness' is much more acceptable, and less likely to lead to any kind of damage, than generating an emotional state such as 'fear' or 'terror'. For this reason, it might not be acceptable to show a clip of a horror film to participants because of the potential damage it might cause. You'll not be surprised to hear that there has been a good deal of research in psychology that might be considered questionable in this respect. For instance, research by Zimbardo (1971) investigated how participants take on the roles of prisoners and guards in a mock prison. The results were quite alarming and the research was brought to an abrupt halt only days in, to protect the participants from psychological

SUMMARY OF ETHICAL CONSIDERATIONS WHEN DESIGNING A RESEARCH STUDY

ETHICAL ISSUE	EXPLANATION
INFORMED CONSENT	Participants must be told what they will be doing and why they are doing it so they can provide 'informed' consent.
DECEPTION	Participants should not be deceived unless absolutely necessary. If deception is required, great care and careful consideration must be given to the project.
DEBRIEFING	After the experiment is complete, participants must be 'debriefed' and informed of the motivations for the experiment. They must be given the chance to ask any questions they have.
RIGHT TO WITHDRAW	Participants should be free to leave the experiment at any time.
CONFIDENTIALITY	Any information and data provided by the participant must be confidential.
PROTECTION	The safety and well-being of the participant must be protected at all times.

and possibly even physical harm. When engaging in research, we have to remember that it is considered both morally wrong and professionally unethical to engage in research which in any way violates the rights and dignity of participants.

Researchers in psychology are guided by a set of ethical principles designed to prevent research from infringing the rights of participants. Drawn up by the British Psychological Society (BPS), these guidelines

> "In all circumstances, investigators must consider the ethical implications and psychological consequences for the participants in their research. The essential principle is that the investigation should be considered from the standpoint of all participants; foreseeable threats to their psychological well-being, health, values or dignity should be eliminated." (British Psychological Society, 1998)

must be adhered to and failure of psychologists to maintain such professional standards can lead to serious reprisals. Psychologists may be ejected from the society or have any licences revoked. Their good name in science would become tainted and the value of their research questioned. If ethical guidelines are not considered or if psychologists simply ignore them in their research then their ejection from the society means that they will no longer be able to carry out legitimate research and their good name will have been blackened. This could mean that employment will be hard or impossible to find and other researchers may not want to be associated with them. The implications of taking an unethical approach can be catastrophic for the researcher.

Informed consent

People must be fully informed about the study before they agree to take part. This need not involve disclosing every single detail of

"Ethical concerns in psychology are a serious business. That aside, they are often a great way of achieving marks! When we mark your papers we look for evidence that you understand a number of issues, and ethical concerns are often really useful ways of criticising a procedure. This is one of those sections that you should spend extra time on. Once learned these principles can be applied to loads of studies, gaining you valuable marks. Remember, you could be asked about ethics anywhere at all in the exam so you really do need to know about it!"

the study, but certainly anything that might influence a person's willingness to take part must be revealed to potential participants. This way, their decision to take part is based on an understanding of consequences and what their contribution means. Later in the book we describe research by Milgram where a lack of 'informed' consent is an important criticism of his work.

One problem with this is that the researcher has to plan very carefully what the participant is to be told. Revealing too much, or revealing information in the wrong way, may influence the participant's behaviour during the study, which can have the potential to invalidate the research. If the participant has an idea of how the researcher wants them to respond then *demand characteristics* have been set up. The results will reflect the participant's desire to respond in a certain way, not necessarily what the research is actually investigating. We'll talk more about demand characteristics later.

In these instances a case can be made to withhold information from participants. Infants sometimes take part in psychological research and, since they are too young to understand the research and therefore give informed consent, special measures have to be taken. If anyone below the legal age of consent is to be used in research, then consent must be sought from their parents or guardians. This rule might also apply to some adults, for example, people who have certain kinds of mental illness or who have learning difficulties, or elderly patients suffering with certain kinds of dementias which may influence their ability to make informed decisions. If the participant might be considered *vulnerable* in any way, the researcher must proceed very carefully.

Debriefing

After the data have been collected, the researcher *debriefs* the participant. The full aims of the research are revealed and the participant is given the opportunity to ask any questions. If a participant reports any reaction or distress because of taking part in research, then the researcher is responsible for correcting these consequences. This might require no more than discussing the rationale for the study and reassuring the participant about confidentiality. Sometimes however more lengthy procedures are needed to ensure that participants are left no worse for their experience.

Whilst desirable, debriefing may not be very effective in practice. For example, it assumes that any reaction immediately follows participation in the research, but in reality this might come much later on, once the experience has been given some consideration. The participant might also be reluctant to discuss their emotions or be unable to clearly express their thoughts. Care and effort is needed by researchers to ensure that debriefing is effective. In the Milgram research, described on page 190, participants in the study were carefully debriefed and told exactly what happened during their research study. In our own research, we have found that debriefing is vital, as it gives participants a chance to ask all sorts of questions, but sometimes they point things out about the research that we had not thought about, and so we can improve things in our next design. Debriefing is vital ethically, and is sometimes useful for researchers. Two reasons to do it!

Confidentiality

Participants have a right to confidentiality, that is, their participation and performance in research is private and not open to public scrutiny. Participants have the same moral and legal rights to confidentiality as everyone in our society, and this is set out in government legislation in the Data Protection Act. However, there can be exceptions. In some cases, participants can waive their rights. *If given permission by the participant* the researcher is free to discuss the participants' backgrounds, where appropriate, and refer to them by name. In some extraordinary cases psychologists might encounter a situation where they have to break confidentiality. It may come about during a debrief, or during the procedure itself, that the participant is in need of specialist care that the psychologist is unable to give. If the participant reveals information of this nature to the psychologist, then the psychologist must seek advice, and possibly reveal information about the participant to someone better situated or more qualified to help them.

In practice, confidentiality is a relatively easy ethical issue to manage. Researchers need only gather personal information about participants which is considered important to the study. Also, participants can be given a unique number, meaning that their personal identities are hidden and comments regarding their performance only referencing this 'anonymous' number. Where research involves studying one person (this is called a case study), it is usual to refer to the individuals by sets of initials, e.g. HM, so hiding a good deal of the information about that person. In the Milgram study we'll see that the behaviour of participants in the study was not as we might have expected, and may not be regarded by the general public as acceptable. For this reason, confidentiality protects the participants from opinions that others may hold, which may not be terribly well informed. For instance, would you want to employ someone who was capable of inflicting on another human being an electric shock that was large enough to cause them serious pain, or perhaps kill them? No? Neither would many people. Milgram's participants were protected from prejudice like this by a confidentiality agreement.

Deception

Deception means that participants are in some way deliberately misled. This usually involves withholding information about the aims of the study, but it can also involve participants being deliberately misinformed. Deception mainly occurs because of the difficulties that informed consent causes.

For instance, a researcher might be interested in the relationship between distraction and memory. The procedure used may involve a conversation outside the door of the laboratory that, unknown to the participant, is staged between two colleagues of the researcher.

Similarly the procedure might involve the participant being interrupted halfway through and given new instructions, the aim here might be to find out how new rules are combined with established ones when completing a task. In both these cases, the researcher would withhold information about the conversation outside the door or the interruption. The participant has been deceived.

Many studies in psychology could simply not happen if there was fully informed consent, so it is perhaps not surprising that deception is the most frequent ethical issue arising from research. The psychologist must make a judgement as to whether the aims of the study justify the deception. Of course, the deception is often a very minor one but even in these cases the participants should be informed, after the event, about what has happened and told that, if they wish, they can refuse to allow data gathered from them to be used. The Milgram study has been criticised for the level of deception used in the experiment.

DEMAND CHARACTERISTICS AND INVESTIGATOR EFFECTS

When people volunteer to take part in experiments they often have no idea at all about what is expected of them. What they *do* know is that scientists are supposed to be very clever people. It may be that the experimenter has unintentionally encouraged the participant to behave in a certain way. This is called an *investigator effect*. It may also be that the participant *thinks* that they are required to respond in a certain way. This is a *demand* characteristic.

Demand characteristics

Psychological research often involves a direct interaction of researcher and participant – it is a social situation. Since people generally alter their behaviour when around others, it is reasonable to assume that behaviour will change in a research situation. Participants may be aware that they are being observed, or

We behave differently when we are alone than when we are in a social situation.

ASK AN EXAMINER

"If you are ever asked about a particular piece of research it's a pretty good bet that 'deception' of some kind has featured in the design. Researchers cannot tell their participants exactly what they are investigating in detail because this could influence the behaviour of the participants. For this reason some kind of deception is often used. That's good for you! It means that you can say that the researchers deceived the participants in some way (explain how) and this could be regarded as ethically questionable."

may think that they are being personally assessed or evaluated in some way. This might motivate them to attempt to find clues, in the research environment or procedure, as to what the study is about and to alter their behaviour accordingly. These features of research, which participants use to change their behaviour, are called *demand characteristics*.

Demand characteristics can seriously affect the findings of research. The extent to which this is a factor, however, varies according to the research method used and the way that the study is designed and conducted. For example, demand characteristics are going to be much more of an issue when people know

that they are taking part in a study, such as is the case with a laboratory experiment.

Although often impossible to eliminate entirely, well-designed research will try, as much as possible, to minimise demand characteristics. For example, if there is to be communication between the researcher and the participant then the verbal and non-verbal content of this communication needs to be controlled by using standard instructions. The setting of the study will need to be carefully considered, especially since some participants may be familiar with the research area. Whether or not the researcher is the right type of person to be interacting with participants also needs consideration, as will be the way in which participants are approached to take part in the study.

It is almost inevitable that the solution to reducing demand characteristics will involve some kind of *deception* – keeping the participants in the dark about the aims of the research might be desirable from a researcher's point of view, since it reduces demand characteristics. This is called a *single-blind* procedure. However, it does raise ethical issues about the deception of participants and this will need to be dealt with accordingly.

Investigator effects

As well as the participants reacting to the research setting, the *researchers* too might *behave in ways that might influence the investigation*. For example, the researcher might have expectations about the study and might unintentionally influence the behaviour of participants. The *age, gender or ethnicity* of the researcher may also influence the behaviour of participants. It should also be remembered that researchers will have put a great deal of time and effort into their research and may unconsciously interpret ambiguous situations in ways which are favourable to their point of view. The amount of influence that a researcher has on the research will vary to some degree according to the research method used – for example, the age, gender or ethnicity of a researcher is likely to have a much greater effect in an interview than an observation – but investigator effects are an issue in all types of research. They have to be identified early in the research design and, as far as possible, eliminated. For example, researchers conducting an experiment might decide that participants should not be made aware of the research aims, and adopt a single-blind control. They might also decide that, for the same reasons, the researchers involved in data gathering should also be kept in the dark as much as possible. This is called a *double-blind* procedure, where both the participants and the researchers involved in gathering data are kept unaware of the research aims.

THE RELIABILITY AND VALIDITY OF PSYCHOLOGICAL RESEARCH

If we get a great result on a Monday morning, have someone rerun the experiment on Tuesday and someone else run it on Wednesday but each person finds different results each time, we can say that the *reliability of our work is in question*. Similarly, it's all very well to find something out in the laboratory, but if that doesn't bear any resemblance to how people really behave in the real world then the work is of limited use. In this case, the *validity of the work is questionable*. Reliability and validity are both very important concepts that need to be considered when reading about people's work.

Reliability

In terms of psychological research, reliability refers to *consistency*. What this means is that if the evidence gathered by research is reliable then anybody else doing the research using the same method would get the same findings. Reliability is very important in

"The following bits (on reliability and validity) are the type of sections that you revise and learn once, but then manage to apply a million times later on. It'll take you two minutes to learn this, and you will then be able to comment on the reliability and validity of every research study you ever read. This means you will be able to gain marks for being able to evaluate or apply the concepts of research methods all over the place. Two minutes learning, loads of cheap marks!"

psychological research as it gives a degree of confidence in both the method of data collection and the findings.

Some research methods are more reliable than others, therefore the reliability of studies will vary to some degree according to the method used to gather data. More importantly perhaps is that it will vary according to the design and conduct of the study. For example, a laboratory experiment, which involves tight control of variables, is considered a more reliable research method than an observational study which employs less control and relies more on the perception of individual observers. However, a poorly designed and conducted laboratory experiment is likely to have less reliability than a carefully planned and well-run observation.

There are a number of techniques available for assessing and improving reliability and they are all based on the same principle – *replication*. For example, if two observers rate a behaviour in the same way then their observations are consistent (or reliable); if an experiment is carried out more than once with the same results then it is consistent (reliable). In other words, if we can replicate something then we can be more certain of the reliability of the study.

Validity

Validity refers to the extent to which a *test actually tests what it claims to*. In other words, validity means that the data collected give an accurate, or 'true', picture of what is being studied.

We can be fairly sure that tools used in the physical sciences, such as thermometers, really are testing what they claim to test – in this instance, thermometers are *valid tools for measuring temperature*. However, in psychology we are often far less sure. For example, IQ (Intelligence Quotient) tests are used to measure intelligence. The problem is that there is considerable debate about whether or not IQ tests really do test intelligence – *their validity is questioned*. This is not a unique case – the nature of the phenomena of interest to psychology means that they can only be brought to light by the methods used to test them. For example, psychologists demonstrate aspects of human memory through the response of participants to particular kinds of memory task. If the test is flawed then it follows that the assumptions which are drawn from the results of the test must also be suspect. The issue of validity is a crucial one for psychology.

A further complication is that a test can be reliable without being valid. For example, a *personality test* might give consistent results but it might not be measuring what we think it is measuring. We'd hope it was measuring how confident someone was, or how shy, but really it might just be measuring how good they are at doing that particular personality test!

Whilst there a numerous methods used for assessing the validity of a test, most researchers rely on their *theoretical knowledge* of the research area to make a judgement as to whether a test is valid. Added to this is *educated common sense* – on the face of it, does the test look as though it is doing what it is supposed to?

PILOT STUDIES

A good deal of planning and preparation goes into good research, and a trial run of a study using a small sample is sometimes a good idea to tidy up the fine details of the design and to see whether the procedure actually does what the researcher wants it to. The reliability and validity of any measurements or tests being used can be tested and it is also a useful way of ensuring that the variables have been appropriately operationalised. For instance, we might be interested in seeing whether the volume of music influences our memory. A pilot study will give us a good idea if the volume levels we are using are appropriate or whether they are too quiet to generate the effect we are interested in. Similarly, we might find out that the sound levels are just too loud for comfort! This is a very important point; we've already said that participants must *not be damaged* in any way, and that includes their hearing!

A pilot study also provides an ideal opportunity to talk to a few participants about their experience of taking part. Such feedback can provide vital information about demand characteristics, investigator bias and the design of the study in general. After a careful check of the procedures and findings, problems can be ironed out and the research design amended, where necessary, before the study begins for real.

METHODS AND TECHNIQUES

Developing ideas and testing out theories is what science is all about.

In this section we learn how to systematically and carefully develop a method for investigating the problem you may have. Methods of research come in a number of forms, and we'll describe them here.

THE LABORATORY EXPERIMENT

A great deal of psychological information has been acquired from experimental research.

The experiment is a method of studying human behaviour which looks to uncover causal relationships, that is, factors which cause us to act in certain ways. It differs from other methods in that it involves deliberately manipulating and controlling variables.

The logic of the experiment is straightforward – if we have two groups of people all doing the same task except that one of the groups does *one* thing differently, then any change in behaviour between the two groups must be due to that *one thing*. For instance, if we had two identical tennis balls, and dropped them using an identical dropping machine from an identical height, except that one ball was wet and one was dry, then if they hit the floor at different times, the thing that is different (the wetness) must have been the thing that caused the change in the speed at which they fell to the ground. See – simple!

● The thing that is different between the two groups is the *variable that we manipulate*, and

this is called the *independent variable (IV)*. In the example we've just used, the independent variable is whether the tennis balls were wet or dry.

● What we *measure or record* as a change in behaviour is another variable, and we call this the *dependent variable (DV)* (because it 'depends' on the independent variable). In our tennis ball dropping example, the dependent variable is 'how long it takes for the balls to fall to the ground'.

An *experiment* is perhaps best understood through looking in detail at an example of one. You may have noticed that some people like to revise for exams with music playing in the background or on their personal music systems. Some of these people are absolutely certain that they must have music otherwise they can't concentrate. Other people prefer to work in silence and are equally as sure that silence is best. As a psychologist you might ask yourself which is best – music or silence? We can't just take a person's preference as evidence of what is best, since we know from other areas of life that what people prefer is not necessarily what is best for them! We need an *objective assessment* of which is best, and this is where an experiment is most useful.

The aim: To investigate whether or not having some kind of noise in the background (e.g. music) affects the retention (memory) of something we have learnt.

We also need to formulate a hypothesis. The results of our experiment will either provide support for our hypothesis or they will lead us to the conclusion that our hypothesis must be rejected.

The hypothesis: The simplest non-directional hypothesis might look something like: 'music affects memory'. This is not quite enough however. Whilst the hypothesis includes our *independent variable* and our *dependent variable* (the IV is the music, the DV is a measure of memory) it is not clear how the variables are being operationalised. A better hypothesis might be:

> '*Music played during learning will influence recall performance on a memory task.*'

This sounds pretty good to us. We are all set for a simple experiment. Of course, experimenting takes a little time and more than a little thought, so it may be the case that your hypothesis may need adjusting a little once you have collected some test data, or pilot data as we call it. That's fine and is not unusual at all.

Before we begin to think about how we are actually going to do this, remember the first and most important rule of research design 'KISS':

KEEP IT SIMPLE, STUPID!

or

KEEP IT SHORT AND SIMPLE!

If you don't keep it as simple as possible, there is a good chance of everything going horribly wrong.

There are a couple of ways we could do this. One way, and it's a nice simple experimental

"We are SO not joking here. You may feel that adding a little bit into your design won't make a big difference. It's not a big deal to add another group of people to test or see what happens when you vary the volume of the music. We've both made some really horrible mistakes by overcomplicating things; a simple elegant design is always (not usually) ALWAYS best. When there's more involved, there's more that could go wrong! KISS!"

set-up, would involve having two *conditions*, each containing a selection of *participants* chosen at *random* to be in one condition or another. Remembering the logic of the experiment, all participants would have the same experience except for one thing – the *independent variable*. The group in which the *IV* appears would be called *the experimental condition*. The other group would be in the *control condition*, against which the scores of the experimental condition would be compared.

EXPERIMENTAL CONDITION (MUSIC)	CONTROL CONDITION (SILENCE)
P1	P6
P2	P7
P3	P8
P4	P9
P5	P10

Table 1: In research, P stands for 'participant'. In our experiment, participants 1 to 5 are in the experimental condition and participants 6 to 10 are in the control condition.

Assuming that all participants have the same experience except for one thing (the IV), then any difference in task performance between the two conditions could only be due to the one thing that varies – whether or not participants listen to music while performing the memory task. It's all looking rather good so far.

We now need to give our participants some kind of task to do. Since we are interested in memory, an important component of learning (which is what revision is all about!), we could give the participants something from a French textbook to learn, perhaps a list of verbs. How well the participants learn these verbs in a given time would be what we measure (this is the *dependent variable*).

Alas, things in psychology are rarely as simple as this. In order to ensure that the experience of participants differs *only* in terms of the IV, we must go to great lengths to ensure that we control experience of the participants. For example, we have given a French verb learning task. Have we controlled for the linguistic ability of participants? Are some of the participants studying French? Indeed, are all the participants students? How do you know whether any of them are French? Have you checked?

What we need is a task which asks the same of all participants. In psychology, *word lists* are often used in these circumstances, consisting of words of equal length and matched for how often those words appear in the language in which you are testing, in most cases the language will be English. Music cannot be used either, because of things like personal tastes, types of music, etc. – one person's music is another person's noise! So, something a bit like music could be used. A steady rhythmic noise played through headphones perhaps.

These factors (things that you need to control for, such as ability in French or music preference) are the *extraneous variables*, and each one could influence the *dependent variable*. For every factor that we fail to control we become less confident that the *IV* alone has produced the *DV*. For each factor other than the sound used (ability at French, whether the person liked the sound or not, etc.) that had an influence on how well they did on the test, the less sure we can be of whether it was the presence of 'music' that really influenced their ability. They could have

been really good at the task because they hated the music and so ignored it as best they could. Similarly, they could have been really dreadful at the task because they liked the music so much they couldn't help but listen and join in with the chorus. In other words, our result has become *confounded*. We need to eliminate as many extraneous variables as possible during the design process.

In our experiment then, we cannot use music as an IV and we cannot use verb learning as a DV. Our variables need to be somehow 'neutral'. This means that our hypothesis is going to need a slight change; 'rhythmic noise played during learning will have a significant effect on subsequent recall'. The IV is whether or not participants have noise played to them whilst learning, and the DV is performance on a word learning task.

Standardised procedure

Another essential control in an experiment is the use of *standardised procedures*. We must describe every step of our experimental procedure beforehand so that each participant gets an identical experience. This will also include *standardised instructions*, ensuring that participants have the same information. This standardisation will also reduce *researcher bias* in that it ensures that we do not unconsciously influence things by varying the procedure.

Hopefully it is becoming clear that, whilst the logic of an experiment is straightforward enough, it takes a great deal of careful thought and planning to design a good experiment. We've got a bit more to do yet. Even though the question is a simple one, we must be really sure that the way we carry out the experiment will provide us with a useful answer.

RESEARCH DESIGN

At the moment, we've decided to randomly put five people in the experimental condition, and five in the control condition (see Table 1).

We do have another option though, and it's one that seems a little peculiar. We could use the same people in both conditions. Sometimes the aims of the study will dictate which *design* we use. For example, if we wanted to see whether women or men were best at a mathematics task we could hardly have the men in both groups! We'd need women in one group and men in another! Often, as in our case, there is a choice and the decision is part of the design process.

Repeated measures design

In this type of design, each of our participants carries out the experiment twice. Once in each of our groups. On one occasion they perform a task while listening to the sound, and on the other occasion they perform the memory task in silence.

The same people do the same task twice. On one occasion they perform in silence, and on the other they listen over headphones.

ADVANTAGES

The two groups are made up of the same people, therefore all individual differences between the two groups are controlled for. Both groups are identical. There are no differences in age, gender, French-speaking ability, how good they are at hearing or whether or not they have beards and wear glasses. They're completely identical.

In this type of design we often say that '*The participant acts as their own control*'. One of your

authors is fabulous looking wealthy, and enormously intelligent. The other is old, overweight, short of cash and is not very bright at all. If we both took part in the experiment and it was designed with a *repeated measures* design, each of us would bring various problems to our performance on the experimental condition, but exactly the same issues would be a feature of our performance on the control condition.

WEAKNESSES

Repeated measures designs create *order effects*. For example, if participants recall more words on the second day (when they return to do the task again) can we be sure that this is due to the noise? It could be that this improvement is due to extra experience with the memory task. This kind of order effect is called a *practice effect*. On the other hand the opposite could happen and performance on the second day is worse than the first. Again, we could not be sure that this was due to the noise – it could be due to tiredness or boredom with the task. This kind of order effect is sometimes called a *fatigue effect*.

Counterbalancing

To overcome order effects we would have to use *counterbalancing*. Half of the participants could do no noise followed the next day by noise (i.e. the control condition followed by the experimental condition). The other half could do noise on the first day and no noise on the next day (experimental condition followed by control condition). In this way, order effects would appear in both conditions and in effect balance themselves out.

Independent groups design

This is the design we originally decided on where we use *different people in each experimental condition*. In this design, each participant is randomly allocated to one condition. In our experiment, one half of the sample would be allocated to the control condition and do the memory test in silence, whilst the other half of participants would be put into the experimental condition and do the test whilst listening to a noise.

The task is completed twice. On each occasion different people take part. One group complete the task in silence and one group wear headphones.

ADVANTAGES

There are no order effects with this design, so things like practice or fatigue will not confound the results. Because each person only provides data in one or other of the conditions it doesn't matter when you carry out the task. You can just grab the person when you see them and ask them to carry out the task there and then.

WEAKNESSES

Because the participants in each condition are *different* we cannot be sure that their *individual differences* are influencing the results in some way. For example, whilst allocation to conditions is random it could be by chance that more people with poor reading skills are in one condition than another (which might be important) or maybe a few people with extraordinary memories are allocated to one condition. In this case, the difference between the two conditions might not be due to the independent variable at all but to the contribution of several 'unusual' participants.

How about an extreme example to make it clear. Imagine you wanted to know whether ability at chess was influenced by how much chocolate someone had eaten (you never know – it might be a factor!). You design an independent samples design. In one room you have ten people, each completing chess problems while eating two chocolate bars. In the other room you have ten people completing the same chess problems, but without any chocolate. Perfect, so you think. It turns out that the ten people in the first room are from the all-UK travelling chess show and the other ten are from the Belgian men's chocolate eating team. It seems that the relationship between chocolate eating and chess ability will not be made any clearer by your experiment after all.

Matched pairs design

This design involves having two separate groups of participants but who are matched on some important variable in order to make them as similar as possible. The ideal participants in a matched pairs design would be identical twins, with one twin in each condition, as they are as matched as two individuals could ever be. If it was always practical, this is the ideal compromise between the independent groups and repeated measures design, as it avoids most of the problems with both and has all their advantages. However, the problems associated with matching (or finding sufficient numbers of twins to participate!) means that this design is rarely used.

The task is completed twice, on each occasion by different, but closely matched people. One group wear headphones, the other participate in silence. In this example we have two different vicars and two different sailors.

ADVANTAGES

Because the participants are matched there is less confounding caused by individual differences. The design is really an independent measures design with practically identical people in each group, so there are no order effects.

WEAKNESSES

Matching participants is very difficult and time consuming and in any case, even with identical twins, individual difference is only reduced rather than eliminated. They may well share a genetic code, and look practically identical, but one twin may have a hobby which makes him reasonably good at simple arithmetic (such as darts, where subtracting numbers is part of every game) and the other may not. In this case, and on this level, they are not very well matched. One has an advantage over the other.

What makes a good experiment?

Taking care and designing the experiment properly is not the fastest process in the world. It's a bit like riding a bike. It takes a while to get the hang of it, and the reason for doing certain things may be unclear at first, but soon it becomes second nature – you just do it. Experimental design is a bit like that. After a while you just know which type of design to choose and why one is better than another. If you do it properly you will be able to have confidence in the results and will not have to go back and do it all again!

A good experiment is one in which:

● Findings are *generalisable* (the findings can be said to apply to others outside the sample).

● Procedures are *replicable* (the experiment can be reliably repeated).

● Findings are *reliable* (if the experiment was done again, the results would be the same or similar). Later on in this section we describe

observation studies and the concept of *inter-rater reliability*. This is where the ratings of one rater are reliably the same as the ratings of another. A good observation study must therefore have a high level of inter-rater reliability.

● Measures are *valid* (the experiment is measuring what it claims to measure).

"There are different types of reliability and validity and you don't need to know about all of them. Just make sure you know what reliability is and why it is important in research methods."

Quasi-experiments

A quasi-experiment is one in which the researcher *cannot manipulate the independent variable*. Quasi-experiments *lack the control* of true experiments. Whilst experimental procedures are used, participants cannot be randomly allocated to conditions. For example, if an experiment is looking at sex difference in some ability or other, let's say creativity, then participants are allocated to each condition according to their sex – males in one condition, females in the other. In the

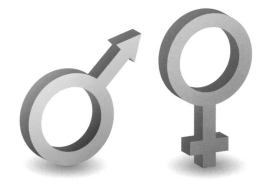

example of sex differences in creativity, the IV is the sex difference and it cannot be manipulated by the experimenter. This means that some studies which, on the face of it, appear to be laboratory studies are in fact quasi-experiments. This also means that natural experiments are quasi-experiments too, since the IV is naturally occurring.

ADVANTAGES

1 Provided that we have carefully controlled our variables, laboratory experiments allow us to establish cause and effect relationships. That is, we can say with some confidence that the *independent variable* has caused the change in the *dependent variable*.

2 If appropriate care is taken in the design and conduct of the experiment, and it has been reported accurately, then it allows replication. That is, it allows other researchers to repeat the experiment with the same findings. A piece of research will have far more credibility if it is replicated and supported.

3 Variables are much easier to control in the laboratory than outside in a natural setting. This gives them a real advantage over the natural experiment as we can be more certain that the results have not been confounded by an unknown factor.

WEAKNESSES

1 The more you control behaviour the less natural it becomes. For example, people change how they act when they sense they are being assessed or watched. Experiments exert a high degree of control, therefore it has been argued that experiments encourage behaviours that are artificial and not like real life we say that laboratory experiments lack *ecological validity*.

2 Not everything of interest to psychologists can be investigated using laboratory experimentation. For example, a psychologist might be interested in understanding the effect that a certain drug has on the developing infant brain but it would not be ethical or practical to do a controlled experiment on this.

3 Biases introduced through such things as sampling, demand characteristics and experimenter expectancy are almost impossible to completely eliminate. This can reduce our confidence in our findings. What we really want to know is whether the IV has influenced the DV. If there are problems of sampling, demand characteristics and experimenter effects, we can't really be sure of the IV/DV relationship.

THE FIELD EXPERIMENT

A field experiment involves the *direct manipulation of variables* but, unlike the laboratory experiment, this is done in what the participant sees as a natural environment. This makes the study *much more realistic* and it is thus argued that it produces data which are more valid. There is still an IV which is being manipulated and a DV which is being measured. A field experiment would be used when it is considered crucial that a natural setting is used to investigate some behaviour. Social psychology makes particular use of the field experiment as it is interested in the behaviour of people in social settings. Since participants should not be aware that they are taking part in a controlled study, their behaviour should be natural. An unrealistic example always helps.

Imagine you wanted to investigate how people behaved in a typical 'Good Samaritan' sort of environment. You might have the idea that people were more 'Samaritan-like' in the north of the country than in the south. You could find yourself a suitable old lady, load her up with shopping, drop her off at the side of a busy road and wait nearby to see what happens. Your IV is whether you are in the NORTH or the SOUTH. Your DV is how many people stop to help the poor, shopping-laden lady across the road.

ADVANTAGES

1 Because of the natural setting there is much greater *ecological validity* with field than laboratory experiments.

2 Because participants are supposed to be unaware that they are taking part in research, *demand characteristics* should be reduced or even *eliminated*.

WEAKNESSES

1 There is less control of *extraneous variables* in a field experiment than there is in a laboratory experiment meaning that the results are more likely to be confounded in some way. Imagine if in our 'Good Samaritan' experiment, just by chance a troop of cub scouts showed up, intent on practising their 'helping people across the road' skills. Our results would have been completely ruined!

2 Field experiments are generally more time consuming and expensive to design and run than laboratory experiments.

THE NATURAL EXPERIMENT

In a natural experiment, rather than direct manipulation, the researcher takes advantage of a *naturally occurring* change in an IV. There is no experimental control other than that which is already in place, and there are likely to be extraneous variables that remain uncontrolled. Because participants are not randomly allocated, natural experiments are really quasi-experiments. However, the behaviour is natural and the situations in which natural experiments arise are usually those in which a laboratory or field experiment would not be possible. For example, you might find that a local hospital has changed its policy on post-operative care for patients undergoing brain surgery. This might provide an opportunity to compare the effects of this post-operative care with another hospital that has a more traditional approach.

The IV would be the kind of post-operative care offered – this has naturally arisen and is not something that you can possibly have manipulated.

ADVANTAGES

1 Because it is natural setting with naturally occurring changes in the IV, there is high ecological validity.

2 Because the researcher has little or no involvement with the situation, and participants would be unaware that they are taking part in a study, there are likely to be few demand characteristics and reduced researcher bias.

3 This type of design allows the researcher to study real-life problems.

WEAKNESSES

1 There is little or no control of variables in a natural experiment. The IV occurs naturally, as will extraneous variables. At best, these can be identified and taken into consideration when causal relations are inferred from the findings. You cannot conclude that one thing caused another, only that in your experiment, there was some kind of relationship between the IV and the DV.

2 Opportunities for natural experiments occur rarely and when they do, they are generally unique events. This means that they are virtually impossible to replicate in order to check the reliability and validity of the findings.

3 The possibilities for confounding variables are endless. Your experiment may be influenced by any number of things beyond your control.

THE OBSERVATIONAL METHOD

As has already been mentioned, all research begins with some form of observation. However, observation is a research method in its own right. The observational method involves systematically watching and recording what people say and do. The behaviours observed are those that naturally occur, meaning that no attempt is made to manipulate variables. The main benefit of this is that we then get natural behaviour, unchanged by the presence of a researcher or research environment.

Observation as a technique

An important distinction has to made here between *observation as a research method* and *observation as a data gathering technique*. Observations can be used as a technique to gather data in a range of research methods. For example, in an experiment on aggression a researcher might show one group of participants a film containing only an aggressive scene. The researcher would then observe the participants some time later to see if their behaviour had changed as a result of the film, compared to the group of participants who did not see it. This is a laboratory experiment, where the dependent variable is derived through observation of behaviour.

Controlled observation is also often used in field experiments where the environment has been deliberately altered by the researcher in some way. Observations are then made of any changes in behaviour as a result of this manipulation. For example, drivers and other road-users behave in a certain way when there are road signs present. Observing the behaviour and carefully noting down important aspects, such as overtaking frequency and speed, might be of importance to your study. Now, remove all the road signs and repeat the observation. You would look to see if the alteration of the environment had altered the behaviour of the road-users.

Observation as a method

Observation as a research method is different in that it involves no manipulation of variables by the researcher – the behaviour being observed is free and natural.

In observational studies a researcher can be either directly involved in the situation being observed (this is called *participant observation*) or can remain outside and unobserved (called *non-participant observation*). Both these methods are sometimes called *naturalistic observation*, since people are being observed in their own environment and will thus behave naturally. For example, a participant observation might be one where the experimenter is part of the sports team in which he is investigating group behaviour. A non-participant observation might be one where the experimenter is observing the play of children from behind a one-way mirror. Observations are being made in both cases, but only in the group-behaviour study is the experimenter actually involved.

Whilst, on the face of it, observation seems to be a natural and straightforward method of gathering data, in reality it requires a great deal of thought and careful planning. Imagine that you are interested in whether or not boys are more physically aggressive than girls. You would need an environment in which to observe the natural behaviour of boys and girls, and an obvious choice for this would be the playground of a primary school. The first practical thing that you would need to do is contact the Head Teacher for permission to enter the school premises, fully disclosing the aims and methods of your research.

Remember, conducting any research involving children carries with it extra ethical responsibilities. The ideal place in which to observe the children would be in the playground during their break times.

Aggression is quite a complex concept and in order to be able to observe it we must *operationalise* it. In this case, we are interested in physical aggression, so shouts and other verbal behaviours – which would otherwise be interpreted as aggressive – do not count. We also use a psychological definition of aggression to clarify our observations further – aggression can be defined as 'any behaviour in which one person is motivated to cause harm which the victim is motivated to avoid'. This would exclude from our observation other behaviours, such as play-fighting and other sorts of rough-and-tumble play. Choosing the variables to operationalise creates *behavioural categories*. It is these that appear on the checklist that the researchers use when observing the behaviour.

Once you have gone through the complicated process of seeking permission and operationalising variables, you will then need to devise some method of recording your observations. For this, you will need an observational checklist.

In its simplest form, the checklist for this study might look like this:

TYPE OF BEHAVIOUR	MALE	FEMALE
Aggressive towards male	卌 IIII	卌
Aggressive towards female	卌 II	卌 II
Friendly towards female		卌 IIII
Friendly towards male	卌 IIII	II

There are many other observations you might want to record however, in which case your observational checklist will need to be adjusted as needed. For example, you might want to record the number of children involved in the behaviour, approximately how long the aggression lasted, any consequences of the act, the response of the victim, and victim and perpetrator relations as in our checklist (whether aggression was male-male or male-female). As you can see, this can get rather complicated and the more complicated the observation checklist the more likely there are to be errors in recording.

Unless we are able to film proceedings for later thorough analysis, it is impossible to record everything. In this case we have to be selective in what we observe. In other words we have to take a sample of behaviours to observe. There are two basic sampling techniques we could use. *Time sampling* involves making observations for short intervals within a given period of time. So, for example, in our study we could watch children for three minutes out of every 15, using the intervening time to clarify our observations and make notes. Our observations of aggression however used *event sampling*, where all clearly defined relevant behaviours are recorded each time they occur.

The problem of bias

One of the greatest difficulties to overcome in observational research is bias. *Observer bias* occurs when observers interpret what they see according to their own beliefs, feelings and expectations. Whilst it is human and natural that biases affect our interpretations, it is crucial in research that everything possible is done to prevent it. The problem is made much worse when there are two or more observers. The first step in doing this is to ensure that we have fully operationalised our variables and that we have a workable checklist where behaviours have been clearly categorised. We also need to check observer reliability; we can get two people to observe the same thing, and if they record events in similar ways then they are showing consistency (or reliability) in their observations. This form of reliability is called *inter-rater reliability*. As with many other kinds of research it pays to conduct a pilot study, which will identify many of these problems and suggest solutions to them. You can relate this to the concepts of reliability and validity that we described earlier in this section.

Awareness of the observer

It is also important of course to ensure that participants *remain unaware* of the fact that they are being observed, in order to ensure that their behaviour remains natural. This, in itself, carries with it all sorts of practical problems. In our study, to have a number of researchers suddenly turn up at the school playground is likely to change children's behaviour, at least in the short term. This problem could be reduced by giving the researchers a rationale for being there (e.g. playground monitors) and not recording observations until the children are used to them being there. The problem could be overcome by sneakily filming behaviour for later analysis. This, however, introduces ethical issues. It has been argued that it is not ethical to observe and record the behaviour of others without their knowledge. This is on the grounds that there is no right to withdraw, no informed consent, no guarantee of confidentiality. Basically, if people do not know that they are being studied then they are being denied their rights. In a partial solution to this problem it has been suggested that only behaviours that occur in situations in which people could naturally be expected to be observed, should be used in observational studies.

The data gathered through observation are going to be highly descriptive (e.g. tallies converted to percentages) and will not offer an explanation for what has been recorded. It is the job of the researcher to make sense of the data, sorting them so that any evidence relevant to the hypothesis is presented clearly.

ADVANTAGES

1 Because observations occur in a natural setting the behaviours occur in their true form. This gives the method high ecological validity.

2 The observational method allows behaviour to be investigated in situations where other methods would not be possible. For example, observing aggressive behaviour in children is possible in the laboratory, but encouraging a child to act aggressively will fall foul of *ethical* considerations. We'll deal with these later.

3 There are few demand characteristics in observational studies because people do not know they are being studied and are not put into a 'false' situation, as would happen in laboratory-based studies.

WEAKNESSES

1 There is a risk of observer bias as it unlikely that researchers will be able to remain completely objective. This reduces the reliability of the data gathered.

2 Unlike observational techniques used in experiments, the lack of control of variables in naturalistic observations means that confounding variables may be introduced. This makes causality difficult to establish and means that replication is going to be more difficult.

3 Observations tend to be rather small-scale so the group being studied may not be representative of the population.

CONTENT ANALYSIS

Content analysis is an observational technique used to *analyse the content of text*. For example, it is used to assess the presence of meanings and concepts in written documents such as newspapers and books. It is not restricted to text however – it can also be used to assess the content of film and television, and is often used to analyse political speeches.

At its simplest level a content analysis is conducted in much the same way as an observational study. The important difference between content analysis and a regular observation study is that in content analysis we produce a *record of the behaviour* not just an observation of the behaviour. Once the aims of the research have been clarified a sample can be chosen although, rather than participants, the sample will be of material. For example, if you are interested in how women are portrayed in tabloid newspapers you need to decide on the newspapers, their frequency and a time period. Then a checklist needs to be developed to record the observations from this sample. Reliability can be checked in the same way as observations, by using more than one rater and investigating if their 'observations' are comparable; this, you'll remember, is called inter-rater reliability.

SELF-REPORT TECHNIQUES – QUESTIONNAIRES AND INTERVIEWS

Self-report techniques involve asking participants a range of questions to which their responses are recorded. The most common self-report techniques are questionnaires and interviews.

QUESTIONNAIRES

A questionnaire is basically a list of prewritten questions. You'll see people administering questionnaires all over the place. Sometimes people come to your front door, but usually you bump into people at the shopping centre or on the high street. You can usually tell these researchers by their clipboards! Some aspects of human experience and behaviour, for example attitudes, would be impractical to investigate using either experiment or observation. A well-designed questionnaire however could provide a wealth of useful information. Because people may feel reluctant to complete questionnaires it is important to reduce the perceived cost of taking part (e.g. avoid asking

for personal information, minimise embarrassment and inconvenience, and make

the questionnaire appear short and easy), and establish trust (e.g. make the questionnaire appear legitimate and important, inform about confidentiality, and offer thanks for taking part).

There are two ways to ask questions – closed and open:

Type 1: Closed questions

These allow limited responses from participants and may take a variety of forms. Whilst restricting the range of answers from candidates, they have the advantage in providing quantitative data which are usually easy to analyse. There are a variety of closed question formats from which to choose:

a. Rank order questions

This is where participants are asked to rate or rank a range of options. This gives information about preferences and degrees of importance, etc. As ranking long lists is difficult, keep the list to about five items. For example:

"Please indicate, in rank order, your preferred drink, putting 1 next to your *favourite* through to 5 for your *least favourite*:"

Coffee/Coke/Tea/Water/Hot Chocolate

b. Likert scale questions

These are statements to which participants are asked to indicate their strength of agreement or disagreement. For example:

"Psychology is so much better than mathematics." Do you agree or disagree on a scale of 1 (strongly agree) to 8 (strongly disagree)?

c. Checklist questions

This is where a list of items is provided from which participants select those that apply. For example:

"Choose three of the following adjectives that most apply to your personality:"

Happy, Grumpy, Friendly, Miserable, Sparkly, Interesting, Quiet, Morose, Sad.

d. Dichotomous questions

These are questions offering two choices. For example:

"Did you do any exercise last week?"

Yes/No

e. Semantic differential questions

With this type of question two bi-polar words are present and participants are asked to respond by indicating a point between the two representing their strength of feeling. For example:

"My home town is..."

Interesting :___:___:___:___:___:___: Boring

Pretty :___:___:___:___:___:___: Ugly

Clean :___:___:___:___:___:___: Dirty

Type 2: Open questions

This is where participants are given the opportunity to respond more freely. Allowing participants to express themselves in this way can help the researcher avoid accidentally biasing the closed questions towards a particular point of view, and can provide a far richer source of information. However, they can produce difficult to interpret qualitative data (data which are hard or impossible to put a value on). For example:

"In the box provided, please describe what it feels like to fall in love."

Many of the problems of questionnaires come from poorly phrased open and closed questions. The following are some of the things that should be avoided:

a. Lack of clarity – questions should be understandable and mean the same things to all participants. They should therefore be written in clear language, avoiding ambiguity and unnecessary jargon.

b. Embarrassing questions – questions that focus on private matters should be avoided. As the questions become more personal then the likelihood of unanswered or wrongly answered questions increases.

c. Social desirability bias – participants will often answer questions in a way that makes them feel better by giving the answers that they think they ought to give, showing them in a better light.

d. Leading questions – leading questions encourage a certain response from participants.

ADVANTAGES

1 Compared to other methods they can be a cheap and efficient way of collecting data.

2 Because large numbers of questionnaires containing lots of questions can be distributed, they can be used to collect large amounts of information relatively easily.

3 Because the participants can remain anonymous and therefore perhaps be more willing to express themselves fully, questionnaires are a relatively reliable method of gathering data.

Designing a simple questionnaire

It might be useful at this point to consider a practical example of the questionnaire method. As a student of psychology you may have noticed that some people are very good at managing their time, whilst others appear to be quite disorganised. This might lead you to further considerations: why some people put effort into time management and some don't, whether this behaviour is related to other aspects of their lives and, indeed, whether or not people believe it is useful.

STEP 1: Define the objectives of the study. Decide upon a research area – "attitudes toward time management in students".

STEP 2: Formulate one or more hypotheses that you would like the questionnaire to address.

STEP 3: Identify a population and determine a way of selecting a sample from this population.

STEP 4: Create a good questionnaire – This is the tricky bit. Selecting the appropriate kinds of closed and open questions and avoiding the pitfalls of question wording are extremely important issues. A great deal of effort and imagination has to be put into creating a good questionnaire. Remember, KEEP IT SIMPLE!

STEP 5: Before administering your questionnaire to your sample it is worthwhile **doing a pilot study**. You need to know if the questionnaire works and you won't know this unless you actually trial it. This will allow you to *get feedback about the length of time it takes to complete, to check that the instructions are clear, to check the clarity of questions and questionnaire layout, and to ensure that the questionnaire is providing you with the kind of data you can analyse.*

STEP 6: Adjust the questionnaire – The information you receive from the pilot study should allow you to adjust the questionnaire and make your research even more effective.

Once you've been through these six steps, you can administer your completed questionnaire. Your questions might resemble something like this:

Male ☐ or Female ☐?

Do you think that time management is important?

Yes ☐   No ☐   Don't know ☐

Please indicate on the scale below, by circling a number, the extent to which you think you manage your time effectively:

Very   Not at all

1   2   3   4   5

If you are given two weeks to do homework do you:

☐ do it straight away

☐ complete it within the first week

☐ complete it in the second week

☐ complete it the night before it is due

☐ miss the deadline

WEAKNESSES

1 Survey data are highly descriptive and as such it is difficult to establish causal relationships. The ability to infer causal relationships will be limited by the quality of the questionnaire. For example, it depends on having asked the right questions to start with.

2 Whilst it is important to select a representative sample it is very difficult to obtain one. Not only is it difficult to identify all members of a population, but even if you could, there is no guarantee that they would agree to take part in the study. It might even be that those who do agree to complete the questionnaire make up a biased sample.

3 There is no guarantee that people will respond truthfully to questions. There are many reasons for this. It might be social desirability, where participants say what it is they think should be said rather than give their own opinion. It might even be that some participants are bloody-minded and deliberately give wrong answers.

INTERVIEWS

Interviews and questionnaires are similar in some ways in that they are both based around a set of questions. Interviews however are generally conducted face-to-face, unlike questionnaires, and the way that information is acquired varies slightly depending on the type of interview. There are many different ways of conducting an interview but the methods are most simply categorised as either *structured, semi-structured* or *unstructured*.

Structured interview

This approach resembles the questionnaire except that rather than write their own responses, participants respond verbally to questions posed by the researcher. The same questions are presented to each participant in the same way and, because of this, it has been described as a 'verbal questionnaire'.

Collecting data in an interview.

Semi-structured interview

Whilst there are no fixed questions here the interview is guided, perhaps, by a predetermined set of topics to be covered. The order in which these topics are covered, or the way in which they are addressed by the interviewer, can vary across participants.

Unstructured interview

With this method of interviewing the participant is free to talk about whatever they like. The interviewer may set the topic, but the interviewee is free to dictate the content by taking the conversation in any direction they wish.

The simplest kind of interview to conduct is the structured interview but, as with all forms of interview, the sex, personality and skills of the interviewer are extremely important variables that can have significant influences on the interviewee. Training is needed for effective interviewing, and the less structured the interview the greater the skills and training needed by the interviewer. This means that, wherever possible, researchers lacking this training should opt for a questionnaire method of self-report.

ADVANTAGES

1 The kind of data you get from an interview is often rich and varied. The information is provided 'off-the-cuff' and is spontaneous and often unexpected. The data are more realistic than you might get in a more formal interview.

2 Standardised interviews are relatively simple to administer and a lot of data can be collected relatively cheaply and quickly. A large sample can be obtained without much difficulty, depending on the subject of the questionnaire, and so the data can often be generalised.

3 The interview can provide a great deal of insight into complicated and difficult individual cases if administered carefully by a skilled interviewer. This can often give clinicians insight into complicated and difficult cases with children or adults who may be suffering with psychological abnormalities of some kind.

WEAKNESSES

1 It might be difficult to find the right sample. Also, some people begin the interview and do not complete it because they find it too lengthy or possibly too difficult to sit through. In these cases the data may need to be rejected from the study.

2 Sometimes people given the same interview provide such widely differing responses that you'd think that they were given completely different interviews! In cases like this, the generalisability of the results is very low indeed.

3 If the interviewer is not sufficiently skilled the participant's responses may not be relaxed and the data will be false and of little use.

CORRELATIONAL ANALYSIS

Correlation is a technique that shows whether or not two variables are associated. As well as being a research method in its own right, correlation can be used to analyse data gathered from any other research method. For example, data from observational studies and questionnaires might be analysed to see if there is a relationship between two or more factors.

Correlations can be represented mathematically as a correlation coefficient. This is a number somewhere between +1 and -1, and is represented by the letter *r*. For example, you may have coefficients that look like r=+0.7 or r=-0.3.

● *A positive correlation.* This is where the *sign* of the correlation coefficient comes in useful! If the sign is positive (+) we say that the correlation is 'positive'. This means that as one variable increases, so too does the other. An example might be the relationship between how many hours you spend studying for an exam and how well you do in it. The more study you do (more minutes) the better your score on the exam. As one goes up, so too does the other.

The more you study, the better you do in exams. The correlation between time spent studying and score on exams is 'positive'.

● *A negative correlation* is one where the correlation coefficient has a negative sign (-). Here we say that the correlation is 'negative'. As one variable increases, the other decreases. An example might be the relationship between the speed at which a driver drives and the amount of petrol they use per mile (miles per gallon – mpg). The faster they drive, the lower the mpg. As speed increases, mpg decreases. One goes up, the other goes down. This is a negative correlation.

● *Zero correlation*. This is where the two variables are not related at all. In this case you would expect to see a correlation coefficient near to zero, or even possibly at zero although this would be very unlikely. There are loads of things that are unrelated; an example might be the relationship between the earnings of deep sea fishermen and the size of the average portion of chips in the UK. One has nothing at all to do with the other. Another example might be the relationship between the number of cups of coffee drunk in the staffroom of your college every day and the amount of cartoons on the telly between 3pm and 5pm. No relationship at all.

The strength of the correlation is given by how near to -1 or +1 the number (r) is. A tip here is just ignore the sign. So, when we see the correlation coefficient r= +0.9 we can say that the relationship between the two variables that made that correlation is stronger than that of two variables with the correlation coefficient r= +0.2. When we talk about the strength of the correlation the sign is not the important bit, it is the number that matters. A correlation of +0.8 is exactly the same strength as -0.8, it is just that one is a positive correlation and the other is a negative one.

The significance of the correlation depends on a number of things including how many people have provided data for your experiment and the size of the coefficient. However, you can be pretty sure that if your correlation is +1 or -1, then it is going to be significant. The nearer the correlation is to -1 or +1, the more likely it is that the relationship between your two variables will be significant. Later in the book (page 167) we describe a study by Rahe et al (1970) who found a significant positive correlation in their study.

Scattergrams are used to depict correlation data. They are also known as scatterplots or scattergraphs. A scattergram is a kind of graph and we'll talk more about these later in a section on graphs.

"The best way to learn something is to really 'own the knowledge'. This means you've got to try and make it fit your own kind of understanding. Read over it a few times, you'll not get it all in one reading. No one is that lucky (and if they tell you they are they are lying!) so when we talk about scattergrams in a minute, come back here and read over the bit on correlations first. Get it set in your mind, so that the new stuff about scattergrams has something to stick on to in your memory!"

Watch out! Correlations and cause

Significant correlation coefficients simply indicate that there is a relationship between two variables. It does not say why or how the two things are related. Care however must be taken when interpreting the meaning of coefficients. Correlation *does not mean* that one variable caused the other to change – only an experiment reveals causal relationships between variables. *Causality* is only one of three possible explanations for a correlation:

1 The relationship is causal (one variable caused the other to change).

2 The relationship is chance (the two variables just happen to be statistically related).

3 There is a third factor involved (another variable is causing the relationship).

For example, let's say that in our questionnaire study on time management in students we are interested in whether or not time management habits are related to subsequent performance in assessments. We could extract the data from the questionnaire which relates to these two factors: how students manage their time and assessment performance (e.g. exam grades). We could then give the data to someone, who knows how to do it, for them to analyse it and produce a correlation coefficient (you don't have to do this at AS level!). Suppose the coefficient is +0.62, and we decide that this is an important (or significant) correlation. It shows us that there is a positive correlation between time management habits and exam grades – the better the time management, the better the grades. We now have to explain this correlation:

(a) Is the relationship causal? (i.e. Did time management cause improved exam grades?)

(b) Is the relationship a chance one? (i.e. the result could be a statistical fluke)

(c) Is there a third variable explanation? (i.e. Is another variable operating which makes the two factors appear causally related?)

In this example, it might be that motivated students manage their time but it is motivation that produces better exam grades rather than the time management itself.

Sometimes the answer is quite clear but often it is not, in which case it is up to the judgement of the researcher as to which explanation is most probable.

ADVANTAGES

1 Allows a researcher to measure relationships between naturally occurring variables, such as height and intelligence, or weight and sleep duration.

2 Correlational studies can indicate trends, which might then lead to further research using experimental means to establish any causal links. They are a really useful and quite a simple way of starting off a research project.

WEAKNESSES

1 It is not possible to draw conclusions about cause and effect. Remember, a significant correlation does not mean cause. Just because there is a significant correlation between the number of sightings of storks and the birth rate, does not mean that we can conclude that storks have caused babies to arrive!

2 Extraneous variables, which may influence the results, are very hard to control. There may be a correlation between two variables but it might be that something else, something you do not know about and have not controlled for, has sneaked into your experiment and 'caused' or influenced the relationship.

3 The coefficient may look like there is 'no relationship' between the variables, as it is near to zero. However, this might hide a really special relationship, a 'curvilinear' relationship or one which shows more than one 'group' in the data. We'll talk more about this when we cover scattergrams later.

CASE STUDIES

A *case study* is a careful and systematic *investigation of a single individual*. A researcher studies a single example either because they are rare or unique in some way, or because they are a typical example of a type of person. Case studies can take a long time to conduct and a variety of data collection methods can be used, therefore detailed in depth information

Bertha Pappenheim, also known as Anna O, one of Freud's most famous case studies.

is obtained. A researcher might use both primary and secondary data in the case study. *Primary* data are those that are gained directly by the researcher, for example from interviews, assessments and observations of the individual or their family, or from information gathered from investigating the environment of the individual. *Secondary* data are those that have already been collected but which are reused by the researcher. Examples of secondary data might include school and medical records, or initial studies of the individual that may have been carried out by other researchers. What information is collected will depend on what the researcher is trying to investigate, on the *aims* of his or her investigation.

ADVANTAGES

1 Case studies produce lots of detail and the depth of understanding acquired through this is useful for understanding the subtleties and complexities of individual behaviour.

2 Although usually a detailed study of one person, the data from several people are often pooled and analysed to give insights into their similarities and differences. This is the case, for example, with neuropsychology where the symptoms of brain damage from a number of individual case studies might be compared in order to give a greater understanding of the causes of the symptoms they share.

3 The case study is the only way to deal with rare and dramatic cases in psychology. For example, insights into the condition of someone who has had extremely harsh childhood experiences could only be gained through a detailed and careful study of his or her circumstances.

WEAKNESSES

1 Because case studies relate to one individual the findings from them cannot easily be generalised to others. Even if generalisations

are made, they may lack credibility in the eyes of other researchers.

2 Case studies rely on retrospective data, that is, information gathered about past events. This information might not be accurate. People have a habit of forgetting things, and our memory for events, especially stressful ones, can be unreliable. Also, memory can change over time, so what really happened may never be known. Relying on this type of data can be very problematic.

3 Because case studies can be very time consuming, involving a lot of time spent with the case, it has been suggested that the relationship that develops as a result, between the researchers and the individual, makes it difficult to rely on the objectivity of the data.

QUANTITATIVE AND QUALITATIVE RESEARCH

Finally, we need to describe the differences between *qualitative* and *quantitative* research. The distinction is actually quite simple, but there are little details that could catch you out, so it is just as well to include a separate section here. Essentially quantitative is to do with assigning numbers to things, and *qualitative* is to do with opinions. It's not quite as simple as that though.

Quantitative research

There is an emphasis in psychological research on gathering numerical data – numbers. In doing this, researchers are being *quantitative* – they are assigning numerical values to things. Quantitative research always involves measuring something in some way – for example, how many times you can hop in one minute, how many cars pass a local school, how far you can go in a car on a single litre of fuel. When these data are collected, statistical techniques are used to analyse them in order to find out if there are any numerical patterns or relationships. For many researchers this approach to investigating behaviour is the right one because it is regarded as the most scientific. It limits the amount of *interpretation* and *opinion* and therefore is *more objective*.

Qualitative research

Qualitative research gathers information which is *non-numerical*. When we described questionnaires, we explained how different types of questions provide different types of data. Open-ended questions provide *qualitative* information. Qualitative research focuses on a person's *experience* and *feelings*, and is more concerned with uncovering the meaning of these things than with measuring behaviour using statistics. Although this kind of information can be converted to quantitative data, it is often left qualitative and summarised. Qualitative research:

● Describes events using words, rather than numbers, and can provide extremely rich and detailed data of emotions and opinions.

● Takes the point of view of the participant, since their responses are not restricted in advance by the point of view of the researcher.

● Is less controlled and structured compared to quantitative research. Quantitative research is more concerned with issues of reliability. It is hard to assess reliability in qualitative research.

● Can be difficult and laborious to analyse, and it is often really difficult to see patterns in the data that would allow you to draw conclusions.

Quantitative or qualitative?

Whether or not a quantitative or qualitative approach is selected depends on the nature of the research and the interests of the researcher. For example, a researcher interested in a participant's subjective experience of some event would prefer a qualitative approach to gathering information.

On the other hand, a researcher interested in measuring some aspect of human memory might prefer a quantitative approach. Quantitative and qualitative approaches are not necessarily exclusive however – one can complement the other. This has led some researchers to use both approaches. For example, quantitative data might be gathered from an experiment, but the researcher might also want to understand something about the experience of the participant. Indeed, as well as having value in its own right, qualitative data can be a very useful source of information about demand characteristics. Because of this, a qualitative approach involving interviews with the participants might usefully form a part of a pilot study during the design process.

Some research methods can actually be used to gather both quantitative and qualitative data. For example, self-report techniques such as questionnaires can gather information which is quantitative (for example, questions that ask for a response on a scale of 1 to 5), and qualitative (for example, questions that ask for an opinion). We've included examples of questions like these in this section where we describe questionnaires.

PRESENTING DATA

Now that we know how to design a study and collect data, we need to know what to do with it. First, we need to look at what we have collected and make it really simple for ourselves and others to see how conclusions might be drawn by summarising the numbers in some way. Next, we need to use techniques to show the data off in such a way that our conclusions are clear and easy to read without too much effort. In short, we need to know something about how to *describe* the data with statistics, and we need to know how to visually represent the data with graphs.

DESCRIPTIVE STATISTICS

Whatever you do in research, you always end up with loads of numbers and a huge amount of information. You can't expect others to spend hours trying to make sense of this 'raw data' so you need to do something with it to make everybody else's life much easier, and bring out the main points in your data.

Just as you can summarise a book or a story in a few words, and just as a cartoonist uses a few important details to describe a whole scene, researchers use descriptive statistics to summarise their findings. Let's use an improbable example! Let's imagine we've given an intelligence test to everyone in the whole world. The postman arrives with a large sack of responses and we need to summarise the huge amount of data we have.

Descriptive statistics allow us to boil down the data and squeeze it into a few handy numbers, so others will not have to spend their time reading all the raw data to try to understand our results.

Descriptive statistics can't do everything!

The clue here is in the name – descriptive statistics. They simply describe the raw data. They do not tell us what you did or whether your findings are reliable (they might be the same if you did the experiment again) and they do not explain the result, or the type and size of the relationship you may have found. They simply allow you to describe the raw data and reduce them to just a few numbers that are easier to manage.

MEASURES OF CENTRAL TENDENCY

Measures of central tendency are sometimes referred to as averages. To find an average of a set of numbers is to calculate a single value that is representative of the whole set. That is, the average is said to be a score which is typical of the rest of scores.

There are *three* measures of central tendency.

1. Mean

This is the best measure of central tendency and is calculated by adding all the scores in a set of scores together and dividing by the number of scores. For example, take the following raw data where we've measured the height of five people.

height/cm: 153 146 151 170 160

STEP 1: Add up all the heights to find the **TOTAL** (153+146+151+170+160)cm = *780cm*

STEP 2: Divide the **TOTAL** by the number in your sample (in this case 5) 780cm divided by 5 (780/5) = *156cm*

THE MEAN HEIGHT OF THIS SAMPLE IS 156cm.

The mean height is quite typical of the heights of your sample. Three people are shorter and two are taller. It is pretty much in the middle. A good 'typical' mean.

STRENGTHS AND WEAKNESSES OF THE MEAN

The mean is the most powerful measure of central tendency because it is the only one which uses all the numbers in its calculation. This however is also its weakness. Because the calculation uses all your numbers, one rogue number has a huge effect on your mean. For example, imagine if one of your five people

was 234cm in height. You now have six people in your sample.

STEP 1: Add up all the heights to find the **TOTAL** (153+146+151+170+160+234) cm = *1014cm*

STEP 2: Divide the **TOTAL** by the number in your sample (now 6) 1014 divided by 6 (1014/6)cm = *169cm*

THE MEAN HEIGHT IS NOW 169cm.

The new mean height is not really typical of the heights of your sample. Five out of six of the people have heights which are lower than the mean. This is why it is a good idea, when using a mean, to also give some indication of how spread out your scores are by including a *measure of dispersion*, particularly the standard deviation, we'll talk about this a little later.

Another weakness is that occasionally a mean is calculated that does not makes sense in the context of the set numbers. Imagine you are interested in how many children a typical family has in Britain. You'd collect a load of raw data, which would show how many children each family has. If you calculated a mean you may end up with a number like 2.4 children. How can someone possibly have 2.4 children? That's two whole ones and almost half of another one, just their legs perhaps. It just doesn't make much sense. In this case, another *measure of central tendency* might be preferable.

2. Median

The median is the central number in a set of scores. In order to find the median, all the numbers in a set of scores need to be put in order and the *mid-point* found. If there is an odd number of scores (Example 1) then the number in the centre of the set, once you have put them in order, is the median. If there is an even number of scores (Example 2) then the median is the number midway between the two central numbers.

Example 1
Ages of employees/years:
21 56 44 34 29

Put them in order (youngest to oldest, or oldest to youngest, it doesn't matter which!).
21 29 34 44 56

The one in the middle is 34 years
The median age of the employees is *34 years*.

Example 2
Ages of employees/years:
21 56 48 44 34 29

Put them in order (youngest to oldest, or oldest to youngest, it doesn't matter which!).
21 29 34 44 48 56

Even number in the sample – two in the middle are 34 and 44 years
The median age of the employees is the midpoint of the two *39 years*.

STRENGTHS AND WEAKNESSES OF THE MEDIAN
The main strength of the median is that it is less affected than the mean by extreme scores. When put in order, extreme scores will be at either end of the list. Being at the centre of the list, the median is likely to be affected only by the extreme scores shifting the centre point slightly. However, it is not suited to being used with small sets of data, especially when these contain widely varying scores. For example:

7 8 9 102 121

The median here would be 9, which is neither central nor typical. A central number might be something between 9 and 102, maybe 60. In cases like this the median does not provide us with a very good measure of central tendency.

3. Mode
The mode is the most frequently occurring number in a set of scores. It's the score that appears most often in your data. For example, if our data is 'days off work because of sickness' we might have a set that looked like this:

3 5 6 6 6 8 9

Here, the mode would be 6 days off sick as it occurred most often (three times in total).

Sometimes a set of numbers gives us two modes, in which case the data are said to be *bimodal*. More than two modes would make the data *multimodal*. For instance, let's enlarge our 'days off work because of sickness' data set:

3 3 3 5 6 6 6 8 9

In this case, the numbers 3 and 6 occur just as often as each other. The data is *bimodal* which means it has two modes, 3 and 6.

STRENGTHS AND WEAKNESSES OF THE MODE
The mode is useful when you want to know how often something occurs. We might want to know how many days off due to sickness most people take for instance. The mode is usually unaffected by occasional extreme scores, because they (usually) only occur once, and so will not be the most typical number and will not affect your assessment of the mode. However, the mode does not always provide a typical score; for example, in a small set of numbers when the most frequent number occurs at either end of a set of scores and is thus far from the central score. For instance, take this set of data showing the number of holiday days taken:

1 1 1 23 24 26 27 30 23

The mode here is 1 day. Not really a 'central' measure, and not really informative about the whole set of data.

Also, sometimes a set of scores does not actually have a most frequent score. Everyone may take a different number of days off perhaps, for sickness or on holiday. In these cases there is no mode. The mode is therefore best used when there are lots of numbers in the set of data and there are likely to be lots of tied scores.

MEASURES OF DISPERSION

Whilst measures of central tendency give us a typical value, *measures of dispersion* tell us something about the spread of scores or how spread out they are. Whenever you give the measure of central tendency, you should also give a measure of dispersion as both scores together tell us more about our numbers than either one alone does.

For example, the mean height of everyone in a large college might be 153cm. This does not tell us anything about how spread out the heights are. If we just give the mean value, we are hiding the true nature of the data. We want to be able to give an idea of how spread out the heights are, how much shorter that 153cm people might be and how much taller.

1. Range

The range is the simplest measure of dispersion and is calculated by finding the lowest and highest scores in the data and subtracting the smallest from the biggest.

For example, if the smallest person in the college is 135cm, and the tallest is 165cm, the range is (165-135)cm = 30cm.

STRENGTHS AND WEAKNESSES OF THE RANGE

Using only two numbers, the range is a very easy figure to calculate. It also takes into consideration extreme scores. However, these

"This might come as a bit of a surprise to you – most psychologists can't stand maths! They use it only as a tool, hardly any of them do it for fun and those that do probably don't have any friends. If you're not that keen on this lot you are not alone!"

are also its main weaknesses. In simply using only two scores, the majority of scores are ignored. These two scores could also be particularly extreme thus distorting the range.

For example, the mean height may well be 153cm, but the tallest may be 190cm and the shortest may be 110cm. Your range here would come out as (190-110)cm = 80cm. This is not really a true reflection. The majority of the heights, which cluster more closely around the mean of 153cm, are ignored; they provide nothing to the range. The range tells us very little about the actual spread of scores, for example, how spread out or clustered they are.

2. Semi-interquartile range

The semi-interquartile range is often preferred to the range because it is less sensitive to extreme scores. It is a measure of the spread of the middle 50% of scores, thus avoiding the extreme scores that might lie in the top 25% and bottom 25%. In our example, it throws away all the really tall people and all the really short people. You're now left with the most typical, most average heights, and it is on these numbers that the semi-interquartile range is calculated.

It's pretty simple to calculate really, but we'll need a set of data first. How about these numbers

1 5 6 5 4 7 7 8 9 9 8 6 6 6 9

There are 15 numbers in total. In research, this is written as 'n=15'.

STEP 1: Order the data
1 4 5 5 6 6 6 6 7 7 8 8 9 9 9

STEP 2: Calculate which one is the LOWER QUARTILE number. To do this, we use a formula (n+1)/4

n=15, so the lower quartile is (15+1)/4, that's 16/4 = 4

The lower quartile number is the fourth one!

Count from left to right until you get to 4. The lower quartile is 5.

STEP 3: Calculate which one is the UPPER QUARTILE number. To do this, we use the formula 3(n+1)/4

n=15, so the lower quartile is 3(15+1)/4, that's 3 x (16/4) = 3 x 4 = 12

The lower quartile number is the twelfth one! Count from left to right until you get to 12. The upper quartile is 8.

STEP 4: Calculate the SEMI-INTERQUARTILE range!
It's now easy. It's the UPPER quartile minus the LOWER quartile divided by 2.
That's (UPPER — LOWER)/2
That's 8 — 5/2
That's 3/2
That's 1.5!

The semi-interquartile range is usually used when the median is employed as a measure of central tendency. This is because of the similarities in their calculation: being the central score, the median divides a set of numbers in half, whilst the semi-interquartile range divides the set of scores into quarters.

STRENGTHS AND WEAKNESSES OF THE SEMI-INTERQUARTILE RANGE

The semi-interquartile range is less distorted by extreme scores than the range. However, it is still only using 50% of the numbers gathered, so much of the data does not add anything to its calculation. It's also quite laborious to calculate by hand. You have to go through all that boring ranking business and if you've got loads of data it can take an awfully long time.

3. Standard deviation

The standard deviation tells us the mean distance of scores from the mean of a set of scores. A *large standard deviation* tells us that scores are widely spread out above and below the mean, suggesting that the mean is not very representative of the rest of the scores. If there is a small standard deviation then the mean is representative of the scores from which it was calculated.

For example:
Take two sets of data, 'set A' and 'set B'
The mean of set A is 72
The mean of set B is also 72

but,

The standard deviation of set A is 14.2
The standard deviation of set B is 3.2

What does this tell us? Whilst the mean scores are the *same*, the standard deviation tells us something about the quality of the mean in terms of how well it represents the rest of the scores. The first mean has a standard deviation of 14.2 compared to 3.2, showing that there is a greater spread of scores around this mean. It is therefore less representative than the mean with a standard deviation of 3.2.

The following formula is used to calculate the standard deviation.

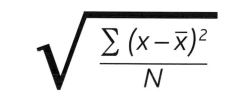

$$\sqrt{\frac{\sum (x - \bar{x})^2}{N}}$$

ASK AN EXAMINER

"Don't panic! In AS you'll never ever have to calculate one of these things. We're just showing it to you here so you know what it looks like. What you will have to know is what a standard deviation is and what it is used for. Why might it be a useful thing to see when you report a mean for instance? Now relax – maths is almost over!"

Just take a closer look at it. It's not that complicated actually, it just seems alarming. What it means, in words, is this.

STEP 1: Calculate the mean. This is written as an x with a line over it. Mathematicians call this 'x-bar'.

STEP 2: Get a sheet of paper. In a column (column 1), write down each value in your data set (in maths, each data value is referred to as 'x') Subtract the mean from it and write this value in the next column (column 2).

STEP 3: Multiply each value in column 2 by itself and write the result next to it in column 4. This procedure is called 'squaring' the value.

STEP 4: Add up everything in column 4.

STEP 5: Divide the value you get in step 4 by the number in your data set (n).

STEP 6: Finally! Take the square root of the value you get from step 5. That's your standard deviation!

Calculation of Standard Deviation

Sample data: 1, 2, 3, 4, 5

Sample size =5

Calculate the mean of the sample data

1+2+3+4+5 = 15 divided by 5 (number of items of data)

Therefore the mean = 3

Column 1 Number (x)	Column 2 Number - Mean	Column 3 (Number - Mean)^2	Column 4 Total of column 3
1	= 1-3=-2	= -2x-2 = 4	
2	= 2-3=-1	= -1x-1 = 1	
3	= 3-3= 0	= 0 x 0 = 0	
4	= 4-3=1	= 1 x 1 = 1	
5	= 5-3= 2	= 2 x 2 = 4	= 10

Sample size = 5-1 = 4

Square root of 10 = 3.16 square root of 4 = 2

3.16/2 = 1.58

Therefore the Standard Deviation = 1.58

It's long-winded but not that complicated if you take each step at a time. There is no hard maths, only adding, dividing and multiplying really, and if you have a calculator with a square root button it's pretty easy to do the last bit.

STRENGTHS AND WEAKNESSES OF THE STANDARD DEVIATION

The standard deviation is the most sensitive measure of the spread of scores as it uses every score in its calculation and it is not heavily distorted by extreme scores. The standard deviation is closely related to the mean. Indeed, the mean is *part* of the standard deviation calculation. It is therefore *the measure of dispersion to use whenever the mean is used as the measure of central tendency*. However, even though it only involves relatively simple mathematics, it is still relatively laborious to calculate.

Which measure of dispersion to use with a measure of central tendency?

A measure of central tendency should always be accompanied by at least one measure of dispersion. The choice of which to use is really down to a careful consideration of the raw data that have been gathered. However, the table below presents a simple 'rule of thumb' which can be followed – but remember, it is only a rule of thumb! Sometimes more than one measure of dispersion is a good idea, and sometimes more than one is asked for!

"WHEN USING A ...	USE A ..."
Mean ...	Standard deviation
Median ...	Semi-interquartile range, or range
Mode ...	Range

TABLES OF SCORES

A simple way to present data is to put them in the form of a table. How you construct a table will depend on the kind of data you have gathered and the research method used. It is usual to use measures of central tendency and dispersion in a table rather than the raw numbers. Which you choose to use will depend on a consideration of both the kind of data you have collected and the advantages and disadvantages of the various options.

For example, in an experiment to investigate the effects of stress on concentration you may have gathered the following data:

PARTICIPANT NUMBER	CONTROL CONDITION (NO STRESS)	EXPERIMENTAL CONDITION (STRESS)
1	6	5
2	5	5
3	7	4
4	9	3
5	8	8
6	5	4
7	6	5
8	7	6
9	8	5
10	6	7

The numbers in the table refer to the number of errors on the task.

It would be okay to use a mean of these data because there are no extreme scores which might affect them. Each condition has a modal score, so this could be used too. The median could be used here too. Since the mean can be used, then a standard deviation should be used here as an indication of spread. The table for these data could therefore look like this:

	CONTROL CONDITION	EXPERIMENTAL CONDITION
Mean	6.7	5.2
Mode	6.5	5.0
Median	6	5
Standard deviation	1.34	1.48

Summary table showing concentration scores in control (no stress) and experimental (stress) conditions. (Standard deviation rounded up to 2 decimal places.)

If it is not possible to use the mean, then either or both of the median and mode can be used. In this case a range would be chosen as the measure of central tendency. *Remember that at least one measure of dispersion and one measure of central tendency should be used to summarise the data in a table.*

Note also that the table has been given a *title*. What makes sense to you when drawing up a summary table will not necessarily be clear to someone reading it. A title explaining what the numbers in a table are and what they represent is essential if the table is to effectively communicate the findings.

Creating clear tables of data is very important, but so is being able to read a table and understand what it means. This is not difficult once you understand what a table of scores is trying to do, and understand the nature of the numbers being used in a table. For example, if a mean is being used, it is essential to be aware of what a mean score is, its advantages and disadvantages and its relationship to other numbers, especially the standard deviation.

The main thing to remember however is that *a table is meant to be a clear summary of data.* Anything which detracts from this goal makes a table less descriptive and therefore less effective.

"In the exam you could be asked to show your understanding of tables by reading information from one. You have to be able to know what each figure in the table means and to what it refers. The best way to remember this, as with other things, is to become familiar with tables. It's another case of practice makes perfect!"

GRAPHS

As well as presenting a measure of central tendency and a measure of dispersion, in order to communicate data to others we could also represent the data pictorially on a graph. The whole point of a graph is to convey information clearly. If this is not done then the purpose of a graph is lost. Therefore, care should be taken not only in choosing the right graph to use, but also in how the graph is drawn. For example, always label and title graphs, and avoid those that put looking good above being clear and simple.

ASK AN EXAMINER

"Graphs are excellent things. They save us so much time! A good graph is worth a 100 words. You'll not get as much credit as you should if you don't choose the right type though, and don't do what some people do and draw as many graphs as you can remember how to do on the understanding that you'll get the right one eventually!"

Data should not be presented in ways that are misleading. For example, the distances between points on a vertical axis should be equal, and the scales carefully chosen so that the data are not exaggerated and distorted by the look of the graph. Since graphs are intended to *summarise* data, it is not appropriate to use individual participant scores unless you are constructing a scattergram, and we'll get to that in a minute.

If data are gathered using the experimental method, then it is a usual convention to plot the dependent variable (DV) on the vertical axis and the independent variable (IV) on the horizontal axis. So, if your study investigates the type of vehicles using a road outside a local school then convention says you plot 'categories of vehicle' (car, lorry, motorbike,

ASK AN EXAMINER

"Practice makes perfect. One really important thing to be able to do, and it's something that we look out for because the exam board requires it, is that you have to be able to interpret a graph. The best way to do this is to spend a little time working out how to draw them! Once you can make them correctly you are much of the way there to interpreting them and understanding why different graphs are used in different situations."

bus, etc.) along the bottom (the x-axis) as it is your independent variable, and 'number' along the side (the y-axis) because that is the one you measure, your dependent variable, the number of each category of vehicle.

The bar chart

This kind of graph uses data which come in categories. Each thing you are counting up for these data can only fit into one category or the other. We call this 'discrete data'. For example, on a trip to a safari park or on holiday in Africa, you may collect data on how many of each animal (elephants, giraffes or lions) you see. Each time you see one of the three you add it to the appropriate column. The data are 'discrete'; a lion can only be a lion, it cannot belong to one of the other categories.

When drawing a bar chart, the vertical axis should show the *score of a variable*, for example the *mean* or *frequency* (how often something occurred), whilst the horizontal axis should show the *individual categories*, or *variables* you measured. The bars on the horizontal axis should be drawn separately with equal width and gaps.

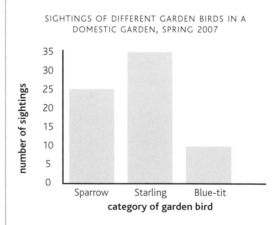

SIGHTINGS OF DIFFERENT GARDEN BIRDS IN A DOMESTIC GARDEN, SPRING 2007

*The **bar chart** need not show all the categories on the horizontal axis; it is acceptable to just show those of particular interest as a comparison. However, being selective in this way can be misleading so care must be taken. Only choosing to show certain categories does not tell the whole story.*

Histogram

Because histograms are superficially similar to bar charts they are sometimes confused. Whilst bar charts deal with discrete data, however, histograms use continuous data. This means that the variable on the horizontal axis is a scale of something, such as length or mass. For instance, your study might be to investigate the relationship between the mass of a person and how many push-ups they can do.

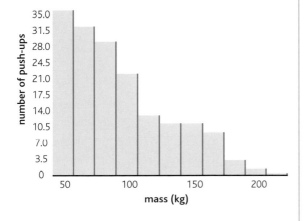

*A **histogram**: Another difference is that, unlike a bar chart, histograms do not have gaps between the vertical bars. This indicates that the horizontal axis has a continuous measure rather than distinct categories.*

The vertical axis represents the frequency of something; that is, the number of times something has occurred. The points on the vertical axis should be equal, as should the width of the columns.

Frequency polygon

A frequency polygon is just like a histogram but, instead of vertical bars, the mid-points of the tops of where the bars would be have been joined by a straight, continuous line. This highlights the continuous nature of the variable on the x axis.

NUMBER OF PUSH-UPS POSSIBLE AT DIFFERENT MASS

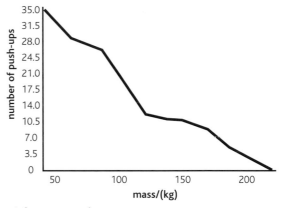

A frequency polygon.

Scattergraphs

Scattergraphs (or scattergrams, or scatterplots) are used to display data when the study is *correlational*. This means that a relationship between two variables is being investigated. Drawing a scattergraph involves plotting two scores – one score is measured along the horizontal axis and another along the vertical one. Where the two plots intersect on the graph an 'x' (plotting point) is placed.

Sometimes a *line of best fit* is added after all the scores have been plotted. This straight line is drawn to show a trend in the plots – it is an estimated line and it doesn't have to pass through any particular number of x's (plotting points). For example, it might not be entirely clear what type of correlation the graph is showing, so a line of best fit clarifies this. Generally speaking, unless there is a specific need to draw attention to this line of best fit, it is better to just leave it out.

The pattern of the points plotted on a scattergraph represents particular kinds of correlation.

Positive correlations

As one variable increases, so too does the other. The more the points resemble a straight line, the stronger the positive correlation.

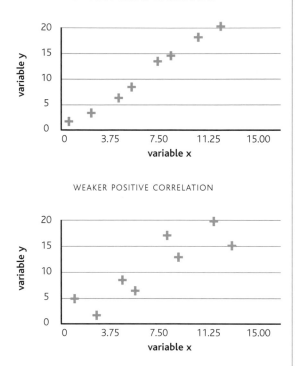

STRONG POSITIVE CORRELATION

WEAKER POSITIVE CORRELATION

Negative correlations

As one variable increases the other decreases. As with positive correlations, the tighter the points cluster around a single straight line, the stronger the negative correlation.

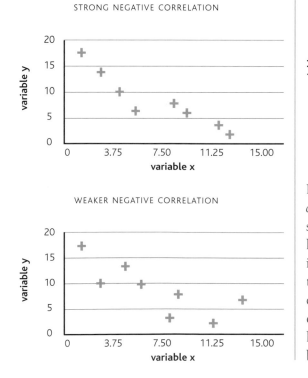

STRONG NEGATIVE CORRELATION

WEAKER NEGATIVE CORRELATION

Zero correlation

There appears to be no relationship between the variables.

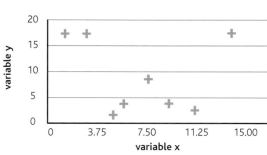

ZERO CORRELATION

Watch out! Dangerous correlations!

Earlier in the section we said that a scattergram can be a very useful in identifying some very important aspects of correlations. They're not really dangerous, but you could be misled into believing something if you didn't draw the scattergraph. Sometimes the true relationship between variables cannot be assumed from their correlation coefficient. Consider the examples given here.

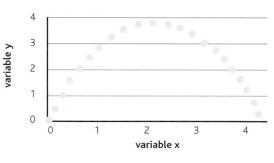

CURVILINEAR RELATIONSHIP

If you calculated the correlation coefficient for a *curvilinear* relationship you'd probably find something close to 'zero'. This is because for half of the time the relationship is positive (as y increases so too does x) but for the rest of the time it is negative (as one increases the other decreases). Taken together they cancel each other out and you get a zero correlation. By looking at the correlation coefficient you may believe that there was no relationship between the two variables at all, but you'd be wrong! There is a very interesting relationship indeed.

In psychology there is a law called the Yerkes-Dodson law. It says that performance on a task will increase as the person becomes more alert. However, if they become too alert, then performance will begin to get worse. You will come across this in Section 4 on biological psychology where we talk about stress. Variable x in this case is 'level of alertness' and variable y is 'performance on a task'. There is another example of this relationship on page 80, in Section 2 on cognitive psychology.

Does eating chocolate always make you feel better?

How about another example. How about the relationship between 'feeling of well-being' and 'chunks of chocolate consumed'? The first chunk always makes you feel much better. The second makes you feel better still and this continues until about the fifth chunk. After the sixth chunk you are surprised to experience a reduction in your feeling of well-being. What can this mean? Perhaps it was a bad chunk, so you take another one, and feel worse and worse the more you eat. At first, your feeling of well-being increases with the amount of chocolate consumed, but eventually it begins to decrease. This is a curvilinear relationship.

AN UNUSUAL RELATIONSHIP

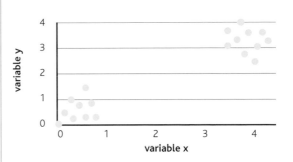

Imagine calculating the correlation coefficient for this relationship! You'd get something close to $+1$, a strong positive correlation. This is because low levels of variable y correspond to low levels of variable x, and the same for high levels (high y means high x). However, there is nothing in between, nothing for medium levels of both variables. Unless you drew the scattergraph you'd not have noticed this. Data like these mean that you really have two separate groups in your experiment. There appear to be categories of some kind here. It might be that variable x is 'ability at chess' and variable y is 'knowledge of chess rules'. If you have a low ability at chess, this corresponds to low knowledge of the rules of chess. High ability at chess means a high knowledge of the rules. There is no in-between. It follows that you need a good knowledge of chess to perform at a high level. Until you have a good knowledge, your performance will not improve.

Presenting qualitative data

Earlier in the section we made the distinction between qualitative and quantitative data. You'll recall that qualitative data is concerned largely with opinion. Qualitative data can be collected in a number of ways, including interviews and questionnaires, and assessed using *content analysis*.

The data collected in an interview can be extremely rich in detail and varied in content. It is likely that you'll have very detailed notes. To present the data you need first to organise your notes into categories that relate to the aims of your research. For instance, if you were interested in collecting data that referred to attitudes to different things, then you need to arrange the comments people make into categories that relate to the attitudes and opinions you are investigating. It might be that you were looking for opinions of ambitions and hopes for the future. These could also be categorised and ordered after the interview has taken place. When reporting the data, you can use examples of comments from these categories or present each comment in a table.

If your data are from open-ended questions that have formed part of a questionnaire you could look at all the responses you have to the open-ended questions together. Next decide on categories on which to score your answers. Just as with interviews, the content of the answers can be fitted into categories you are investigating in your research. Once this has

been done, examples of responses can be presented as they might be for interview data.

In both interviews and questionnaires the number of responses in each category you are assessing can be counted up and put into a table. These numbers can also be plotted into a bar chart. For instance, if you were using interviews or questionnaires to assess people's opinions of living in London, you may have 12 responses that say it is a great place to live, and five that say London is a horrible city to live in. You could plot these numbers on a bar chart with 'nice place to live' and 'unpleasant place to live' as categories.

"Right, Research Methods is over. Do yourself a favour though. Make sure you know this section. You are expected to apply this knowledge all over the place and we will be looking out for that ability in the examinations. A proper understanding of this lot will really help us give you marks."

Section 2

Cognitive Psychology
— Memory

WHAT YOU WILL LEARN ABOUT

The aim of cognitive psychology is to explain behaviour by understanding our 'higher' mental processes, such as memory. The word 'cognition' refers to the mental process of thinking. Because we can't directly observe thinking, it is normal for psychologists to develop what they call models of how the various cognitive processes work. Cognitive psychology is a dominant approach in contemporary psychology. You will be learning about one aspect of cognitive psychology, namely human memory.

WHAT YOU NEED TO KNOW

Cognitive Psychology is in Unit 1 of the specification. As you learn, you are expected to develop your knowledge and understanding of Cognitive Psychology, including concepts, theories and studies. This also includes a knowledge and understanding of research methods and ethical issues as they relate to this area of psychology. You also need to develop the skills of analysis, evaluation and application. Rather than just recall and reproduce information, you are expected to be able to apply your knowledge and understanding. The subject content is split into two parts:

Models of memory

- The multi-store model, including the concepts of encoding, capacity and duration
- The strengths and weaknesses of the multi-store model
- The working memory model
- The strengths and weaknesses of the working memory model

Memory in everyday life

- Eyewitness testimony, including the effects of anxiety and age on eyewitness accuracy
- Misleading information and the use of the cognitive interview
- Memory improvement strategies

Models of Memory

Tying knots in things, like a handkerchief, or tying ribbons or string around a finger is an old 'mnemonic', or memory aid. Each time they look at it, it reminds the person that there was 'something they had to remember'!

Simplifying something very complicated can help us try to understand it. In psychology we use models to help us do this.

A 'model' is something used in psychology to help us think about a hard-to-visualise phenomenon, in this case 'memory'. Models have assumptions and rules which we can test by comparing them with other models. We may also develop experiments and studies to look at how well our model explains how something works. In the section that follows we discuss two such models.

THE MULTI-STORE MODEL OF MEMORY

Where would we be without memory? Trying to remember the phone number someone has just given you or how to make a cup of tea would be impossible. Your life would be very confusing indeed. The multi-store model was the first that attempted to explain the structure of memory. Developed by Atkinson and Shiffrin (1968), it proposed that memory was not a single process but involved more than one stage and more than one kind of memory. The different stages in memory operate together, giving us the rich memory nearly all of us are lucky to have.

There is a flow of information through the memory system. First, information enters our sensory memory. Some of the information in the sensory memory is selected for further processing in the short-term memory, a temporary hold area for information that might be transferred to a more permanent, long-term memory.

SENSORY MEMORY

This part of the memory system receives and stores information from the environment through our senses.

Although there is probably a sensory store for each sense, most of what we know about sensory memory comes from research on vision and sound. The sensory store for sight is the *iconic* store.

> **ASK AN EXAMINER**
> *"The multi-store model is one of those things in psychology that lends itself rather nicely to a neat diagram. Our advice is to learn how to draw the diagram in Figure 1. It will help you remember how the different parts of the model relate to each other as well as acting as a rather good memory aid(!) in your examinations."*

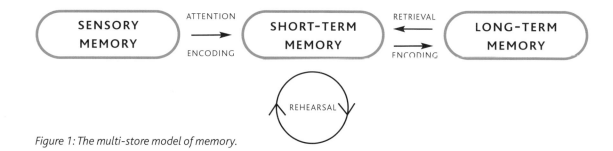

Figure 1: The multi-store model of memory.

Iconic memories last a very short time (about half a second) before the information decays and is lost.

Sensations received through our auditory sense (hearing) are stored in the *echoic* store. Research suggests that iconic and echoic memories operate in similar ways, with the main difference being the length of time it takes for information to *decay* – it can take several seconds for an echoic memory to decay and be lost.

Sensory memories last just long enough for them to be transferred to the slightly more permanent short-term memory (STM) store which we will talk about in a moment. *Attention* is an important factor in this transfer. We are bombarded with a great deal of sensory information – far more than our memory system could consciously handle. Therefore there is an attention mechanism which selects out a small proportion of the information in our sensory stores for further processing. Information which is not selected (or 'attended' to) decays and is lost. We are not aware of this selection process – it occurs at a level below our conscious awareness.

SHORT-TERM MEMORY

Material that is selected from the sensory store is transferred to the short-term store. This part of the memory system holds the information an individual is consciously thinking about at any one time.

Encoding is the process of changing information to be remembered into a form which makes it suitable for the memory to deal with. STM prefers to encode information according to its sound. For example, when we look up a telephone number from a directory, we see the number (this is visual encoding). We might also encode the number semantically, by giving it meaning (for example, it resembles an important date in our calendar). However, in both cases we have also encoded acoustically – we tend to either explicitly verbalise the material (the phone number in this case) by saying it to ourselves out loud over and over, or we may subvocally verbalise the material, repeating it to ourselves silently. This preference for sound was demonstrated by Conrad (1964) and it still remains an important study. Take a look at the Study Outline on this page for more information.

STUDY OUTLINE

Sound matters in short-term memory Conrad (1964)

Conrad used strings of **letters** to investigate short-term memory. A typical string might be 'AKJBSL'. These were presented extremely quickly on a screen for approximately three quarters of a second. The errors in recall were very interesting. B and V were muddled with P but the letter S was only very rarely muddled with P. Conrad said that it was the sound of the letters that mattered in encoding in the STM. Even though presented on a screen, the visual information must have been changed into sound (on the way to the subjects' memory) for the errors to have occurred.

Capacity is the amount of information that can be held. In his famous paper 'The magic number $7+/-2$', Miller (1956) suggested that STM could hold between five and nine items of information. For example, we would have no problem remembering a six-digit telephone number. We would, however, have difficulty remembering the telephone number

"A lot is talked of how best to pass your exams and there are a few good tricks. In this area of the specification you may be required to know the difference between the different parts of the multi-store model. A good way to do this is to talk about the differences in encoding, capacity and duration. You'll find a table on page 65 that summarise these."

CHUNK IT!

- Try this for yourself. Get a string of numbers, how about 579642356862.

- Next, find a willing participant. Ask them to try and remember the string and repeat it back to you.

- Now, reorganise the string into the following 'chunks' 579 642 356 862.

- Find someone else and test their memory for your chunks. You should find that their memory surprises even them!

if it also included the dialling code for the town in which you live. This is because the dialling code makes the number longer than 7+/-2 items (see Study Outline below).

It is not always clear what constitutes an 'item' in memory. For example, a list of 'items' could be six digits making up a telephone number or six verses of a song. The amount of information in each 'item' can be very different. We can even change the size of items by reorganising information. This process is called *chunking*. For example, we might have difficulty remembering 12 separate numbers or letters, because this is too much information for our limited capacity STM. However, if we can meaningfully 'chunk' together some of these then the task becomes much easier because it now falls within the capacity of STM. In effect, chunking increases the capacity of STM.

The length of time or *duration* that information can be held on to in the STM is also limited. If a memory is not in use, it will quickly disappear. We hold on to information in STM by *rehearsing* it, that is to say repeating it. By repeating information we are in effect re-entering the information into STM. Rehearsal then prevents information from disappearing and allows us to hold on to it for longer.

Research suggests that without rehearsal, information will be forgotten within seconds. For example, Peterson and Peterson (1959) presented the participants in their study with a trigram (three letters of the alphabet, e.g.

PMW) and then required them to count backwards in threes. It was found that after 18 seconds of counting backwards they could not remember the trigrams.

The study by Peterson and Peterson demonstrates clearly that STM has a limited duration. If we do not use information in our short-term memory it will quickly decay and be lost. It also tells us something else very important about STM – it is sensitive to *interference*. Whilst rehearsal is essential for

STUDY OUTLINE

The capacity of short-term memory is limited
Jacobs (1890)

The old ones are often the best ones and this research is certainly old! The **capacity** of the STM has been investigated by a number of people since Jacobs, including Miller in 1956 in part of his famous paper 'The magic number 7+/-2'. Jacobs investigated the **serial digit span**. He used letters and numbers but not W or 7 (they have two syllables in English). Using a metronome, he could be sure to present an item every half a second. His findings were surprising. The average digit span (numbers) was just over nine whereas the average span for letters was just over seven. He also found that as we get older we get better at remembering both digits and letters. The capacity of STM is rather limited then. From Jacobs' research we can estimate it as between five and nine items but it depends to some extent what it is we are trying to remember.

STUDY IN FOCUS

The duration of short-term memory
Peterson and Peterson (1959)

STM was studied by Brown (1958) and by Peterson and Peterson (1959) and the method has become known as the 'Brown-Peterson' technique.

What they were doing and why? The researchers wanted to know how long information remained in their STM when there was no rehearsal. In order to ensure that they were really measuring duration of STM, participants had to be prevented from repeating information to themselves (i.e. rehearsing it). The Brown-Peterson technique overcomes this and stops people engaging in this maintenance–rehearsal behaviour.

How did they do it? 24 participants were found from the student population at a university. Letter strings of three letters (called 'trigrams', e.g. ZPS) were presented over headphones – they were presented auditorily. After hearing the trigram, participants were either told to repeat what they heard or told to count backwards in threes (i.e. 100, 97, 94, 91, 88 ...) for a set amount of time, which the experimenters called the retention interval. Once the retention interval was reached participants were told to recall the trigram.

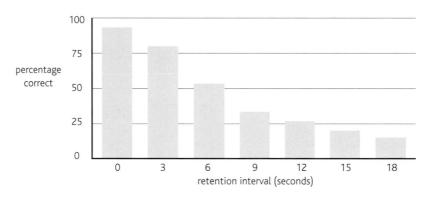

Figure 2: Data redrawn from Peterson and Peterson (1959).

What did they find? The graph shows what happened. The results are very clear. Recall was extremely good with short retention intervals but more mistakes were made the longer the person had to retain the information. At 0 (zero) seconds, retention interval, where recall was required immediately, performance was over 90%, which is extremely high. This dropped off to below 5% when the interval was 18 seconds. They concluded that without rehearsal, the length of STM (its duration) was approximately 18 seconds, and if a second task (a distractor task) is used, the duration is reduced if rehearsal is prevented; very little information remains in STM for very long.

Take a closer look
- The link between this experiment and real life is unclear. Trigrams remembered in a laboratory are not really reflective of the type of tasks our memory usually carries out.

- Using students means that the results may not relate to the general population. Students at university are, hopefully, of above average intelligence so a memory task may show different results with them than if another group of people had been chosen.

holding on to information in STM, the rehearsal process is itself easily disrupted – if we are disturbed when rehearsing, the information is, again, lost.

Some researchers distinguish between maintenance and elaborative rehearsal in short-term memory. *Maintenance rehearsal* just keeps information in the short-term store, for example by repeating something over. With *elaborative rehearsal* the information is used and changed in some way. The way that information is rehearsed is important to whether it will ultimately be made more permanent. It is through elaborative rehearsal that information is passed into the long-term store.

LONG-TERM MEMORY (LTM)

Long-term memory is where information is held for some period of time, beyond that of sensory and short-term memory. This could be anything from a few seconds to a lifetime. It is where all our knowledge of the world is stored – every skill, every piece of knowledge, no matter how mundane, is stored here. Without the ability to hold on to information for a period of time, we would not be able to do even the most simple everyday task.

Information in LTM is encoded in terms of its meaning rather than sound. This can be seen in the kinds of errors we make with everyday memory. For example, if we are trying to remember the word 'barn', we are much more likely to remember, by mistake, words which are meaningfully related, such as 'shed' or 'hut', than we are to recall the word 'born', even though it is only one letter different and sounds similar. This would be a sound-based error and is a very unusual mistake to make in LTM. Another word for 'meaning' is semantic and many researchers refer to long-term memory as *semantic memory* because of the tendency for memories in LTM to be organised in terms of their meaning.

The *capacity* of our long-term store seems unlimited. Estimating an upper limit is impossible – the amount of information

	STM	LTM
ENCODING	Mainly based on sound (acoustic)	Mainly based on meaning (semantic)
CAPACITY	Limited (7+/-2 pieces or chunks of information)	Unlimited
DURATION	Short (less than 30 seconds without rehearsal)	Long (potentially a lifetime)

Table 2: A summary of the differences between the short and long-term memory stores.

which LTM can hold is certainly greater than the size of the brain and number of brain cells suggests. There is plenty of evidence from research that, under the right conditions, people can remember a great deal of information, far more in fact than they would ever predict they could remember.

A study by Bahrick et al (1975) suggests that long-term memories may last a very long time. However, although often described as our permanent memory store, information in our long-term memory is not necessarily 'permanent' (although some researchers believe that information never really disappears, it just becomes harder to find or retrieve).

STRENGTHS

1 The distinction between STM and LTM has been supported by studies of people with amnesia. For example, Shallice and Warrington (1974) found that one such person, whom they called KF, could do no more than recall one or two items in a digit-span test. However, he appeared to have no problems with his LTM. An LTM/STM distinction can also be seen in people with Korsakoff's syndrome (a memory disorder caused by long-term alcohol abuse). People suffering from this have problems with their LTM but have reasonably intact STM. For example, they might hold perfectly normal conversations with you but have no memory of them later. Evidence from brain-damaged people seems to clearly suggest that STM and LTM are independent from each other.

2 The multi-store model offers a good explanation for the *serial position effect*. Murdock (1962) found that when asked to remember a list of words, participants can generally remember the first few words (the *primacy effect*) and the last few (the *recency effect*) more easily than those in the middle. The multi-store model explains the primacy effect because the words learned at the start are more likely to have been rehearsed and transferred into LTM, whilst the recency effect occurs because the words are still in STM.

3 Many of the features of the three stores are supported by research. For example, Conrad (1964) supports the idea of acoustic encoding, Peterson and Peterson (1959) support the idea of a limited duration in STM, whilst Bahrick et al (1975) support the relative permanency of LTM.

WEAKNESSES

1 The assumption that there is one single short-term store is inaccurate. For example, it assumes that STM operates using sound-based information, i.e. information is encoded acoustically. Investigations of patient KF by Shallice and Warrington (1974) however showed that this is not the case. They found that his STM problem was restricted to verbal material, such as words and letters. His performance in short-term memory tests for non-verbal sounds, such as a door bell or telephone ringing, was normal. This suggests that the short-term store must have at least two different sound-based mechanisms – one for dealing with verbal and one for non-verbal sounds.

2 The multi-store model suggests that there is one long-term store. However, other researchers have suggested that this is not the case. For example, Tulving (1989) has made a distinction between episodic and semantic memory. Episodic memory relates to a particular experience you may have had, for instance, whether there was a number 7 in the telephone number you were trying to remember. Semantic memory is the memory for what we can recall in the form of general information, for instance whether a dog is a mammal. Similarly, procedural memory (our memory of how to do things) is also long-term. The multi-store model does not distinguish between these different types of LTM.

STUDY IN FOCUS

How long is long-term memory?
Bahrick et al (1975)

What were they doing and why? Bahrick et al were interested in the duration of long-term memories. They used participants from the US because of a tradition there of producing a 'yearbook' with pictures of and a statement about all those students who left school in the same year. Many previous studies had shown that much of what we need to store is rather unmemorable and therefore difficult to retrieve. By using meaningful information from their participant's past, they hoped to avoid this problem and tap into what they called very long-term memory (VLTM).

How did they do it? The experiment contained three main tasks. **First**, participants had to remember as many names of their ex-classmates as they could (free recall). **Second**, some pictures were taken from their yearbook and mixed with others that the participant would not previously have seen. This set of photos was then given to the participant to identify those which they recognised (visual recognition). **Third**, participants were asked to recognise names of people from school (verbal recognition).

What did they find? The findings were interesting. In all cases free recall was not great, with those having left school within 15 years being only 60% accurate and only 30% accurate for those having left 48 years previously. They found that verbal and visual recognition was highest (about 90% accurate!) in those who had left school less than 15 years previously. 48 years after leaving school, accuracy had dropped off to 70% verbal (names) and 80% visual (faces). We can conclude from this that long-term memories can last a VERY long time. It also shows however that long-term memories are not permanent since, with the passage of time, they get worse. The study also illustrates something which is already familiar to us all – that we remember something better by recognition than recall. Recognition involves being given some kind of clue which aids the search for information in LTM. Recall is more difficult because it doesn't have this advantage.

Take a closer look
- This study shows that memory can persist (last) for much longer than had been previously shown. This could be because this study used more meaningful stimuli, allowing a more realistic measurement of long-term memory than if artificial or meaningless stimuli were used.

- When you meet old school friends the first thing you do is talk about, well, school and old school friends! It might be that the participants had rehearsed their recall of names and faces and had reviewed their old school photographs many times before the study took place. This lack of control could have meant that the results were not terribly reliable and so the very long-term memory found could be because of this regular rehearsal.

- Pictures were taken from a yearbook in the study. It is unclear whether people gave their permission for researchers to use these pictures. This could be considered an ethical infringement on the part of the researchers.

3 According to the multi-store model, rehearsal in STM is essential for information to be encoded into LTM. However, the model may be exaggerating the role of rehearsal. Shallice and Warrington (1970) showed that some brain-damaged subjects who have lost STM can still have LTM of events that occurred after the damage so information must be reaching LTM without passing through STM. Everyday observations of how our memory works also suggests that rehearsal is not necessary for information to become established in long-term memory. For example, we often seem to be able to recall information at a later date with no obvious rehearsal having taken place earlier. You might remember something you heard on the radio in the morning or a conversation you had with a friend on the bus last week. It appears that STM does not have to come between sensory memory and long-term memory for material to be retained long term.

WORKING MEMORY MODEL

The working memory model was developed by Baddeley and Hitch (1974), partly in reaction to what they saw as an underestimation of the complexity of STM in the multi-store model. For them, STM was a much more active and important part of memory, since it was this that, on a moment-by-moment basis, does all the work in the memory.

The working memory model is the one which has attracted most interest from researchers in recent years, and as a result the model has undergone quite a few changes. In this section we will give you a good overview of the basic features of this important theory.

According to Baddeley and Hitch (1974) the multi-store model of memory underestimated the importance of short-term memory (STM). They claimed that STM is not just a passive storehouse of information; it is more complex and active than a temporary 'waiting stage' for information before long term memory (LTM).

Working memory is that part of the memory system where new information is held temporarily and combined with knowledge from LTM. Roughly speaking, working memory holds all the material that you are thinking about at any one moment. For many psychologists working memory is our 'consciousness'.

The idea that working memory is an active system can be seen when we do relatively simple tasks like mental arithmetic. For example, if we are asked to add two simple numbers like 43 and 29 we must first get some information from our LTM for knowledge of the meaning of numbers and the rules by which numbers are added. The result of the sum 3+9 will need to be stored whilst we work on 40+20, then the outcome of both of these mini-calculations will need to be combined. It is also very likely that the visual memory is being used – numbers are conjured up in our mind's eye and perhaps manipulated on the equivalent of 'mental rough-paper'. For instance, you might imagine yourself or someone else doing the sum on a piece of paper, or on a whiteboard in a classroom.

It is clear then that not only do apparently simple mental tasks require complex

ASK AN EXAMINER

"There are only so many questions we can ask you in the exam and we can only ask you what the specification allows us to. Here's a tip. The specification tells you that you MUST know about the multi-store model AND the working memory model. Remember, you need to know about BOTH."

processes but also that working memory sends and receives information to and from LTM. For the majority of people these mental maths tasks need to remain rather small – our working memory system rapidly struggles to cope with mental arithmetic of more than a few steps and digits. This suggests that the system has a limited capacity – it keeps active a small amount of information for a limited time whilst it is processed. Because information in working memory is fragile and easily lost, it must be kept activated to be retained. For example, other tasks demanding working memory will interfere with the mental calculation if allowed and, after the calculation, the information about it in the working memory will rapidly fade. There are, of course, individual differences in our use of working memory – for example, the size or capacity, or the use of visual imagery differs from person to person and these differences can result in people demonstrating very different memory abilities.

The working memory model developed by Baddeley and Hitch is a multi-component system. Unlike the single STM of the multi-store model, working memory has several separate but connected, parts (or modules). This means that the components can either work together or independently. If two tasks make use of the same component, they cannot be performed successfully together. If two tasks make use of different components, it should be possible to perform them as well together as separately.

THE CENTRAL EXECUTIVE

This controls the activity of working memory. It has a 'supervisory' function, hence the name 'executive'. It 'manages' what goes on, just as a manager in an office decides what work should and should not be done at any one time. Just as in an office some jobs are often given priority, in memory the central executive will direct attention towards the most important

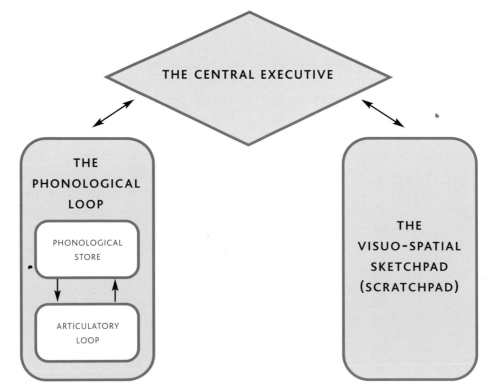

Figure 3: The working model memory.

information at the expense of other, less important information. The other modules are 'slaves' to this one. It integrates the actions of the other systems so that our thinking processes appear coordinated. It is also modality-free, that is, it works independently of the senses.

THE PHONOLOGICAL LOOP

This component is an auditory store, rehearsing sound-based information to prevent the rapid decay (loss) that would otherwise occur. It has two subdivisions, both of which hold a limited amount of verbal information for a short amount of time. The phonological loop has two parts.

1. Phonological store

This is often referred to as the 'inner ear' and, as this suggests, it deals with the perception of sounds and, in particular, speech.

2. Articulatory loop

This is linked to speech production, often referred to as the 'inner voice'. It is a verbal rehearsal system, used to prevent the decay of verbal material by saying things over and over and in order to hold on to verbal material until it is spoken. According to Baddeley (1986) the articulatory loop is a rehearsal system of up to about two seconds duration. That is, we can hold as much information here as we can rehearse in two seconds.

THE VISUO-SPATIAL SKETCHPAD (SCRATCHPAD)

The visuo-spatial sketchpad (sometimes called the 'scratchpad') is often referred to as the 'inner eye'. This component can be considered a visual and spatial version of the articulatory loop. It's called a visuo-spatial sketchpad because it deals with information by visually organising it, rather as you would by laying items on a table or drawing them on a piece of paper. It maintains visual information in working memory. For example,

it is the 'mental rough paper' we conjure up in our mind's eye when we do a mental sum, or it is the mental map we use when we want to find our way around.

STRENGTHS

1 The working memory model has received support from studies of the effects on memory caused by brain damage. Farah et al (1988) reported that a patient (LH) was good at spatial tasks (ones that involved organising things due to their spatial or physical relationship) but not very good at tasks that required visual imagery. This shows that visual and spatial tasks require a separate system, just as the working memory model tells us they do.

2 Brain imaging studies have suggested that the components of working memory are related to distinct areas of the brain.

For example, Cohen et al (1997) found that there was higher brain activity in a part of the brain known as the prefrontal cortex during a task when the central executive was working. The phonological loop is related to activity in completely separate parts of the brain that deal with two different parts of our language system. These are Wernicke's area, which is involved in speech perception, and Broca's area, which is involved in speech production. Also, the regions of another part of the brain (the *occipital lobe*) involved in visual processing become active during tasks which require the visuo-spatial sketchpad. It seems that tasks needing different parts of the working memory model use different areas of the brain, giving us evidence that there really are separate systems at work.

3 The role of the phonological loop in rehearsal has been supported by studies of the word-length effect. This refers to the tendency to immediately recall short words better than long words. The working memory explains this phenomenon by saying that the articulatory loop has a very limited time-based capacity (i.e.

as much as we can rehearse in two seconds), and so because small words take less time to say we therefore remember more of them than long words. Baddeley et al (1975) found that they could make the word-length effect go away by using up the articulatory loop, that is, preventing it giving an advantage to short words. They did this by getting participants in their study to repeat simple word sounds over and over whilst learning short or long-word lists. This repetition fully occupied the articulatory loop, so that no advantage was gained by a word being small.

4 As the model predicts, it seems that if we do two tasks at the same time and those tasks need the same systems, then our performance will suffer. Baddeley and Hitch (1976) showed this experimentally. Take a look at the Study Outline opposite for more information.

WEAKNESSES

1 Most of the research into the working memory model has focused on the 'slave' components rather than the central executive. The result is that the central executive which, remember, governs the whole system, has relatively little experimental support. For example, the central executive is said to have limited capacity but the actual capacity has not been established. Also, it is not clear how it functions 'modality-free'. Much of the terminology used to describe the central executive is vague and it may turn out that the complexity of it has been greatly underestimated.

2 Research suggests that there are individual differences in working memory, for example, in attention, capacity and duration. Engle (1994) suggests that differences in abilities such as reading, spelling and writing are directly related to these individual differences in working memory function. It is not clear from the working memory model, as it is currently understood, why these differences

exist. This has opened up a rich area of research though, with Barrett et al (2004) suggesting that working memory capacity can play a very significant role in many areas of social, personality and cognitive psychology.

3 Working memory is said to be a temporary holding area which contains information taken from LTM, as well as new information. Information from working memory may be made more permanent by being encoded in LTM. Although most researchers agree that the theory provides a useful explanation of how working and long-term memories communicate and work together, it is not clear really how the communication is managed.

STUDY OUTLINE

Doing two things at once
Baddeley and Hitch (1976)

The working memory model says that memory is made up of different components. Baddeley and Hitch (1976) showed that if two tasks require different components then performance on each will be reasonably OK. If however, the two tasks require the same component then performance suffers.

In their experiment, Baddeley and Hitch had two tasks:

Task 1: Two statements (A then B) were given to the participant. The participant was then given a screen with statement B followed by statement A, or statement A followed by B. Participants were required to state whether the order was true or false as quickly as possible. This occupies the central executive.

Alan Baddeley

Task 2: This could be one of three different 'tasks'.

1. Participants were required to repeat 'THE THE THE THE THE' over and over again. This occupies the articulatory loop.

2. Participants had to say random digits out loud. This occupies both the articulatory loop and the central executive.

3. Participants were not required to complete a second task.

The results showed that when task 1 was combined with version 1 or version 3 of the second task, performance on task 1 was not affected. Participants were just as fast at making the true or false decision. When combined with version 2 of task 2, speed dropped significantly. This shows that doing two tasks that use the same component of memory causes difficulty. When different components are used, performance on the tasks is not adversely affected.

Memory in Everyday Life

How observant are you? Do you notice every detail of those things that go on around you? Can you remember what everyone in the queue at the cinema was wearing last time you went? Memory is an extremely useful tool that relates to many things that happen in our daily lives. A shopping list is just a memory aid, but one you may find that you use very often, perhaps even on a daily basis.

In our daily lives, we take memory for granted. Regular routes, favourite songs and exams all involve our memory. In the section that follows we look at an application of memory research and we also look at how we might go about improving our memories or at least use them more effectively.

EYEWITNESS TESTIMONY

It's all very well us talking about different theories but what use can we make of them? In this section we'll introduce an area of study that is a direct application of memory research: eyewitness testimony. Being vigilant and taking in the details of your surroundings is more difficult than you think.

"Take your time."

Our daily lives are full of distractions that hold our attention and we often miss rather significant events going on around us. Occasionally, very startling events occur, such as accidents or robberies, and people are called upon by the authorities to say what they saw. The implications of providing inaccurate information can be catastrophic. Innocent people may go to jail or, in some parts of the world, they may be put to death, just because inaccurate testimony has been given. In this part of the book, we investigate the accuracy of eyewitness testimony and look at how a personal memory of an event might be reconstructed.

EYEWITNESS TESTIMONY

Human memory is not a passive and inert system but an active and dynamic one, constantly changing and updating itself. Stored material is reorganised and transformed because of new knowledge and the passage of time. New information is put into the right format for storage, and memories can be modified and changed as they are encoded. Cognitive psychologists agree that most memories are, at least in part, reconstructions of events, rather than exact versions. It seems that when we remember something, say an event from several years ago, we do not replay in our minds a faithfully recorded version of it. Rather, we retrieve some accurate fragments and then fill in the gaps around this using common sense and logic.

We don't 'record' everything. We tend to be selective about what aspects of events around us we attend to and thus commit to memory. Our expectations also play a big part, causing us to memorise and recall things as we expect them to be, rather than as they really are. According to Loftus (2003) "memories are the sum of what (people) have thought, what they have been told, what they believe." We are generally not consciously aware of the reconstructive nature of our memory and only occasionally is it brought to our attention. For example, sitting with a group of friends remembering a shared experience from some years ago you might notice considerable variations in how different people recall the same event. Some versions might be so at odds with your own that you might even begin to wonder if you were there at all!

STUDY IN FOCUS

Reconstruction of automobile destruction:
An example of the interaction between language and memory
Loftus and Palmer (1974)

What were they doing and why? Loftus and Palmer wanted to find out whether memory could be influenced by the type of questions people were asked, so they ran two experiments to see if this would happen.

What did they do in Experiment 1? In their first experiment Loftus and Palmer showed a series of car crash videos to 45 students. They asked each student to fill in a questionnaire after they had seen a video. The questionnaire had lots of questions. One of them was important. It asked:

- **'How fast were the cars travelling when they .... into each other?'**

The blank space was filled with one of:

- **'Smashed, Collided, Bumped, Hit, Contacted'.**

The participants were split into five groups. Each group received a sentence with a different verb.

What did they find? The results were very interesting indeed. As you can see from Figure 4, the word placed at the end of the sentence made a huge difference to the estimated speed of the cars. The sentence 'How fast was the car going when they smashed into each other?' drew the fastest estimate of all.

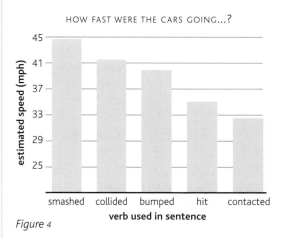

Figure 4

Averages of estimated speed
'Smashed' – 40.8 mph
'Collided' – 39.3 mph
'Bumped' – 38.1 mph
'Hit' – 34.0 mph
'Contacted' – 31.8 mph

It is clear that information presented after an event can significantly influence our perception of that event. Here, the word used in the question influenced people's perception of speed. Loftus and Palmer concluded that this alteration may be one of two things. It could be *distortion* (where memory is changed) or it could be a *response-bias* (where the word influenced a judgement, perhaps because they were not sure of the speed, so the word 'suggested' a speed of some kind).

What did they do in Experiment 2? In a similar experiment, 150 students were shown videos of cars crashing and then they were presented with the questionnaire. This time the question hidden in the questionnaire only used the verbs 'hit' and 'smashed' (so there were only two experimental groups). A third group was not asked about the speed at all. In addition to this, participants were asked another question a week after the experiment. That question was:

- Did you see ANY broken glass?

There was no broken glass in the film used.

STUDY IN FOCUS

What did they find? Average estimates of speed depended on the verb used in the sentence, just as in Experiment 1. The estimate of speed with 'smashed' was higher than that for 'hit'.

The result of the 'broken glass' question can be seen in Figure 5.

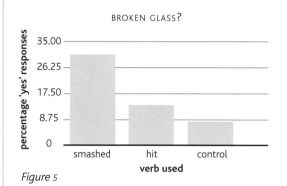

Figure 5

Percentage of those indicating they had seen broken glass
'Smashed' group - 32%
'Hit' group - 14%
'Control' Group - 12%

It is very clear that questions following an event can influence our memories, so much so that those who were asked about the speed of the cars using the word 'smashed' felt that there was indeed smashed glass. Those not asked about the speed, and those in the group where the word 'hit' was used, were much less likely to remember seeing glass. Using the word 'smashed' builds the concept of 'broken glass' in memory and, as a result, people really felt that they had seen broken glass in the film they had watched the previous week.

This supports a **reconstructive memory hypothesis** where information retained at the time of an event can be altered or influenced in some way by information presented after the event. Once all this information is linked together, separating it becomes at worst impossible, and at best extremely difficult indeed.

Take a closer look

● The experiment was very well controlled. The participants in each group were well matched and the images they saw were the same, allowing the researchers to present exactly the same stimuli to each of their many participants. In the laboratory, researchers do not have to rely on chance to ensure that each participant gets the same stimuli. They use skill and great care to control the situation.

● Watching a video is not the same as seeing an event in real life, so the experiments lack validity. In a real life situation participants would experience a much richer perceptual scene. There would be different smells, noises and distractions, all adding to the experience and all likely to add to the type of memory they may have for the event. In a laboratory, we cannot possibly expect researchers to develop the experience like this. What's good about a lab study is that it is carefully controlled (see earlier evaluative point).

● You can't really tell if a memory is 'distorted'. It could be a 'demand characteristic' where participants respond in a certain way because they think they should.

● Loftus and Palmer, like so many other academic researchers, used participants who were university students. It may be that these students were very good at remembering things and that they would not want to look silly in front of teachers and researchers by responding in a certain way. The result may have been influenced by this and so may lack validity because the sample used was not from the 'general population'.

RECONSTRUCTIVE MEMORY

Sometimes psychology really seems to have something to say about what is happening in the world. In this, the early part of the twenty-first century, the news seems to be full of stories of knife crime and gun crime, and anyone would think that all people under the age of 19 are going about ready to stab or shoot anyone who comes near them. Of course this is nonsense, but because it's in the news, people will think that when they witness a violent incident, a gun or a knife is more likely to have been involved. Think back to an early memory, perhaps the first time you rode a bike or went to the park on your own. Your memory of this event will be a reconstruction of many snippets of information that may have changed or altered over time. The details of these snippets may change because when you recount the event to a parent, they may help you fill in the gaps. 'Then I cycled down the path without my stabilisers' you may say, but your father might reply, 'No you didn't; you went on the grass. I made sure of that just in case you fell off!' The next time you recall the event, your memory may be of riding, not on a concrete path, but on the nice soft grass.

ASK AN EXAMINER

"Memory is a very odd thing. If you ask someone about an event you shared many years ago, it's really strange how your two memories will often be very different. When you answer questions in the exam, you might think about giving examples in your writing. This illustrates your answer and shows that you really understand. You could use something from your own experience. We've used the example of learning to ride a bike here but you may have a better example. Don't be afraid to use it but make sure that it illustrates the problem you are working on. If it doesn't, it won't get you any marks!"

"RONNIE BULLOCK was sentenced to 60 years in jail for kidnapping and raping a young Illinois girl. Edward Honaker spent a decade in a Virginia prison for sexually assaulting a woman at gunpoint. Kirk Bloodsworth was shipped off to Maryland's death row for raping and strangling a 9-year-old girl. All three of those men were convicted in part because eyewitnesses or victims firmly placed them at the scene of the crime. But not one of them was guilty. They were among the first convicts to be exonerated by DNA tests proving that someone else was responsible." (Miller 2000)

We have the impression that vivid memories are true and authentic even though they may be only partially accurate. On a day-to-day basis the reconstructive nature of memory doesn't really impact upon our daily activities. However, it does have an impact in situations where accuracy of memory is of vital importance. One area where psychologists have studied this impact is in the effect it has on eyewitness testimony in the courtroom. It is crucial to the legal process that eyewitnesses to crimes give testimony that is both accurate and reliable as there are major consequences otherwise. For example, Cutler and Penrod (1995) estimate that as many as 4,500 people are wrongly convicted in the US each year because of faulty eyewitness testimony – 0.5% of the annual convictions for serious crimes.

How reliable are the testimonies of eyewitnesses? Loftus and colleagues believe that the memories of eyewitnesses are prone to all sorts of influences and distortions and in many circumstances are very unreliable. Loftus and Palmer (1974) demonstrated that even subtle changes in the wording of a question can produce changes in responses to

"If you've not noticed already, we'll spell it out for you: psychology progresses by people doing experiments and making observations. We can use our knowledge of research methods to help us understand what they were doing and why, and better still (it gets you marks!) evaluate the work. In Loftus and Palmer's 'smashing experiment', as we like to call it, some of the evaluative points come straight from an analysis of research methods. Take a look and see. Revise it thoroughly once for one topic and then use it everywhere else! Easy."

a witnessed event. Take a look at the Loftus and Palmer study, one of the most famous studies in 'modern' psychology, to see how simple it is to alter a memory by altering a single word in a question.

THE INFLUENCE OF ANXIETY ON EYEWITNESS TESTIMONY

Anxiety is a sense of unease and worry and is an entirely normal feeling to have occasionally. You may not be surprised to hear that people who witness a criminal event often experience some degree of anxiety. The event might involve some threat to their personal safety or they might empathise with ('relate to') a victim. Giving evidence can also cause anxiety, not just because the witness has to recall possibly unpleasant events but also because it is a serious, pressured situation. Given that it is well-established that high levels of anxiety can impair the ability to both encode and retrieve memories, this has implications for eyewitness testimony.

Peters (1988) conducted a study in a health clinic where people were receiving inoculations (an anxiety-causing event). The experience of participants was manipulated so that they met a nurse (who gave the injection) and a researcher for brief but equal amounts of time. One week later the participants were asked to identify the nurse and researcher from a selection of photographs. It was found that the researcher was more readily recognised than the nurse. Whilst it was suggested by Peters that the anxiety of the injection directly affected the accuracy of memory it has also been suggested that the attention of the eyewitness was drawn away from the nurse and other details of the situation by the syringe that she was holding. This indicates that witnesses to a crime might be distracted by specific aspects of a scene, in this case something that could be interpreted as a weapon.

Loftus et al (1987) monitored the gaze of participants and found that, when shown a film of a crime, they tended to focus their gaze on the gun used in the robbery. When questioned later, these participants were less able to identify the robber and recalled fewer details of the crime than other participants who saw a similar film minus a gun. This phenomenon is called 'weapons-focus'.

A number of studies support the idea that the presence of a weapon increases anxiety, focuses perception on only certain aspects of a scene and ultimately makes a person a less reliable eyewitness. Mitchell et al (1998) on the other hand suggest that, rather than being threatening and anxiety-inducing, the presence of a weapon is seen as unusual and it is this novelty that creates the weapons-focus effect.

The violence of an event can also be a cause of anxiety. Loftus and Burns (1982) made participants in their study watch a film of a crime. Some participants however saw a version with an extremely violent scene (a young boy being shot in the face). When questioned about the events in the film, those participants who saw the non-violent version of the film recalled much more detail of the crime than those who witnessed the more violent crime. It seems that the shock of the event disrupted storage of other details, both before and after the actual violent scene.

It may be however that many of these findings are, at least to some extent, the result of the way in which the data were collected. These were, after all, artificial experimental situations and not adrenaline-fuelled natural conditions. Naturalistic studies have provided some contradictory evidence. For example, Yuille and Cutshall (1986) interviewed 13 witnesses to a real-life shooting incident in which someone had been killed. Despite the anxiety which the experience must have caused, their accuracy of recall did not seem to be significantly affected. The witnesses appeared to be resistant to leading questions, they stuck to their original impressions of the event and there was little evidence of memory reconstruction.

The influence of anxiety on memory could be said to follow the *Yerkes-Dodson law*. This suggests that there is an ideal or optimum point at which anxiety actually helps memory. Above and below this optimum, anxiety causes more harm than good, interfering with our memory processes, with very low and very high levels of anxiety impairing our memory.

THE INFLUENCE OF AGE ON EYEWITNESS TESTIMONY

Research has consistently shown that the age of an eyewitness is an important factor when considering the reliability and accuracy of eyewitness testimony. As we grow older, the amount of memories we have to store increases. Our memory size itself does not increase, so we work out ways of storing these new memories. Our experiences in life can influence the types of things we remember and the types of things we forget. For instance, older people may pay more attention to some aspects of a scene whereas younger people may be drawn to pay attention to other aspects. Memory then, may not be a constant thing; it can change as we age and the way in which we use it can change also. Whilst adults of all ages have traditionally been

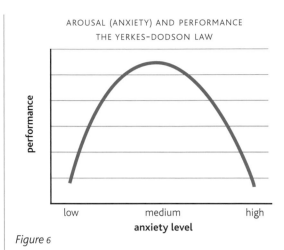

Figure 6

"*The Yerkes-Dodson law relates to all sorts of things. How about arousal and exam performance? If you are not bothered at all, then you'll not be motivated and you'll not do very well. If you are so bothered and anxious that you can't stay out of the bathroom for more than two minutes, you'll also fail. If you are bothered by just the right amount, you'll be motivated and alert and will perform at an optimum level. It's the 'three-bears phenomenon' all over again. Too much or not enough won't do it for you; it's got to be just right. Remember that when you come to revise!*"

required to give testimony, children are increasingly being asked to give legal testimonies as witnesses to events they have seen or experienced.

Eyewitness testimony from young children

There has been considerable research in recent years on factors which might influence the reliability of the testimony of a child witness. It is not always the case, but generally speaking, the younger the child, the less information they provide spontaneously. Because of this, interviewers need to encourage children to give more detailed or specific responses. Unfortunately the danger is that the child is likely to be influenced by both *cognitive factors* (the way that the questions are asked affects how they are answered) and *social factors* (the child is more suggestible because of the power and status of an authoritative adult). Many factors have been found to influence child testimony and three are considered here – suggestibility, language abilities and memory processes.

Suggestibility

Research seems to suggest that children are more sensitive than adults to leading questions and that the younger the child the more likely they are to be influenced. Ceci et al (2000) found that in children aged 3 to 12 years, 3 and 4 year olds were most susceptible to having their memories altered by leading questions. They argued that the memories of 3 to 5 year olds are both weaker and fade faster than those of older children and that this makes them more uncertain about the detail of events. This leaves children more suggestible and their memories vulnerable to reconstruction. Warren et al (2005) gave children and adults a story to read and then asked them 20 questions; 15 of these questions were misleading. They showed that children were more likely to be influenced by the leading questions than were adults. In a second experiment the participants were told that the questions were 'hard' and that they may make 'mistakes'. When asked the questions again, the effect of the misleading questions was reduced in all age groups tested, including the children.

Language abilities

A child's ability to comprehend and answer the interviewer's question is also a factor likely to affect their recall. This is clearly demonstrated in a study by Goodman and Schaaf (1997). They found that the more complex the question, the more likely a child was to give an inaccurate answer. For example, a question such as 'The pirate engaged in blowing bubbles during the course of the puppet show, is that not true?' was less likely to result in an accurate response than one phrased in a more child-friendly way (e.g. 'The pirate blew bubbles, didn't he?'). This suggests one aspect of ensuring the accuracy of a child's eyewitness testimony is not to test them on skills that they do not have at their developmental level. Complex language skills come with age and by avoiding complex language or long sentences the child's weaker language ability need not get in the way of their testimony.

Memory processes

Young children tend to recall less complex memories than do older children and adults. This might result in testimonies that appear incomplete and unconvincing. Goodman and Reed (1986) conducted a study whereby 3 and 6 year olds and adult participants took part in a simple game (a variation of 'Simon says') with an unfamiliar adult male researcher. When they were questioned five days later about this event it was found that whilst the 3 year olds recalled less detail, it was no less accurate than the recall of the 6 year olds or adults. It does seem however that whilst the accuracy of child testimony is approximate to other age groups, the types of error made do seem to differ. Saywitz (1987) asked children in her study to listen to a description of a crime recorded on audiotape. They then had to recall the incident as best they could and then repeat this after five days. The recall of the youngest children (8 years) was less detailed but just as accurate as older children (11 and 15 year olds). However, the 8 year olds were more inclined to embellish their recall with contradictions and exaggerations.

Eyewitness testimony and the elderly

Research seems to suggest that, as with very young children, the elderly are especially susceptible to the effects of leading questions when recalling eyewitness events. In one study by Cohen and Falkner (1989) young adults (average 35 years) and elderly participants (average 70 years) were shown a silent film-clip of a kidnapping. Ten minutes later, participants were given one of two versions of a written summary of the crime to read: one was an accurate account whilst the other contained inaccurate information. Later on, all participants were tested for their memory of the event. It was found that elderly participants were much more likely to be influenced by the incorrect information and to include some of the incorrect material from the written account in their own recall of the film.

The increased suggestibility of elderly eyewitnesses is not supported however in a study by Coxon and Valentine (1997). In their study, participants were shown a video recording of a staged crime. Both young children (7 to 9 years) and elderly people (60 to 85 years) were less accurate in their recall of events than young adults (16 to 18 years). Coxon and Valentine put this down to immature cognitive development in children and advancing age in the elderly. However, whilst children were found to be more suggestible to misleading questions, the elderly participants were found to be no more susceptible to misleading information than young adults. These findings suggest that testimonies from elderly people are less reliable but this is due to *less complete* recall rather than increased susceptibility to leading questions. Searcy et al (1999) indicate that this diminished memory for events can result in lower accuracy and more false-positive identifications in a line-up. It seems that eyewitness testimony is not, perhaps, as accurate as people sometimes make out. In the elderly, for instance, the accuracy of their performance in a task where a culprit is picked out of a line-up may be very different from that of a child or of a younger adult.

THE COGNITIVE INTERVIEW

It is essential in criminal investigations that accurate information is gathered. Kebbell et al (2002) reported that 36% of 159 UK police officers surveyed, believe that eyewitnesses are 'always' or 'almost always' the most important source of leads in an investigation. However, the same survey revealed that 53% of officers believe that they 'never' or 'rarely' got as much information from witnesses as they wanted. One method developed in recent years to improve the amount of accurate recall from witnesses is the *cognitive interview*.

According to Waddington and Bull (2007), the cognitive interview is an approach to interviewing that seeks to encourage accurate and thorough recall of specific events. It is based on two basic principles of memory:

1 Information is *organised* such that memories can be accessed in a number of ways. For example, there are many ways to arrive at the memory for what someone was wearing – you might get to thinking about fashion, shops and types of clothes. These might provide you with a route to your memory trace. Or it might be a good idea to recall a series of actions, such as thinking of a morning routine, in which you choose clothes to wear for the day, taking a jacket from a hook before you leave. This may help you remember what a person was wearing when they committed a crime you had witnessed.

2 Memories are *context-dependent*, meaning that retrieval will be more effective if the cues present at the time of storage are reinstated. We'll talk a little more about how to do this in a moment.

MEMORY FOR A FACE

Photofits often seem to look rather unrealistic. I mean, would you trust the man in this photofit? Have you ever seen anyone who really looks like this? Just for a second, think about someone you know very well, take a piece of paper and describe their face. Use as much detail as you possibly can from memory. Now get a photo of them and see what details you've missed. Even with extremely familiar faces, the amount of detail is really hard to describe to someone else, so imagine how difficult it would be if you'd only seen a stranger for a few seconds. It's no wonder these photofits often look like aliens!

This is a 'photofit'. Sometimes the police use photofit software or get artists to draw a face that a witness describes. Getting the information they need in enough detail might be done using a cognitive interview. Careful interviewing may be needed to extract enough information.

Cognitive interviews have no standardised questions; they are not time-limited (witnesses must feel confident that they have time to think, talk and repeat themselves as they need), and the interviewer remains silent during witness recall (for example, the interviewee is not interrupted and asked to clarify something). Whilst the interviewer will be recording proceedings and may be taking notes, clarification and elaboration is sought only after recall has seemingly ended. Even then, this must be phrased in *open-ended* and *non-leading* ways. For instance, you cannot ask the witness something like, 'He was wearing a green jacket, isn't that right?' because this leads the witness to a conclusion and, as we already know, the language used in the question can influence our memory of the event itself. We want the real memory, not one that our badly-worded question has planted!

The cognitive interview uses four techniques:

1. Reinstate the context
The interviewee needs to be returned, in their mind, to the situation (the context) in which the event occurred. Recreating the exact conditions in which the witness experienced events is not practicable but if something resembling the original mood and environment can be conjured in the imagination of the interviewee, then more details of the event might be recalled. An interviewer might do this by asking the interviewer to think back to before, during and after the event and recall their environment (where they were, what they were doing) and their mood (how they were feeling – frightened, bored, cold, hot, etc).

2. Change sequence
Whilst traditional interviews might ask a witness to recall events in chronological order, the cognitive interview differs. A witness would be asked to recall events in all sorts of different orders. For example, a witness might be asked to begin their witness account at any point in events, or to repeat their account but this time reversing the order of events. This ensures that the witness is not skipping details which might be important and might help to

fill in any gaps which might exist in a story told chronologically.

3. Change perspective

The interviewee is asked to recall events from another perspective. For example, witnesses might be asked to think what another observer would recall of the event, or be asked to consider the event from another point of view. It is important however that the witness is encouraged to report what they actually know and not to be overly imaginative or inventive, so as to avoid inaccurate material being inserted into the account.

4. Report everything

Regardless of how fragmented or irrelevant thoughts might seem, eyewitnesses are encouraged to report everything. Whilst it is likely that this unrestrained recall will produce a lot of irrelevant material, it is likely to throw up details which might otherwise be inadvertently mentally 'edited out'.

Some research indicated that the cognitive interview was not as effective as it could be, due to poor communication between the interviewer and interviewee. This led to the development of the enhanced cognitive interview. This new version includes the techniques of the original cognitive interview but with added instructions to interviewers. In the enhanced technique, the interviewer is encouraged to help the interviewee speak slowly and carefully; they are told not to overload the interviewee but leave pauses between questions and answers. Perhaps, most interestingly, the new technique encourages the interviewer to tailor their language so that the interviewee feels more comfortable with it. For instance, a young witness may use different language than an elderly one and this can make the difference between accurate and misleading evidence. Fisher et al (1987) found that this enhanced cognitive interview was more effective,

> ### STUDY OUTLINE
>
> ## The cognitive interview
>
> According to Geiselman et al (1985) the cognitive interview is a more effective method of gathering information from eyewitnesses than other methods that might be used. They found that the cognitive interview produced an average of 41.1 correct statements from eyewitnesses, compared to 29.4 using a standard police interview and 38.0 correct statements using hypnosis.
>
>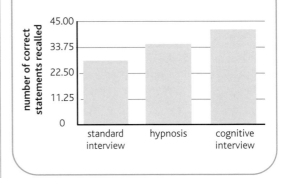

producing more correct eyewitness statements than the original cognitive interview (57.5% compared to 39.6%). This has even been replicated in naturalistic settings. Fisher et al (1990) trained Miami police officers to use the enhanced cognitive interview and found that 46% more information was obtained using this, with over 90% of this material proving to be accurate.

EVALUATION

1 The cognitive interview can be used with relatively little training. Compared to a no-training control group, Geiselman et al (1986) found that 35% more correct information could be obtained with relatively brief guidance on cognitive interview procedures given to interviewers, without loss of accuracy. However, to be effective the quality of training in cognitive interviewing is crucial. Stein and Memon (2006) introduced the cognitive interview to Brazil, a developing country where witnesses are likely to have very low income and education. The interviewers were trained in cognitive interview techniques for three days and practised the techniques over a three-month period, receiving feedback during this time. It was found that, compared to standard interview procedures, the cognitive interview produced more recall with at least as good accuracy. It seems that even in quite challenging environments, the cognitive interview is a robust enough technique to show benefits over other methods in gaining reliable eyewitness evidence.

2 As Milne and Bull (1999) pointed out, the cognitive interview is a form of effective communication and its success depends on the skills of the interviewer. Whilst interviewers can be trained, it is difficult to assess their competence as they are doing more than simply following a set of learned technical skills. Similarly, it is very easy for an inexperienced or slightly clumsy interviewer to ask questions that might be considered as 'leading' the witness. The accuracy of information from the cognitive interview may be subject to the same problems as regular interviews where the wording of the question might play a very significant role.

3 Eysenck and Keane (2005) point out several limitations with the cognitive interview. For example, although there is greater recall with the cognitive interview, several studies have suggested that this produces a small increase in erroneous recall. Another problem is that because context does more to improve recall than recognition, the cognitive interview does not help with the recognition of a culprit, for example, from photofit evidence. Thirdly, the cognitive interview is most effective when the interview follows shortly after the event. It becomes less effective as the passage of time between event and recall increases.

IMPROVING MEMORY

Some people will tell you that they have a terrible memory.

Memory could be regarded as a tool: the more you use it, the better you get at using it. There are good ways and bad ways of using any tool, and in this section we look at how different techniques might be employed in improving memory, possibly the most important tool of all.

Think of memory as a pile of boxes, each containing some information from our past. A teddy-bear perhaps or the smell of cut grass on a summer's day. How the information is arranged might help you find it if you need it. If all the boxes are just thrown into the attic of your mind, then retrieving the correct information could take a very long time and may sometimes be impossible as the information becomes mixed up and decays. A better idea might be to think about what memories go together when packing the boxes and to carefully categorise the boxes when storing them. You might also use a sensible, organised method to search through them when trying to find something. Memory is not, of course, this simple but the analogy of boxes in an attic is useful here. In this section we will discuss various methods that have been proposed for improving memory.

ORGANISATION OF MEMORY

There is hope for those of us who think our memory is not very good. Ericsson (2003) has shown that the brains of those with particularly good memories do not differ significantly from others' brains. It seems that it is the skill employed in organising our memory that counts. Human memory is highly organised. When we put information into long-term memory it is normally done in such a way that it is relatively easy to find. If this was not the case then we would not be able to search such a vast store of information as efficiently as we usually do. However, our frequent experiences of being unable to recall information when we need it suggests that our memories are not as well organised as they could be. Material that is well organised is easier to learn and remember than 'random' bits and pieces of information. It follows then that the more organised information is, the better memory will be. Although research appears to consistently support the idea that there is a relationship between organisation and memory we cannot say that organisation causes good memory. It may be that a good memory causes organisation!

Evidence to suggest that information is organised at storage comes from De Groot (1966). Chess players, ranging in ability from 'grandmaster' to 'beginner', were shown a set of chess positions for a few seconds. Each was then asked to reconstruct them as accurately as possible. It was found that the more accurate memories belonged to the players with the most experience. Apparently, the more experienced chess players had an existing memory for chess which organised the new information at storage.

Once information is put into long-term memory in an organised way it tends to stay for some time – from minutes, to years, to a lifetime. However, to use information it must be retrieved from storage. That this can be a problem is an everyday experience – for example, when we know that certain information is in LTM but we can't easily recall it (this is the 'tip-of-the-tongue' phenomenon). It follows then that memory will be improved by anything that makes the retrieval process more effective, regardless of whether or not information is organised during storage.

> **ASK AN EXAMINER**
>
> *"This area of the specification lends itself rather nicely to examples. It will help your revision and your question answering if you include analogies. Think of memory as a warehouse full of crates. How would you organise it to make everything easy to find? Well, when a new crate arrives to be stored, you'd need to have experience to know where that type of crate should go. It's the same with organisation of memory."*

Retrieval cues

One way to improve retrieval is to narrow down the search – to have information about the location of information in memory. Knowing the likely whereabouts of a piece of information in our vast permanent memory store will make the search for it much more efficient. When we commit something to memory, we also encode along with it other information, such as where the information fits in with existing knowledge, our mood and physical state. These are the retrieval cues that help us locate the information during retrieval. Retrieval cues can be sounds, sights, tastes, smells or indeed anything that helps you find information.

Research has demonstrated the importance of retrieval cues. For example, Tulving and Pearlstone (1966) found that participants who were given words to remember could recall more words when given their categories than participants who were not given categories. In this study the word-list category acted as a *retrieval cue* and allowed the participants to remember more words.

State-dependency

Other important retrieval cues are the physical or emotional state you were in when you learned the information. Memories can be state-dependent, meaning that information can be more easily recalled when you are in the same physical or mental state as when it was encoded. For example, Bower et al (1981) found that the participants in their study could recall more sad than happy information from a story read whilst in a sad mood. It seems that a person's emotional state can act as a cue to memory. The kind of mood state is irrelevant, as long as there is a match between the mood at encoding and mood at retrieval. This is an example of something called the *encoding specificity principle*. However for retrieval cues to be effective, they must be encoded at the same time as the information that is to be later recalled.

STRATEGIES FOR IMPROVING MEMORY

There are many techniques for improving memory. Using a *mnemonic* can be an effective way to make memories more permanent. Mnemonic is the word given to something which improves memory. They help to integrate new information with information already in memory. In one way or another, mnemonic techniques help to improve the organisation of memory, either at the storage or retrieval stage. In the section that follows we will describe a number of these mnemonic methods and evaluate their usefulness.

Mnemonic 1: The method of loci

'Loci' is Latin word meaning 'places'. This method of improving memory works by first imagining a very familiar place – such as the town where you live or your house. Each item in the to-be-remembered list is then 'pegged' or 'hung' on various locations. When you want to remember the items you take an imaginary walk around the location – you will pass the memories hung at various places. The method was apparently invented by an ancient Greek called Simonedes while at a dinner with a number of guests. He stepped out of the building during the dinner, and while away from the table the roof collapsed, killing everyone inside. Simonedes used the method of loci to remember who was there and where they were sitting during the recovery of the bodies of the dinner guests.

The 'method of loci': Visualising a familiar place such as your house and pegging things to be remembered around it can help us to recall them later.

Clearly, this method relies on the power of visual imagery – how well you can 'use' pictures in your imagination will dictate the extent to which the method of loci is effective. Although it might appear that the loci method is only good for lists, with good imagery it can be used to remember more difficult material. The words in a list can serve as aids to memory by triggering further memories – they are in effect acting as retrieval cues. Also, by making the imagery more complex and meaningful, more detailed information can be recalled when imagining the location.

DOES IT WORK?

1 The use of mental imagery to assist memory and improve understanding is well established; one might even call it ancient. For example, relatively few people in ancient Greece and Rome could read or write. In order for people to remember things it became usual to become very skilled with their memory and the loci method was one of the favoured techniques. In ancient Greece, politicians used the method to great effect in remembering their speeches.

2 In linking verbal pieces of information with visual images the loci method is using two coding systems – verbal and visual. According to the *dual code* theory our memories are encoded using both visual and auditory codes. The use of two codes in the method of loci creates a much stronger memory than by using a single one.

3 Research shows that significant improvements in memory can occur when this technique is used. Crovitz (1971) reports one study where two groups of participants were required to memorise a list of 32 words. One group used rote learning, whilst the other used the loci method. Much greater recall was observed in the latter group (78%) than the rote group (25%). To this day it is the favourite method used by those involved in memory competitions.

4 When we get older our memories often begin to malfunction or do not work quite as well as they used to. Yesavage and Rose (1994) have shown that the richer the visual image in the method of loci, the better the memory. So if we make the image personal to us, perhaps even of emotional importance, then our memory for it will be better. The research shows that the method of loci not only works but it can be developed and improved!

"Sometimes students tell us that they don't see the point of studying something. Algebra or Shakespeare may sometimes seem a little detached from real life. This bit of psychology is about as useful as anything can possibly be. Try the method of loci or one of the other mnemonics next time you have to remember something, when you are revising perhaps. Tell all your friends. They'll thank you for it when you've helped them pass their exams. Remember though, like any skill, practice makes perfect, so you'll need to work at it a bit."

Mnemonic 2: Narrative chaining

Narratives are short stories that contain the information that has to be remembered. Unlike memorising by repetition (rote), the narrative puts the unorganised information into a meaningful context. The first item to be memorised is connected to the second, the second with the third and so on through a story or 'narrative'. In combining the elements to be remembered you end up with a 'chain' of information, where one item or element is associated with another in a series.

DOES IT WORK?

1 Research suggests that the narrative technique is a very useful method for improving retention. Bower and Clark (1969) asked participants in their study to learn 12 lists of disconnected words, each list containing 12 words – 144 words in all. Participants were either told to use the narrative method (where short stories were created using the 12 items in each list) or were given no special instructions. It was found that participants in the 'narrative' group recalled an average of 94% of their items, whilst the other 'non-narrative' group recalled an average of 14%.

2 Narrative chaining is another technique that uses mental imagery to some extent. In this case, there is a meaningful interaction between separate items represented in the narrative. Bower (1970) suggests that this kind of interactive imagery is far more effective than other methods where images are used with no interaction between them.

Mnemonic 3: Acronyms

An *acronym* is a word that is formed out of the first letter of a string of other words. These words are typically difficult to associate. For example, **ROY G BIV** can be used to remember the colours of the rainbow – Red, Orange, Yellow, Green, Blue, Indigo, Violet. Another kind of acronym forms phrases out of the first letter of each word in a list. For example, **Richard Of York Gave Battle In Vain**, does the same job with colours of the rainbow as ROY G BIV. Those of you who have ever eaten a famous brand of confectionary, or who live in York, may like to know that **Rowntrees Of York Gave Best In Value** does the job just as well!

DOES IT WORK?

1 Although acronyms can be very useful memory aids, they do have some disadvantages. Just because something is memorised it does not mean that it is understood – remembering is not the same as knowing. Acronyms are very useful for *rote* memory, that is, for information that is going to be recalled exactly as it is learned. The most permanent memories however are based on understanding and meaning.

2 It isn't always easy to form an acronym – not all lists of to-be-remembered things lend themselves to this technique. It may be that in order to form the acronym you have to change the order of items in a list. This is not always helpful when the order is an important factor.

3 Even if an acronym can be formed, it needs somehow to be committed to memory or it will be forgotten. The amount of effort this sometimes takes means that the costs of using acronyms might not be worth the benefits you receive.

4 Research suggests that not all acronyms are equally as effective. Bower (1972) showed that if you make material meaningful and form a visual image then it is easier to remember. For instance remembering the word-pair DOG-BICYCLE is easier to remember if you visualise a dog on a bike. For the same reason a meaningful acronym that can be 'visualised' is better than an acronym that is not meaningful. For instance, the acronym for notes on a musical score F, A, C, E – (face) is meaningful and can be visualised, perhaps as a face drawn over a piece of music, or a face made out of musical notes. The acronym for the International Union of Pure and Applied Chemistry is IUPAC, impossible to visualise and tricky to recall.

Mnemonic 4: Keyword technique

This technique was developed by Atkinson (1985) and can be used to effectively increase vocabulary in a foreign language. We can think of it as a three-stage process.

Step 1: The acoustic stage

A sound is recognised in the pronunciation of a foreign language word that has an English equivalent. This isolated sound is the *keyword*.

Step 2: The visual-image stage

An image is formed combining the English sound and the translation of the foreign word – the visual image links the keyword and the *to-be-remembered* word.

Linking the things to be remembered into a story provides a useful form of organisation which can significantly improve memory. In this story, a number of items on a shopping list are linked into a simple narrative.

A TRIP TO THE SHOPS

The shopping centre was busy and he decided to have a coffee. Why not, he deserved a treat, and chose a muffin to go with it. The muffin had chocolate flakes, his favourite. The man next to him was smoking a cigarette, which made him sneeze. He reached to his inside pocket for a tissue, and found that he had left them at home on the table, in the hall, next to the fruit bowl. Once he had finished his coffee he called in at the chemist and bought some more, taking the opportunity to buy some toothpaste at the same time.

Things to remember from the story:

Coffee, chocolate, cigarettes, tissues, fruit, toothpaste.

Step 3: Rehearsal

The image is then *rehearsed*, which helps commit it to memory. When we encounter the foreign word again, the image comes to mind which then generates the English meaning.

Here's an example of how it works with remembering vocabulary. The French for bottle is 'bouteille'. It sounds a bit like 'boot'. You could visualise an old boot with a bottle in it.

Although keywords are most often single words, they do not have to be. Nor is the method restricted to foreign language vocabulary. It can also be useful for remembering less familiar plant names, Latin names for things in medicine or chemicals you may use in chemistry. For instance, 'forsythia' is a shrub that has lovely yellow flowers in early spring. 'Bruce Forsyth' is a well-known British entertainer. 'Forsythia' may be remembered as a 'Bruce Forsyth bush'. You may visualise Bruce Forsyth next to the bush, conducting a game show perhaps. The sounds of the names are almost identical, providing a perfect keyword.

The method has also been used to help people remember names. A name that sounds like something – for instance the British cognitive psychologist Philip Beaman may be visualised as a delivery lorry filled with bees; just as a milkman would carry milk, a Beaman would carry bees! If you knew Dr Beaman, you might visualise him driving the lorry. Now you can associate his name with his face.

DOES IT WORK?

1 Roberts (1985) gave participants ten minutes to learn 20 unfamiliar words. Some participants used the keyword method whilst the remainder used a more traditional rote method. Immediate recall of the words did not significantly differ between the two groups (69% and 62.3% respectively). However, one week later the members of the keyword group were found to have retained nearly twice as many words in their memories (40.6% against 21%). It seems that the keyword method improves the longer-term retention of information.

2 One problem with the keyword method is that it does not work well in situations where it is difficult to identify keywords. Put simply, many ideas and words do not lend themselves to this system.

3 It has been suggested that if keyword is used to learn a language then it is useful only in the early stages where building a vocabulary is important. It has less application to the development of grammatical skills, for example.

4 The keyword technique might also be more useful for some languages than others. For example, Zhang (2005) suggests that keyword is a useful method for Chinese students learning English as a foreign language, whilst Atkinson and Raugh (1975) indicate that it has only limited usefulness for American undergraduates learning Russian vocabulary.

5 Wang and Thomas (1995) have suggested that if learners are given the keywords then vocabulary learned using this technique may be more readily forgotten than vocabulary learned in other ways. The memory links provided might not match the type of knowledge that the learner already has (their knowledge base) – it seems that the technique works best when learners themselves generate the keywords and images.

Mnemonic 5: Elaboration

In a previous section on the multi-store model of memory we learned that information remains in our short-term memories only for a very brief time unless it is used in some way. We can hold on to information longer by rehearsing it. One type of rehearsal is *maintenance rehearsal*. This is where information is simply repeated so that it is maintained in short-term memory. For example, we might repeat a telephone number we have been given over and over until we use it. This type of rehearsal does not normally lead to a long-lasting memory for the information. Curiously though, it can lead to the experience of rehearsal entering our long-term memory. This can lead to a 'false impression' that we can remember. For example, we can remember the experience of repeating the telephone number so believe that we should also remember the number itself. In reality, material in short-term memory is quite easy to disrupt so when maintenance rehearsal is interrupted in some way the information can be lost very easily. Clearly, if you want to remember information, even a short time later, something more effective than maintenance rehearsal should be considered.

ELABORATE!

We often use 'elaboration rehearsal' without thinking about it. Consider the telephone number 911350. Take two friends. Give one of them the number for 20 seconds and tell them to try and memorise it. Tell the other the number but tell him to remember it as 350 Porsche 911 cars, and that reversing the numbers gives the correct telephone number. Leave it for a day or so then ask your friends what the telephone number was. The person who elaborated is more likely to give you an accurate response.

A second and more effective form of rehearsal is *elaborative rehearsal*. Here, more attention is given to information. Rather than simply repeating information, we use and change it in some way. We 'organise' the information, relate it to information already in our memory store, and make the information more meaningful. For example, with the example of the telephone number, rather than repeating the number over we could make it more meaningful – maybe it is like a friend's number already in memory but with the last two digits switched, or maybe a rhyme could be added to it. This kind of elaboration not only keeps information in short-term memory longer (increasing the chance for permanent storage in long-term memory) but also builds extra links to existing knowledge (increasing the number of retrieval cues)

It seems that if we want to improve our memories, that is, to increase the chances that we remember something, we need to make the information as meaningful as possible. One method is to perform elaborative rather than maintenance rehearsal.

DOES IT WORK?

1 Elaborative rehearsal involves processing information in the memory system at a deeper, more semantic level. Craik and Tulving (1975) found that giving the information to be remembered more meaning and more links to other things will help people recall it later on. This is called the 'levels of processing' approach. The deeper the level, the more elaborately it is encoded and the more secure it is.

2 Elaboration occurs as a result of already existing interest and knowledge. Therefore, the success of elaboration will be affected by the motivation of the learner. For example, Morris et al (1981) found that football fans recalled a list of football results far better than did non-football fans.

WANT TO KNOW MORE?

If you'd like to read a little more about the areas covered in this section, you should be able to find these books without too much trouble.

Baddeley, A (1997) *Human Memory: Theory and Practice*, Psychology Press

Baddeley, A (2004) *Your Memory: A User's Guide,* Carlton Books Ltd

Brown, D (2007) *Tricks of the Mind*, Channel 4 Books

Higpee, K (2001) *Your Memory: How it Works and How to Improve It*, Marlowe and Co.

Section 3

Developmental Psychology – Early Social Development

WHAT YOU WILL LEARN ABOUT

Developmental psychology focuses on changes to behaviour and mental processes that occur from conception, the moment at which development begins, to old age and ultimately death. Some psychologists emphasise the role of the environment and learning experiences in shaping behaviour, whilst others prefer to focus on biological forces that shape behaviour such as hormones, genes and evolution. These assumptions influence a vast range of behaviours such as personality, language, aggression and emotions. The effect of early social development on later behaviour has received particular attention. A consideration of how development is affected by interactions with others is also important. It is this area of developmental psychology that is the focus of this section.

WHAT YOU NEED TO KNOW

Developmental Psychology is in Unit 1 of the specification. You are expected to develop your knowledge and understanding of Developmental Psychology, including concepts, theories and studies. This includes a knowledge and understanding of research methods and ethical issues as they relate to this area of psychology. You also need to develop the skills of analysis, evaluation and application. Rather than just recall and reproduce information, you are expected to be able to apply your knowledge and understanding. The subject content is split into two parts:

Attachment

- Explanations of attachment, including learning and evolution
- Types of attachment, including secure and insecure attachment
- Attachment and culture
- The disruption of attachments, including privation and institutionalisation

Attachment in everyday life

- The impact of day care on social development
- Implications of research for child care practices

Attachment

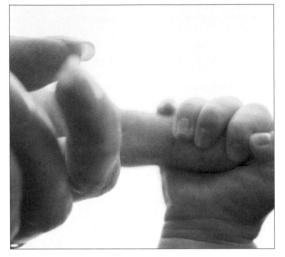

Developing from a tiny fragile newborn into a grown adult can be a difficult process.

Development does not stop at adulthood. We go on developing from infancy to adolescence, through adulthood until eventually we reach old age. The traditional understanding of developmental psychology is as 'child psychology', whereby infants mature, gaining abilities we usually take for granted as adults. An aspect of developmental psychology that is of great importance is the relationship the newborn has with the person, or people, caring for them. These relationships are described in terms of attachments, and it is to this area that we now turn.

EXPLANATIONS OF ATTACHMENT

One of the most important events occurring during the first year of life is the development of attachments.

An attachment is an emotional connection or bond between the child and the principle caregiver, characterised by mutual affection, frequent interaction, a desire for proximity (to be close) and selectivity (the child wants to be with the caregiver rather than anyone else). Whilst the caregiver is usually the mother, attachments can also form with the father or some other person.

Whilst caring for the physical needs of the child is important (e.g. food, comfort, security), attachments involve more than this and are important in the emotional and social growth of the child. Children who receive consistent and responsive caregiving have been found to develop an attachment that is suggested to have advantages for intellectual, social and emotional development throughout childhood and early adolescence.

A number of theories have been developed to explain why attachments occur. One early theory suggested that attachment is, as with any other behaviour in infancy, something which is learned through reward and punishment. Another approach suggests that attachment behaviours evolved because they increased the infants' chances of survival. This approach sees humans as complex animals and therefore human behaviour is governed by the same principles of evolution that apply to other animal species. This means that findings from animal research might offer useful insights into the origins of some aspects of human behaviour.

THE EVOLUTIONARY PERSPECTIVE

Much of human behaviour is explained using the theory of evolution, therefore the theory is very important to psychology.

The idea here is that as one generation develops into the next through reproduction, those reaching the age at which they have children will be those who have managed to survive development and will have the opportunity to pass on their genetic make up to their offspring. *Attachment* is part of an animal's instinct. Forming an attachment may give a newborn an advantage over a newborn that does not form an attachment, by ensuring a good source for food and protection from harm. Similarly, a *biological parent* who is careful to form an attachment is more likely to see their child develop into adulthood. It is their instinct to form an attachment. If this happens, then the child (who carries their parents' genes) will hopefully reproduce and pass these genes on to the next generation. By this reckoning,

EVOLUTION: NATURAL SELECTION

The theory of evolution was developed by Charles Darwin. Actually, the idea had been around for a little while, but it is Darwin who really developed it into a theory and it is he who is traditionally credited with this hugely influential approach. Very briefly, the theory says that all species evolve. We'll concentrate on 'man' because that's what we are really interested in here. The theory says that we have developed over the centuries from early man to the complex creatures we are today. Our brains have increased in size, our bodies have become more upright. It is the evolution of our cognitive abilities that have given us the wheel and satellite navigation, the farm and the refrigerator. Darwin sets out some basic 'rules' which explain how evolution progresses – and how it is that species change over the years to become ideally suited to their current situations – one of which is **natural selection**.

The idea is rather simple and elegant. Animals produce many young, more than could possibly survive. Each time they reproduce, the offspring are all very slightly different from the parent and from one another. These young vary in their abilities to cope and reach maturity. Those without these abilities perish, and it is the strong, clever ones who reach adulthood. They are the strongest of their generation. When they breed, and produce more young, the process continues. As the generations go by, the aspects of the animal that help them survive (called traits) are passed on, and become widespread in the population. This is the basis for the idea of **the survival of the fittest**, not a phrase Darwin himself used, but one which was used later. In evolution fitness does not refer to your ability to look good on a Saturday night, or how fast you can run a marathon. Evolutionary fitness is a measure of how successful an animal is at passing their genes on to the next generation. The more offspring that carry their genes, the fitter they are.

there is an evolutionary advantage to forming attachments.

Research with animals

Some of the most famous work in this area has been done with animals. Studying animals in the wild and in captivity can help us develop theories and ideas of how attachments are generated and maintained.

The work of Konrad Lorenz

Biologist Konrad Lorenz (1935) noted that the young of precocial species (that is, animals that are mobile soon after birth) had a need to quickly recognise and follow a caregiver if they were to survive. For example, ducklings are mobile and able to feed themselves soon after hatching. This however is not enough and in order to help them survive a very vulnerable time in life they will need to stay close to an adult. The 'parent' will provide some direct protection from predators and the elements,

Konrad Lorenz

and the ducklings will learn many skills necessary for later life, such as evading predators and interacting with other members of its species. An essential requirement for a duckling therefore is the ability, very early on in life, to recognise which particular object in its environment is its caregiver. The ability to develop this recognition is innate (inborn) and is called *imprinting*. As well as individual survival, imprinting is important for the survival of the species. It enables animals to recognise members of their own species and to learn species-specific behaviours. This ensures that when it comes to mating, sexual behaviour is directed towards other animals of the same species.

Imprinting. Lorenz was interested in how young animals recognise their caregiver.

According to Lorenz, there is a *critical period* early in life during which this imprinting occurs. He demonstrated this by hatching goose eggs in an incubator and presenting the goslings with various objects for differing periods of time. He found that the goslings had a tendency to imprint on the first large moving object that they were allowed to follow for more than ten minutes. In one study Lorenz allowed some goslings to imprint on him. He then mixed up these goslings with others that had properly imprinted on a mother goose, and others that still had not imprinted. Lorenz found that when they were released from an enclosure, the goslings made straight for the 'parent' to which they had imprinted – some went to him and some to the mother goose. The goslings who had not imprinted on anything wandered about, seemingly without purpose.

His studies also indicated that this imprinting had to occur within the first 36 hours of life. According to Lorenz, the effects of this critical period are irreversible – with appropriate imprinting the young would recognise and follow its parent, but outside of this critical period imprinting would not happen. If the young did not properly imprint then they would be unlikely to survive for long by themselves without an adult to guide and protect them. Inappropriate imprinting would also have long-term consequences even in circumstances where survival was not at risk. For example, Lorenz claimed that imprinting determines the choice of sexual partner in adulthood – he found that goslings which had imprinted on him showed a preference for humans over other geese when it came to mating!

EVALUATION OF LORENZ'S THEORY OF IMPRINTING

1 Research has shown that imprinting can occur outside of the critical period. Because of this, many researchers prefer to use the term *sensitive period* to refer to a time when an animal will more readily imprint. For example, Sluckin (1965) showed that if young birds are hatched and reared in isolation then the normal critical period can be extended.

2 The effects of imprinting may not be as permanent as Lorenz suggests. Kendrick et al (2001) demonstrated that if sheep and goats are cross-fostered at birth, many of their behaviours grow to resemble those of their foster species. For example, male goats fostered to sheep very soon after birth show a strong preference later on for socialising and mating with sheep, even when raised around other members of their own species. However,

"Take a look at point 2 in the evaluation of Lorenz's theory. There are differences in the nature and consequences of imprinting both within the same species and also between species. We need to be careful to consider this when we apply the findings of these animal studies directly to humans. Whenever you read an animal study ask yourself whether there are problems of application to humans. It's a good evaluation point if you apply it properly!"

their study also showed that the effects of this early experience are not necessarily permanent. Males kept in mixed flocks for three years persisted with their preference, but females kept in similar conditions tended to revert to preferring their own species in one to two years.

The work of Harry Harlow

Harry Harlow

The importance of this early attachment can also be seen in studies of monkeys reared in isolation. Harlow (1962) removed infant monkeys from their mothers soon after birth and kept them in cages with two artificial substitute 'mothers'.

These 'mothers' were similar wire models except that one was covered with cloth. Harlow found that the infant monkeys became quite attached to the cloth-covered 'mother', using it as security when stressed or to cling to when in need of comfort. Given a choice between a bare wire mesh 'mother' with milk and a cloth covered one without, infant monkeys preferred to spend all their time clinging to the cuddly 'mother', only going to the wire alternative to feed. The infant monkeys, it seems, considered tactile comfort to be more important than having a nearby food supply.

One very important finding from Harlow's studies was that this early experience with surrogate mothers had long-term consequences for the monkey. The physical health of the monkeys was not affected by their experience, but they did show problems in their emotional development. The monkeys developed into timid, fearful adults with poor

social skills; they were clumsy and often unsuccessful during mating, and seemed to lack normal monkey parenting skills. For example, females were observed to lack basic nurturing skills and often behaved very cruelly towards their offspring. Harlow concluded that these behaviours were due to the monkeys having been deprived of maternal care when they were young, something which Harlow called *maternal deprivation*.

Further studies by Harlow however suggested that it wasn't necessarily *maternal* deprivation that the monkeys were suffering from, but *social* deprivation (being deprived of the company of other members of the same species). He raised monkeys in almost total isolation, allowing them only 20 minutes a day to play with other monkeys of the same age. Unlike monkeys who were not given this opportunity to interact, these monkeys appeared to grow up to be normal adults.

It seems that monkeys need physical contact with a live, affectionate caregiver during a critical period in infancy (the first six months) in order to develop normal social

Harlow used two 'mothers' in his research: a soft cloth-covered mother, and a more basic wire mother. In this picture the monkey is standing on the cloth mother.

and emotional skills, and that some contact with other monkeys helps to limit the negative effects of this deprivation. If they did not attach during this period then there would be permanent social and emotional damage to the monkey.

EVALUATION OF HARLOW'S STUDIES

1 It has been suggested that it is not true to claim that Harlow's monkeys had suffered maternal deprivation. Deprivation means that something you once had has been taken away. This is not what happened to the monkeys in Harlow's study however – they had no maternal care at all. Strictly speaking then, Harlow's monkeys did not suffer deprivation at all, but *privation* – that is, never having had something.

2 The idea that contact comfort is important has been supported in some studies with humans. For example, Klaus and Kennel (1976) found that mothers in hospital given extra time in physical contact with their newborn babies during the first weeks of life showed stronger attachments one month later than those who did not have this experience. This is evidence that early contact helps us form attachments.

3 For Harlow, contact was important but he failed to acknowledge that there are different kinds of contact. In humans at least it seems that it is not the *quantity* of contact with a mother figure that is important but the *type* of that contact. For example, Fox (1977) suggests that Israeli children who have most contact in their upbringing with nurses still have the strongest attachments with their mothers.

4 Whilst Harlow's findings are useful they are, nevertheless, the result of research with monkeys which are quite different from humans in evolutionary terms. It is debatable whether or not the findings of these studies could or should be directly applied to humans. Humans have an intellectual and emotional life above that of other animal species and it is to underestimate human abilities (and overestimate animal ones) to say that behaviours in one species (in this case 'monkey') are directly comparable to behaviours in another (in this case 'human').

Human attachment

According to the evolutionary view, for much the same reason as other animal species, human babies also have an innate tendency to establish a bond with their caregivers. Influenced by the work of other researchers like Lorenz, John Bowlby (1958) applied the principles of imprinting to the human infant–caregiver relationship.

John Bowlby

According to Bowlby, an infant has a biological need to form an *attachment* to its main caregiver. (The term 'attachment' is used rather than 'imprinting' since attachment is a more complex social and emotional bond than that seen in the imprinting which occurs in simpler animals). This attachment to one person is called *monotropy*, and although this person is usually the biological mother, it needn't be. This bond with the mother is a special one which is different from any other bond that the infant might develop and the quality of this bond is important in healthy psychological development.

Bowlby saw attachment as *reciprocal,* i.e. a two-way process. Babies are programmed to engage in behaviours that will encourage the main caregiver to stay close and provide protection and sustenance. These signalling behaviours are called *social releasers* and include such things as crying, smiling and gurgling. Because the infant is carrying half of her genetic material, the mother is motivated to look after this 'investment'. Consequently, the caregiver responds to these social releasers and behaves in ways that ensure the infant's survival. This proximity then leads to the development of strong emotional bonds between the two.

The kind of emotional relationship that an infant has with its mother provides it with a set of expectations about relationships which stays with the baby throughout life. This is called an *internal working model*. In effect, this is a kind of template, or 'blueprint', for all future relationships. For example, an adult who has strong needs for close and loving relationships would, as an infant, have had a similar relationship with his or her mother. Similarly, a 'poor' or unsatisfactory relationship as an infant with the mother figure would lead to unsatisfactory relationships with others later on in life.

For Bowlby, attachments develop in a fixed sequence:

1 *Non-focused orienting and signalling*
For the first few months of life an infant engages in indiscriminate *signalling behaviours*. For example it will smile and cry for the attention of whatever adult might be present. They develop a distinct preference for the company of people and can be easily comforted.

2 *Focus on one or more figures*
By about 3 months the infant begins to demonstrate recognition of those who most often provide care. For example, the infant will direct signalling behaviours more at caregivers than they might at a complete stranger.

3 *Secure base behaviour*
By about 6 months, signalling behaviours become increasingly directed towards its main caregiver (usually the mother). Infants will start to become visibly upset at the departure of the caregiver, a phenomenon called *separation anxiety*. An infant will also begin to show suspicion and sometimes fear at the approach of someone unfamiliar, a behaviour known as stranger anxiety. As an infant grows older and more mobile it will move about in order to stay close to the caregiver and avoid the proximity of the stranger. Attachment behaviours are harder to see after about 2 or 3 years of age, although the attachment to the main caregiver remains strong.

The critical period for this attachment to develop is the first three years of life, otherwise it may never do so. If this attachment is broken or never develops then there will be serious consequences for the social and emotional development of the child. If, on the other hand, there is consistent, responsive and sensitive care then a successful attachment develops which, as a consequence, will have longer term benefits for the child's social competence, including for example increased autonomy, independence and self-efficacy. This is known as the *continuity hypothesis*. The benefits of attachment continue to show themselves in later life.

The quality of early attachment relationships then is largely due to the experience that the infant has with its primary caregivers. Especially important is the extent to which the infant feels that it can rely on the caregivers as sources of support and security, in other words the extent to which the caregiver provides a safe haven. Infants that feel sufficiently comforted by the caregiver's presence are likely to explore their environments more, encouraging the development of, for example, autonomy and independence. This is called the *secure base hypothesis*.

EVALUATION OF BOWLBY'S THEORY
1 There is some doubt about the accuracy of the monotropy concept. Research suggests that, far from having a primary attachment figure, many infants form *multiple attachments*. For example, Schaffer and Emerson (1964)

found that, whilst many of the infants in their study did indeed form an attachment to one particular person, some had no obvious preferred attachment figure. Indeed, some of the infants showed clear signs of attachment to someone other than the mother, for example, to a father or sibling.

2 Bowlby placed a great deal of emphasis on the role of the mother in the attachment process. The father was thought to be important only in supporting attachment by providing an appropriate environment for the mother and infant, e.g. through working and earning money. Whilst it is true that in Western societies the mother usually bears responsibility for child-rearing, fathers are more significant figures than Bowlby suggests. For example, infants not only occasionally have a primary attachment to their father but often show preference for certain kinds of activity with them, especially play. Whilst fathers on average spend about a third of the time that mothers do with infants, it has been suggested that this may be due in part to the attitudes of the mothers themselves: they resist attempts by the father to assist in caregiving due to their strongly socialised role of caregiver.

3 There is research support for many of Bowlby's ideas. For example, his continuity hypothesis is supported by research which shows that securely attached infants continue to be more emotionally and socially competent than insecurely attached infants. There is also general agreement with Bowlby's concept of separation anxiety. Indeed, the idea fits in with another established aspect of intellectual development called *object permanence*. Object permanence is the understanding that when things are out of sight they still exist, something which develops at about the same time as separation anxiety. For instance, when a toy train is moved into a 'tunnel' the child with object permanence will expect it to reappear from the other side of the tunnel. The child

without object permanence will regard the train as having disappeared on its entrance to the tunnel. Similarly, a child with object permanence realises that the caregiver is a permanent figure so that when they are separated they will continue to be upset at the absence. Before object permanence, where there is an 'out-of-sight out-of-mind' attitude, the infant can be passed around people and barely notices the absence of the main caregiver.

4 Bowlby's theory has been very influential. It has stimulated a great deal of research and many of the ideas have been applied in a wide variety of situations, for example to the understanding of loneliness and adult romantic love, the experiences of children in care, and in institutions like hospitals and foster homes.

LEARNING THEORY

The evolutionary explanation says that attachment is biological and part of an animal's instinct. An alternative is learning theory which says, as the name suggests, that attachments are learned

Learning theory recognises that humans have *drives*, such as hunger and thirst, which we are motivated to reduce. In other words, if for example we feel hungry we will want to get rid of this feeling by finding food. Drives related to biological needs like food are called *primary drives*. A baby has several primary drives, for example comfort and security, but the main one is hunger. Because the mother is most often the one providing food, she becomes associated with the satisfaction of this primary drive. This kind of association learning is called *classical conditioning*.

Through the same conditioning processes, the baby learns to enjoy other behaviours associated with the mother during feeding, such as physical contact and verbal communication. Basically then, the mother becomes associated with providing food, satisfying hunger and providing other comforts.

CLASSICAL CONDITIONING

This explanation of learning says that people and non-human animals learn because of the associations they make. The initial research was carried out by Pavlov. He demonstrated that dogs salivated to the sound of a bell because they 'associated' the sound with the presentation of food. Each time the dogs heard the bell, food was presented. Eventually, the bell itself could make them salivate. Salivation is a reflex action and requires no thought. It is a response to a stimulus. Here, the response is to an unusual stimulus. It is a conditioned reflex. A similar relationship can be said to happen in the learning of attachments. For instance, the caregiver acts caringly towards the child. This is called the **unconditioned stimulus (UCS)**. In response to this, the infant feels content. The feeling of contentment is called the **unconditioned response (UCR)**. After a while, and after the UCS has been presented a number of times, making the child feel content, the infant learns to associate feeling content with the actions of the caregiver. Classical conditioning can be regarded as a three-stage process, and can be summarised as follows.

STAGE 1 Pre-conditioning	**STAGE 2** Conditioning	**STAGE 3** Post-conditioning
The caregiver's actions (unconditioned stimulus – UCS) produce a feeling of contentment in the child (unconditioned response – UCR).	The caring behaviour is presented over and over again, making the infant feel content each time. The infant begins to associate the feeling with the stimulus.	The feeling of contentment has been learned (conditioned). It is a 'conditioned response – CR' to the now 'conditioned stimulus – CS' (the caring behaviour).

Once a baby has made the association between the mother and food, it will engage in behaviours which encourage the presence of the mother. For example, babies that smile at their mothers are likely to get some kind of response from her. This is rewarding, or reinforcing, for the baby who is now more likely to smile in the future in order to get the same reward – a response. This reinforcement process is reciprocal, meaning that the mother and child are, by their behaviours, reinforcing each other – for example, the mother finds the actions of the baby rewarding (or reinforcing) and is likely to repeat her behaviour. This kind of learning through rewards is called operant conditioning.

There may also be an element of *social learning* in attachment. According, to *social learning theory*, learning occurs through a process of observation, modelling and imitation: someone is observed engaging in a particular behaviour. We call this person the 'model'. This behaviour is imitated. If there is imitation we can say that learning has occurred.

Whether or not imitation occurs depends on a number of factors; for example, the consequences for the model of the behaviour, or the status of the model. Applied to attachment, this theory suggests that children watch their parents (models) engage in loving and affectionate ways and copy this behaviour. Furthermore, this kind of imitation is encouraged through reinforcement by parents who clearly value this kind of caring behaviour themselves. Thus, children are developing attachment through *observational learning*.

EVALUATION OF LEARNING THEORY

1 According to learning theory, whilst reinforcements increase the likelihood of behaviours occurring again, punishment will

OPERANT CONDITIONING

In operant conditioning, we are said to learn because we are either rewarded for our behaviour, or the way we feel, or punished for it. If we do something and it makes us feel happy, then that behaviour is reinforced. We are more likely to do it again. If we do something and it makes us feel unhappy, or uncomfortable, for instance putting a hand in a candle flame, then our behaviour will not be reinforced. In operant conditioning we talk about the unpleasant result of an action (the finger in the flame example) as punishment.

Touching something very hot, like a fire or a flame, results in an unpleasant feeling and the behaviour is not reinforced.

Eating sweeties results in a happy feeling and it is reinforced. The child is more likely to want to eat lovely treats again than place their hand into a flame.

do the opposite and reduce the likelihood of behaviours reoccurring. However, this is contradicted by the observation that children continue to show strong attachment behaviours towards parents who have been very cruel to them, for instance parents who have been punishing rather than reinforcing.

2 Learning theory predicts that in the absence of reinforcements, learned behaviours will eventually die away (the term for this is *extinction*). In this case, absence for a period of time from the caregivers that provide reinforcement should result in the strength of the attachment diminishing. Even everyday observations of children who have been separated from their parents for a length of time show this not to be the case.

3 Learning theory would predict that the infant's strongest attachments would be to the person who most often provides food, comfort, etc., that is, the person who has the greatest impact on drive reduction. Schaffer and Emerson (1964) however found that less than half of the children in their research had attachments to people with this kind of caregiving responsibility. Furthermore, research by Harlow on rhesus monkeys suggests that other factors, such as physical and social contact, are important in attachment formation.

4 For learning theory, feeding activity is crucial to the emergence of the infant–caregiver attachment. It also suggests that the infant is a passive participant in this process. Provided that it has an appropriate environment, the infant will learn to attach because of the rewarding activities of the caregiver. However, the findings of Harlow contradict this. Harlow's infant monkeys put contact comfort from a surrogate mother ahead of nourishment. Even when Harlow introduced a frightening stimulus into the cage, such as a toy spider, the infant monkey ran for security to the cloth-covered 'mother' rather than to the one providing food.

TYPES OF ATTACHMENT

A child forms close bonds or attachments with those around them.

Theorists generally agree that the first attachment the child forms is the most important one. This is, more often than not, with their mother or primary caregiver. However, studies have shown that attachments vary from one individual to another – they can be weak or strong, secure or insecure.

According to Ainsworth's *caregiving hypothesis*, the quality of an infant's attachment depends largely on the kind of attention the infant has received from the primary caregiver. Based on her observations of infants, Ainsworth and Bell (1970) extended some of Bowlby's ideas on attachment and developed a procedure for measuring it. According to Ainsworth, the quality of a child's attachment to the mother could be seen in the use of the mother as a 'secure base' and the response of the child to both separation and reunion in the home. The test that Ainsworth developed to assess attachment between an infant and mother is called the *Strange Situation* test, a standardised test which takes place in a laboratory setting. It involves a sequence of episodes, each a few minutes long, in which the mother and child and a stranger engage in a series of introductions, separations and reunions. Researchers discreetly observe the child's behaviour in response to the events. Two aspects of the infant's behaviour in particular are observed, namely reactions to separation and reunion and the level of exploration throughout the procedure. An example of the procedure can be seen in the Ainsworth and Bell Study in Focus box.

From the assessment of studies that used the 'Strange Situation' test Ainsworth et al (1978) estimated the proportions of children showing each of the three types of attachment.

Main and Solomon (1990) noticed that some children did not seem to fit the attachment categories identified by Ainsworth et al and added a fourth, which they called *insecure or disoriented attachment*. Although this category is estimated to account for 5–10% of babies, the percentage is greater in children who come from homes with parents who suffer mental illness or where the children are ill-treated.

EVALUATION OF THE STRANGE SITUATION

The Strange Situation has been widely acclaimed as a method for identifying and measuring infant attachments. It has generated a large amount of research which has substantially increased our understanding of the social and emotional development of children. However, a number of issues have been raised about the use of the Strange Situation to measure security.

Table 3: Attachment types described by Ainsworth et al (1976) and Main and Soloman (1990).

TYPES OF ATTACHMENT	HOW DOES THE CHILD BEHAVE IN THE STRANGE SITUATION?	APPROXIMATE % OF CHILDREN IN THIS CATEGORY
Secure Attachment Type B	• Explores the environment • Shows distress on separation • Greets mother warmly • When mother is present, is outgoing and friendly with strangers	60–65
Insecure Attachment (Anxious/Avoidant) Type A	• Shows little or no interest in exploring • When separated shows little distress • Avoids contact. When mother returns child avoids contact • No nervousness around strangers	20
Insecure Attachment (Anxious/Resistant) Type C	• Appears to be anxious • Shows much distress when separated • When mother returns the child shows ambivalence (no strong obvious feelings one way or the other) • When mother is present child is nervous of strangers	12
Insecure Attachment (Disorganised/ Disorientated (Main and Solomon, 1990) Type D	• A mixture of other two types of insecure attachment (types A and C) • When mother returns the child shows confusion over whether to approach or avoid her	5–10

1 The Strange Situation involves subjective evaluation. Because it is the same observer who both observes the mother's behaviour and classifies the infant attachment, it has been suggested that perhaps there is an element of *observer bias*. For example, if researchers are aware of the hypothesis and have a detailed knowledge of the research area (as they would certainly do) they may be inclined to observe behaviours and record them in ways which support expectations. This is especially likely to happen where behaviours are unclear and require some judgement on the part of the observer – there could be slight misinterpretations of actual events.

2 If the Strange Situation is a *reliable* measure of attachment then children should be classified in the same way whenever they are tested and retested. However, studies which have retested children suggest that the second Strange Situation test is a different experience for the infant. For example, infants often indicate that they remember the first experience well and as a result alter their behaviour, for example they become upset more quickly. Consequently, not all infants are classified in exactly the same way on the second occasion, thus casting doubt on the reliability of the Strange Situation test.

Because of this problem it is recommended that the Strange Situation should not be administered to the same children within four to six weeks. Unfortunately, this may not be an effective solution. Four to six weeks is a considerable time in the life of a rapidly developing infant and there is a possibility that attachment could be affected by life

STUDY IN FOCUS

The Strange Situation
Ainsworth and Bell (1970)

What were they doing and why? The researchers wanted to see how a child behaved towards strangers and their caregiver under controlled conditions of stress, in which the infant might seek comfort, and also conditions of 'novelty' where the infant might be encouraged to explore their surroundings. The researchers would then use 'exploration behaviour' and 'comfort-seeking behaviour' as indicators of type of attachment.

How did they do it? 100 middle class American mothers and their children took part. The researchers employed a *controlled observational* technique, which means that the researchers controlled the activities in which the mother and child took part.

The following procedure was used, and is made up of eight episodes. Each episode, apart from the first one, lasts about three minutes, the whole procedure lasting not more than half an hour.

1. Mother and child enter the room.
2. Mother responds to child if baby seeks attention.
3. Stranger enters the room, speaks to mother and slowly approaches baby, mother leaves room.
4. Stranger lets child play, encouraging play with toys if child shows inattention. If child becomes distressed the procedure ends.
5. Mother enters room. Stranger leaves. Child settles again. Mother leaves infant alone in room.
6. If infant is distressed, procedure ends.
7. Stranger enters, and repeats procedure outlined in step 3.
8. Mother returns. Stranger leaves.

During the procedure, the researchers noted down how much the following behaviours were exhibited.

• The infant's unease when the mother left the room – '**separation anxiety**'
• The infant's willingness to explore
• The way the infant greeted the mother on her return – '**reunion behaviou**r'
• The infant's response to a stranger – '**stranger anxiety**'

What did they find? The results led the researchers to conclude that there were three main attachment types that they described as Type B (secure) and Types A (insecure-avoidant) and Type C (insecure-resistant). These are outlined in Table 3. In this study the researchers concluded that the type of attachment formed by the child depends upon the responsiveness and sensitivity of the caregiver.

Take a closer look
● The standardised procedure is a really strong point of the Strange Situation. It means that others can replicate it easily and accurately.

● It might be that the behaviour of the child in the Strange Situation is unnatural because the situation is extremely unusual and unfamiliar to the child. This means that the Strange Situation may not be a very realistic measure of attachment.

changes occurring during this time. Even changes which might appear small to an adult can be big for a child, such as a change in child-minding. This could mean that whilst the Strange Situation is measuring the stability of attachment (in that it can be categorised), it may not be the best measure of the consistency of attachment over time.

" Think about the procedure itself. This is a chance to flex your research methods knowledge! An observational study, where researchers mark down different behaviour when they see it comes with certain problems. What if the behaviour is not noted for some reason, perhaps if there isn't a category for it on the observer's recording sheet, or perhaps if the observer just misses it? Have a think here about problems associated with observational methods to refresh your memory, have a look back at the research methods section."

3 Some researchers question the *validity* of the Strange Situation. For example, Lamb (1977) claims that the Strange Situation only assesses attachment to the person the child is with at the time (usually the mother). Evidence suggests that a child might have different attachment relationships with the father and another again with the grandmother, etc. Main and Weston (1981) found that the behaviour of children varied in the Strange Situation depending on which parent they were with at the time. It seems that the Strange Situation might be assessing specific attachment patterns rather than an overall attachment type.

4 Concerns about the validity of the Strange Situation have led to the development of alternative methods for measuring attachment. For example, the Attachment Q-Sort (or AQS) is thought by some researchers to be a more satisfactory way of assessing attachment. It involves a trained observer watching parent–child interactions for several hours, followed by a task whereby

100 statements about child behaviour are ranked from 'least descriptive of the child' to 'most descriptive of the child'. The sum of these statements is then compared to a profile of a typical securely attached child to give an indication of the degree of secure attachment. An advantage of AQS is that it does not require the set-up of the Strange Situation so it is more flexible, and can, for example, be used to assess the security of attachment in more varied (and more natural) environments. It is also less stressful to the child than is the Strange Situation. A further benefit of the AQS is that it can be used with children up to the age of 48 months, unlike the limit of 18 months with the Strange Situation.

5 The Strange Situation is highly artificial and places the baby under enormous stress. It is actually designed to see how infants react under conditions which are increasingly stressful. Many researchers argue that this is not an *ethical* practice – that is, putting very young infants under deliberate duress can never be justified. This concern has led some researchers to develop alternative methods of assessing attachment (for example, the AQS) or to rely on naturalistic opportunities to assess infants' reactions. For example, True et al (2001) adapted the Strange Situation for use during a weigh-in at a baby clinic for infants in Mali.

" The Strange Situation is pretty unpleasant to observe sometimes. We've seen it actually performed and hearing children in distress, and sometimes having to really encourage mothers not to break down the door of the laboratory to get back to their child, is very difficult to watch. Think about ethics here. It's a good chance to show your knowledge and evaluate. If you're unsure, flick back and have another look. Does the child consent to the procedure? Can the child give consent at such a young age? What might be the psychological consequences to the parent and the child and how would you make sure there was no long-term harm?"

The stability of attachments

The types of attachment identified by Ainsworth are thought to persist and can be seen in the behaviour of children throughout infancy. Indeed, most research does seem to suggest that the attachment seen during infancy is moderately to highly stable. For example, using the Strange Situation, Waters (1978) found that 96% of the infants in his sample belonged to the same attachment category at 12 and 18 months. The infants in this study however all had very stable caregiving experiences.

A somewhat different picture emerges from research on the attachment patterns of children who experience change during infancy. Vaughn et al (1979) found that changes in the quality of parent–child relationships resulted in changes to attachment patterns. They found that, over a six month period, the degree of life stressors experienced by low–income families was related to infants shifting from secure to insecure attachments. Mothers of infants who remained secure during this same period experienced fewer stressful life events. These findings indicate that attachments remain stable when there is consistent caregiving and are likely to change when infants experience significant change.

There have been few studies which have investigated Bowlby's claim that attachments developed in infancy remain relatively stable over a lifetime. One reason for this of course is that attachment theory and methods of assessing attachment are relatively recent ideas. However, Waters et al (2000) retested adults for their attachment style 20 years after having first been assessed when 12 months old. They found a high degree of stability, with 72% of adults receiving the same classification from adult attachment tests as they did in infancy from the Strange Situation. Lewis et al (2000), on the other hand, reported much lower attachment stability from their longitudinal study. They compared the attachment classification of children at 1 year of age with their classification at 18 years of age. With a stability of 42%, no strong evidence for consistency over time was found. Whilst these two studies disagreed on the amount of change, they did agree that change, when it occurred, was most often associated with negative life events. For Lewis et al (2000) the key life event was parental divorce. The effect of divorce on the child was not linked to any specific attachment classification, so that divorce had an impact regardless of whether an infant was securely or insecurely attached.

Factors influencing the development of secure and insecure attachments

There has been a considerable amount of research into how both secure and insecure attachments develop. Whilst many factors have been suggested which contribute to this process, a number of influences consistently emerge:

1 *Maternal sensitivity*

For Bowlby, maternal sensitivity in responding to the needs of the baby was a crucial factor contributing to the development of attachment relationships. Maternal sensitivity refers to a range of things, but includes a mother's positive emotions, responsiveness to the child's needs and gentleness of behaviour. The more sensitive the caregiver is to the needs of the child then the more likely it is that a secure attachment will develop. There have been many studies on the relationship between maternal sensitivity and attachment. In one study, Ainsworth et al (1978) investigated 26 infant–mother relationships, in the home and in a Strange Situation, when the child became 12 months old. Of the many aspects of maternal behaviour observed, the one most strongly related to attachment was sensitivity to the signals and communications of the infant.

However, whilst Ainsworth's findings have been supported by other studies, many other studies have failed to find such a strong link between sensitivity and attachment, and others still have found no relationship at all. Some studies have suggested that other aspects of maternal behaviour such as positive parental attitude and emotional support are equally as important. It appears that whilst maternal sensitivity is essential, it is only one of a number of factors contributing to the development of secure attachments.

2 Emotional availability

Whilst similar to maternal sensitivity, emotional availability refers specifically to the quality of the *emotional* interactions between parents and children. According to Biringen et al (2005), emotional availability is an *exchange* of interactions. This means that it is not just about emotional communication by the child to the parent and vice versa, but also about the parent's ability to *understand* the emotional experience of the child and to respond appropriately. A parent can look as though they are 'doing the right thing' such as interacting with the child and responding to cries, but can still be insensitive to the emotional needs of the child. So, a parent can appear dutiful but be emotionally negative or detached from the interaction. This is supported by Martin et al (2002) who found that mothers of 2-year-old children who had less positive emotional experiences when interacting with their children (for example, they found the experience stressful, emotionally difficult or unrewarding) were also less sensitive to the emotional needs of their children.

Biringen et al (2005) suggest that children who have emotionally available relationships with their parents develop more secure attachments which, in turn, benefit their wider social development. Such children have better peer relationships, are less likely to be the targets of aggression from other children, show less aggression themselves and have generally better social skills.

3 Temperament of infant

One factor affecting the responsiveness of the caregiver is the temperament of the child. Temperament is an aspect of personality describing emotionality and sensitivity. According to studies by Thomas and Chess (1977), infants can be categorised into three groups according to their temperaments.

Easy babies:
Are moderate in their reactions and predictable in their behaviour, tend to adapt well to new situations and are generally positive.

Difficult babies:
Tend not to adapt well to new situations, they can be unpredictable and are generally negative.

Slow-to-warm-up babies:
Are slow to adapt to new situations, are relatively inactive and withdrawn.

Difficult babies and slow-to-warm-up babies are harder for parents to cope with, and this might affect the emotional bond between them. For example, it is easy to imagine how 'easy' babies, who are positive and happy to be cuddled and played with, are not going to be as difficult to look after as a 'difficult' baby who is unpredictable and resistant to being comforted. The nature of this relationship is likely to be an important factor in shaping the attachment process.

Different babies can have different temperaments.

According to Kagan (1984), the temperament of an infant plays a key role in the development of attachment to the mother. His *temperament hypothesis* states that the quality of attachment depends primarily on the temperament of the child. For Kagan, the Strange Situation measures temperament rather than attachment, and the *attachment behaviours* displayed are a reflection of this infant temperament. For example, securely attached babies have easy or 'good' temperaments, whilst insecurely attached babies have 'bad' temperaments, so that anxious/avoidant have 'slow' and anxious/resistant have 'difficult' temperaments. This is supported by Hsu et al (2006). Infants in their study had their temperaments assessed at 12 months of age and the quality of the attachment relationship with their mother at 30 months. They concluded that the type of attachment a child forms is partly determined by their temperament and temperament is a very important factor in how a child develops relationships and acts towards others as a toddler. The positive aspects of a child's temperament were related to the security of the attachment they form later on. The more positive the temperament, the more secure the attachment.

However, whilst there has been some support for Kagan's theory, most research seems to suggest that, whilst temperament is an important contributor, *caregiving* is the primary determinant of infant attachment. Vaughn and Bost (1999) looked at the findings of 54 published investigations (collecting and analysing studies together like this is called a meta-analysis) and found only small and inconsistent links between attachment security and temperament. They argue that individual differences in temperament do not directly cause differences in attachment security but is rather an additional stressor on an already stressed caregiver.

CULTURE AND ATTACHMENT

One aspect of psychology that continues to stimulate research and thinking is the study of what makes people different from one another. Culture is a set of learned values, beliefs and behaviours shared by the members of a society. It is complex and is likely to have many influences on attachment. Cultures vary in different ways, and it is to these variations that we now turn.

The *culture* in which people live and in which they develop contributes to individual differences. In this case *culture* refers to all the things that make our society what it is. These may be rules and laws, and less obvious things like social norms and customs.

We can think of cultural differences in broad terms. An *individualist culture* for instance, is one where the importance is placed upon the individual; Western cultures such as the UK or the United States fall into this category. A *collectivist culture* on the other hand is one where importance is placed on the group as a whole, such as in Japanese society. It is also possible that there are different pockets of culture within the broad categories of collectivist and individualist. For instance, the culture of the super rich in the United Kingdom may very well be different from the culture experienced by the majority of us! These distinctions within cultures are called *subcultures*.

CULTURAL VARIATIONS IN ATTACHMENT

Bowlby developed his theory of attachment on the basis that the features of attachment are *universal* – that is, they apply to all human beings in all *cultures*. However, the world is made up of many different cultures with many different ideas of ideal parent, child and caregiving behaviours. So, whilst all children might, according to Bowlby, need responsive and sensitive parenting, how children go about getting this through their attachment behaviours and how parents encourage attachment through their child care practice is going to vary widely.

Cultural differences in long-term goals of child rearing

Cultures vary in the *long-term goals* that they have for their children's development. For example, some cultures (collectivist) encourage social cooperation, obedience and compliance whilst others (individualist) emphasise individual achievement and independence.

Carlson and Harwood (2003) studied mother–infant attachments in Puerto Rico, one of the Caribbean Islands. One particularly important cultural value in Puerto Rico is a strong sense of community. This sense of belonging to a wider social group is so important that things like respect towards others, sense of duty and obligation are valued personal traits. Carlson and Harwood noted that such values had a major influence on child-rearing and attachment.

For Puerto Rican mothers attachment involves the development of interdependency in children, for example '…respect, obedience, calmness, politeness, gentleness and kindness' towards others in the community. This is in contrast to more Westernised ideals which emphasise encouraging independence in infants through sensitive caregiving. Carlson and Harwood point out that teaching infants to be calm, attentive and well-balanced requires a much more direct approach to child-rearing than it does to foster self-confidence and assertiveness. Consequently, there is much more physical contact and control in Puerto Rican child-rearing. However, whilst Ainsworth's studies show that physical control is related to *insecure attachment*, in contrast to this Carlson and Harwood found that physical control was related to *secure attachment* in Puerto Rican families. For Carlson and Harwood, this "highlights the need for culturally specific definitions of sensitive caregiving".

Cultural differences in the ways that parents respond to their children's needs

How a caregiver feeds, responds to and shows affection for their child is heavily influenced by culture. These *child-rearing practices* are passed down through many generations because they satisfy both the beliefs and the needs of that particular culture. These child-rearing practices are likely to influence

the relationship that is built between the caregiver and the child.

The *Dogon* people of Mali in West Africa are subsistence farmers living in relatively small social groups. Dogon mothers are extremely attentive to their children's needs. The infants are in constant proximity to their mothers and receive immediate breast-feeding when they show any sign of distress, or else have constant physical contact with an adult, especially in the presence of a stranger. True et al (2001) suggest that this closeness explains why they did not see any insecure avoidant attachment behaviours in Dogon infants. They did however observe an unusually high rate of insecure disorganised

Dogon woman and child.

attachment, with 25% of the infants showing this behaviour. True et al suggest that this is due to the extremely high infant mortality rate amongst Dogon infants, with at least 10% dying in the first 12 months and 25% dying before the age of 5 years. Understandably, a mother's experience with, or fear of, bereavement is seen in their behaviour, with mothers frequently showing frightened or frightening behaviours in front of their infants when they were separated from them. It is this parental behaviour that lies behind the high rates of disorganised attachment.

Cultural differences in how children and caregivers are valued

Cultures place different values on children and the role of the caregiver. For example, in some cultures the relationship between the child and a specific caregiver is highly valued, whilst for other cultures this is less significant and the importance of multiple caretakers is emphasised.

Tronick et al (1992) studied mother–infant attachment among the *Efe* people, a semi-nomadic people who have a basic subsistence lifestyle in the African rainforest of Zambia. Efe families live in close proximity to each other and it is normal that during the day infants receive more care from other adult women in the social group than they do from their own mothers. This even extends to breastfeeding. They noted that as much as 60% of an infant's day is spent with someone other than their biological mother with, on average, over a dozen different caregivers. Infants are rarely if ever left alone, being held and carried at all times. Even as toddlers, when the infants are mobile and like to explore their environment, they are never out of sight and earshot of several adults. The Efe infants develop close bonds with these *multiple caretakers*, but still develop a strong preference for the company of their mothers by the end of their first year. According to Tronick et al, these emotional ties with a number of caregivers are as strong as those

found in more Western cultures between infants and fewer caregivers.

The Strange Situation – cultural differences and similarities

Although nearly all research on attachment is North American or European, the Strange Situation has been used to measure attachment across a range of cultures. Van IJzendoorn and Kroonenberg (1988) gathered together the results of 32 separate studies conducted in eight different countries, all of which used the Strange Situation to assess attachment. (This kind of research, where data are gathered together from different studies, is called a *meta-analysis*).

One of the most important findings to emerge from their analysis was the *consistency of secure attachment* – it appeared as the most common attachment type in all eight countries. Van IJzendoorn and Kroonenberg suggest that this supports one of the most central ideas within attachment theory – that a secure attachment is best for healthy social and emotional development. It is the most common form of attachment across cultures because it is the norm. One of the most important cultural differences to be seen in the findings was the relatively high proportion of insecure-avoidant attachments, especially when compared to, for example, Japan. Grossman et al (1985) suggest that the high rate of insecure-avoidant relationships is due to the high value placed on independence and self-reliance in German culture. It is seen as desirable, for example, that children do not get particularly distressed at the absence of the mother (as seen in insecure-avoidant behaviour), whilst some of the behaviours that other cultures might see as acceptable as indicators of a secure attachment are not. It is arguable therefore that the use of the term 'insecure' to describe the behaviour of German infants is not exactly fair or strictly accurate, having, as it does, a qualitative element. In Japanese culture, dependency is highly valued – it is a normal part of Japanese child-rearing practice that mother and child are rarely apart for the first 12 months. It is then not surprising perhaps that Japanese infants show a relatively high proportion of insecure-resistant attachments. One aspect of this attachment type is the extreme distress that an infant shows over the absence of the mother.

Another significant finding to emerge from the Van IJzendoorn and Kroonenberg analysis was the one-and-a-half times greater variation within culture than between culture. This means that there were greater differences in attachment patterns in studies from the same culture than there were in the attachment patterns of studies from different cultures. One implication of this is that it may be wrong to use the term 'culture' to generalise and refer to all members of a culture as though they act in the same way in some regard. Even within cultures there are important and identifiable subcultures and it is difficult to assess where the limits of

cultural influence end. The alternative is an over-simplified view of cultural influence.

EVALUATION OF THE VAN IJZENDOORN AND KROONENBURG STUDY

1 Care should be taken about drawing too many conclusions from the data because of the limited variety in the studies used. For example, whilst 18 studies are used from the US, there is only one study from China – a single study which involved observing the behaviour of only 36 infants. Many more studies need to be conducted in cultures other than the US to allow meaningful comparisons.

2 Some researchers have questioned the use of the Strange Situation in different cultures. This test and its classifications were largely developed in the US, based on observations of American infants, and therefore reflect the values and customs of this particular culture

COUNTRY	No of studies	Secure (Type B)	Avoidant (Type A)	Resistant (Type C)
UK	1	75	22	3
USA	18	65	21	14
NETHERLANDS	4	67	26	7
WEST GERMANY	3	57	35	8
ISRAEL	2	64	7	29
SWEDEN	1	74	22	4
JAPAN	2	68	5	27
CHINA	1	50	25	25
Average		65	21	14

Table 4: Results of Van IJzendoorn and Kroonenberg (1988) showing the number of studies from each country and the proportions of children showing each type of attachment.

with regard to the forms of attachment and child-rearing practice considered best.

3 It is important to note that all 32 studies were either 'Western' or 'Westernised', and the parents would all have been exposed to similar messages in the mass media about child-rearing practices. What we might be seeing in these studies is this influence of the norms and values of Western industrialised cultures from which this media emerges. There have been relatively few studies of infant–caregiver attachments in cultures which have not been exposed to such influence.

Cultural bias – a Japanese perspective

Rothbaum et al (2000) argue that most research on attachment assumes that the basic principles of attachment theory apply to all cultures and therefore focus on factors that influence variations in attachment classification. There is insufficient regard for the importance of culture and the significant cultural differences in child-rearing attitudes and behaviours. They suggest that the

Akiyo Shibuya, a friend of Nigel Holt, as a young girl growing up in Japan.

concepts which make up attachment theory are "deeply rooted in a Western-perspective". This means that the theory was developed in a Western industrialised country and focuses upon the values and customs of this particular world view. This makes the basic concepts of the theory culturally biased, and any attachment research which accepts the universal nature of these concepts is also therefore culturally biased.

For Rothbaum et al, three aspects of attachment theory demonstrate particular bias towards a Western way of thinking. They use comparisons with Japanese child-rearing and culture to illustrate this.

1 *The sensitivity hypothesis*

It has been argued by Ainsworth and others that secure attachment patterns result from sensitive and responsive care. However, what is considered sensitive and responsive is likely to reflect a society's values and goals. In the US, this means that emphasis is placed on a child's *autonomy* – that is individuality, wilfulness and personal satisfaction. These views are basic to attachment theory and the assessment of sensitivity with the Strange Situation. In Japan, very close contact between mother and child, especially during the first 12 months, is considered a key element of sensitive caregiving. The Japanese view then is at odds with this. Responsiveness and sensitivity have more to do with encouraging a child to control their emotions and increasing *dependency* on the mother.

2 *The secure base hypothesis*

For attachment theorists, such as Bowlby and Ainsworth, a healthy attachment means that a child has a secure base, giving them a sense of protection and comfort. The presence of a caregiver therefore encourages a child to explore the environment, which in turn promotes greater *individuation*, a term used to encompass things like individuality, separateness and self-awareness. In Japan however, individuation is less desirable than *dependency*, encouraged through close contact with the mother. Indeed, a number of studies have observed less exploratory behaviours in Japanese than US infants. A lack of willingness to explore (regardless of the presence or absence of the caregiver) is a key indicator of anxious-resistant attachment.

It is hardly surprising then that Japanese infants are more likely than US ones to be classified as such. Rothbaum et al point out that many of the features of insecure-resistant attachment are considered good and desirable in Japan and, in fact, resemble normal relationships described as *amae*, the term used in Japan to refer to a particular emotional bond shared by a child and its mother. There is no direct equivalent elsewhere, but it is complex and resembles feelings of dependency and need for love and indulgence. It is important in Japanese culture, and it may be the key factor which distinguishes Japanese child-rearing from that of other cultures. Rothbaum et al (2007) interviewed mothers from the United States and Japan and found that, whilst there were fundamental similarities in how both sets of mothers viewed attachment, there were

important cultural differences. For example, in the interpretation of desirable and undesirable attachment behaviours, Japanese mothers were likely to attribute the stressed behaviour of children in the Strange Situation to *amae*, with US mothers attributing it to a child's need for attention and control.

3 The competence hypothesis

According to attachment theory, one consequence of early secure (and therefore successful) attachment is social competence. Securely attached children show a number of behaviours related to competence (e.g. self-expression, exploration, emotional openness and autonomy). Rothbaum et al point out however that in Japan social competence is not viewed in this way. For example, group accomplishment and reliance on others are favoured and emotional openness frowned upon because of the negative effect it could have on social harmony. Clearly, what counts as competence can vary considerably between cultures. In this instance, using a definition of competence drawn from Western values will increase the likelihood of an attachment being labelled as insecure.

STUDY IN FOCUS

Attachments in Japan and the USA
Rothbaum et al (2007)

What they were doing and why? The researchers investigated the similarities and differences in perceptions of secure attachment in caregivers from the United States and Japan, with a particular focus on the relationship between attachment and amae (see page 119).

Interview methodology was used because researchers were interested in mothers' understanding of the meaning of their children's behaviour and the motives underlying mothers' behaviour towards their children.

How did they do it?

A pilot study was conducted in order to make the interview as culturally fair as possible. According to Rothbaum et al, a common problem in cross-cultural research is that most measures are borrowed from the West, making comparison between cultures unfair.

Previous research had indicated that the Strange Situation produced particularly strong stress reactions in Japanese infants. The purposes of the pilot study were (a) to develop a measure of amae and (b) to find out what constituted equivalent levels of separation anxiety in the two cultures.

The sample consisted of 28 mothers: 14 Euro-Americans from Boston in the United States and 14 Japanese from Tokyo. All mothers had children aged 3–4 years (taken on advice as an age when amae is most evident). The interview was conducted by a native-speaking female graduate student in each country.

To maximise cultural fairness the interview was translated into Japanese and checked for accuracy by other people fluent in both languages. The translated interview was then translated back into its original language by someone unfamiliar with the research and the outcome compared with the original. As a result, changes were made in both the US and Japanese equivalent interviews.

The interview was *semi-structured* and consisted of ten questions. Four issues were addressed:

1. desirable and undesirable behaviours
2. attachment security
3. amae
4. maternal responsiveness

The interviews, which took about an hour to complete, were conducted at times convenient to the participants in their own homes.

STUDY IN FOCUS

What did they find? Findings provide support for cross-cultural importance of attachment theory. For example:

Most mothers in both cultures perceived children with desirable characteristics as securely attached and children with undesirable characteristics as insecurely attached.

The children seen as most socially desirable were believed to have mothers who were maternally responsive.

However important cultural differences emerged:

In describing socially desirable and undesirable behaviours, Japanese mothers focused on social roles, cooperation and harmony as desirable whilst US mothers focused on personal attributes and individual achievement.

In perceptions of children's Strange Situation behaviour, Japanese mothers were less likely than US mothers to see exploration as desirable, and expected to see much more distress than US mothers in the reunion episode.

Compared to US mothers, Japanese mothers were much more likely to attribute a child's demanding and difficult behaviour in stressful situations to needs for security and interdependence. US mothers were more likely to view this behaviour as attention-seeking behaviour. This may be due to Japanese mothers seeing through the behaviour and interpreting it as an expression of a child's desire for amae.

Take a closer look

● The *size of the sample* used in the research was relatively small. Also, the researchers did not select the families randomly. Instead they actively approached mothers with young children to ask them to take part, and in Japan, friends of one of the researchers participated because of a difficulty in finding participants. Because of this there may be *sampling* problems. The people who agreed to take part may have really wanted to help the researchers, and so their answers may not have been as honest as they could have been. Also, the families were not *matched*. All were from cities and were of similar backgrounds socially and financially, but the researchers did not take account of any other possible differences, such as child care differences, employment of families or presence of other family members, such as grandparents or siblings, who may have had an influence on the mother–child relationship. Similarly, experience of schooling was not considered. The children may have attended pre-school or kindergarten at some stage, which may have influenced their behaviour.

● The study consisted of *interviews* which asked mothers how they might respond or how they expected their children to respond. This means that a full picture of attachment was not gained. It may have been more accurate to *observe* mothers and children responding in an actual Strange Situation. Just because a mother thinks a child would and should behave in a certain way does not mean that they would do so.

● The researchers themselves point out that they did not go far enough in their questioning. For instance, Japanese mothers mention self-assertion as a desirable characteristic. However, on reflection, the researchers point out that this may be because Japanese mothers may regard 'putting your hand up in class' as assertive, but American parents may have had rather different behaviour in mind when they describe self-assertiveness. What the researchers might have done is probe the mothers more, asking them what they mean by such a characteristic, perhaps asking them to give examples of the behaviour in question.

DISRUPTION OF ATTACHMENT

If a child fails to form an attachment there could well be serious consequences for their development. Attachment is an important component in laying the foundations of a healthy individual. If attachments do not form, or if they are disrupted in some way, the child may find themselves growing up outside the traditional family environment.

According to Bowlby (1951) an infant must form an attachment to its mother, or a true mother substitute, during the *critical period* of 6 months to 2½ years. If this did not happen, or the infant experienced disruption to an existing attachment, then it would suffer both *emotionally* and *socially* in later life.

> "*Mother-love in infancy is as important for mental health as are vitamins and proteins for physical health*"
>
> J. Bowlby 1952

This is called the *maternal deprivation hypothesis*. This was based partly on Bowlby's own studies of juvenile delinquency. Many of the *juvenile delinquents* in his study had what he called 'affectionless psychopathy', which is basically an inability to have feelings for others. He noted that most of these affectionless psychopaths had experienced some kind of separation from their mothers in their early years of life.

Bowlby's maternal deprivation hypothesis stimulated a great deal of research and attracted a lot of criticism. Most of the subsequent research supporting the maternal deprivation hypothesis, however, has not been convincing, either because of flawed methodology – the studies were badly controlled with lots of confounding variables

STUDY OUTLINE

The 44 thieves, Bowlby (1944)

Bowlby provided support for his **maternal deprivation hypothesis** by asking whether early separation from the mother could be related to behavioural problem later on life. 88 children who had been referred to a child guidance clinic were investigated. 44 of them were reported to be 'thieves'. The findings were quite striking. A portion of the 'thieves' were diagnosed as 'affectionless psychopaths' and of these 86% had experienced 'early and prolonged separations from their mothers'. Of the other thieves only 17% had experienced such separation and of the other 44 children, the control group, only 4% had experienced such early childhood experiences. Bowlby concluded that there may be a link between early separation and later emotional and social problems. However, we must bear in mind that the research was **correlational**, so no causal relationship between early separation and later behavioural problems can be implied, and the information about the separations was collected retrospectively, that is to say, after the event, and it may not have been terribly accurate. Similarly, we do not know what kind of care and attachments the children may have experienced during these periods of separation, and this may have added to their later social and emotional problems.

– or because the research wasn't necessarily focused on maternal deprivation.

There have been studies which appear to directly contradict this theory. Freud and Dann (1951) studied the development of a group of six children rescued from a Nazi concentration camp where they had spent their early life. In the absence of any adults to provide care, the six children became very close and developed attachments to one another. According to Bowlby, these children all suffered maternal deprivation and as a result should have developed affectionless psychopathy. However, they showed no clear signs of this, suggesting that it isn't the lack of an attachment to the mother which is important, but the inability to form any kind of attachment at all.

In a major review of maternal deprivation research, Rutter (1981) suggested that there should be a distinction drawn between the *distortion* of attachments (for example, when the mother is present but the family relationships are affected by such things as illness and divorce) and the *disruption* of attachment (for example, when the mother has died). The maternal deprivation hypothesis would predict that the loss of a mother would have a far greater impact on an infant than a disturbance to the bond. Rutter points out however that distortion can be far more harmful to the child than disruption – the poor quality of family relationships can have a greater impact on a child than separation from an attachment figure. It is far too simple to say that separation as such causes harm – the nature and consequences of separation need to be taken into account.

According to Rutter (1997) one of the most important contributions of attachment theory has been the attention it has drawn to the importance of early stable and dependable care for children, and the significant impact that disturbance to this process has on young children. There are many ways in which deprivation may occur, for example death of a parent, hospitalisation or divorce. Two further examples are discussed in more detail below.

Foster care

Sometimes children are removed from their home and given to the care of foster parents when it is thought that remaining with their natural parents would threaten their own well-being. Unlike adoption, where there is no contact with natural parents and parental rights are given to the adoptive family, fostering is often a more temporary situation. There is no permanent commitment to stay with the foster family and there may still be contact with the natural parents. Whilst foster care adequately provides for the physical care and protection of children, some researchers have raised concerns about the implications of foster care for the healthy emotional development of young children.

Stovall and Dozier (2003) suggest two reasons why foster children may have difficulty forming attachments to new caregivers:

1 Even very young children have experienced inappropriate care before fostering and this may have resulted in the development of resistant, avoidant or disorganised attachments. This insecure attachment is likely to influence the relationship with the new carer.

2 Being placed in foster care means that children are experiencing a serious disruption to their primary attachment relationships. Research has shown that being separated from the primary caregiver can lead to a variety of short- and long-term problems. Withdrawal, depression, resistance to being soothed and excessive clinginess have all been observed in such children. These behaviours are likely to interfere with the development of a secure attachment.

One very important factor influencing the infants' ability to develop a secure attachment with foster parents is the age at which they are fostered. Attachment bonds are not present at birth, but take time to develop. Whilst infants appear happy to receive care from anyone for the first couple of months of life, they soon begin to show preferences. At about 6 months of age babies begin to resist separation and, in normal circumstances, infants develop an attachment to a caregiver before their first birthday. The timing of separation then is clearly crucial. Tyrrell and Dozier (1998) interviewed foster parents about attachment-related difficulties with children placed before and after 6 months of age. They found that although foster parents reported problems with children placed after 6 months, the greatest problems were reported with children placed after 12 months of age. They found that these older infants all developed insecure attachment relationships with their foster parents. This is supported by Stovall and Dozier (2000). They conducted case studies of ten foster parent–infant relationships and found that age at placement was relevant to the child's attachment classification. Those placed before 12 months of age were more likely to be classified as securely attached while those placed after 12 months were mostly insecurely attached.

Another factor is the foster mother's attachment style. Infants placed in foster care have often experienced abuse and neglect, and need more responsive and sensitive care than typical infants in order to develop a secure attachment. Research suggests that the strongest predictor of infant attachment is the caregiver's *state of mind*. This refers to the way in which an adult processes thoughts about their own attachment experiences. Adults who process their own attachment experience coherently are said to be *autonomous*, and parents with this state of mind are most likely to create secure attachments in their infants. Dozier et al (2001) found that the foster mother's state of mind was related to the attachment of her foster infant in similar ways as birth mothers to their infants. Foster mothers classified as autonomous were much more likely to have foster children who were

securely attached, while those mothers with non-autonomous states of mind were more likely to have foster infants who were insecurely attached. Furthermore, the age of infant and attachment style of the foster mother interacted. Autonomous foster mothers were more accepting of infants placed before 12 months and more negative toward later-placed babies, a relationship not found among non-autonomous foster mothers.

Premature birth

Recent medical advances have meant that children born prematurely have a far greater chance of surviving than they once did. Whilst the normal gestation time is about 40 weeks, medical technology can now help infants born at 25 weeks to survive. Because of their early birth the babies are likely to be smaller and more fragile, their

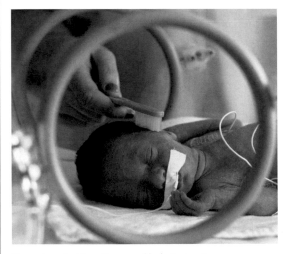

Premature babies often need help to survive.

cries weaker and they tend generally to be less alert and responsive than full-term babies. Another consequence of being born so early is that, unlike full-term babies, premature babies do not display the social releasers normally used to encourage and maintain contact with the mother. So for example, whilst premature babies readily cry, they are hard to comfort; they do not smile or reach or cling. These behaviours will not emerge until they are developmentally ready to do so which, in the case of premature babies, will take a considerably longer time after birth than for full-term babies. Furthermore, the medical complications usually associated with premature birth means that a long-term stay in hospital is required. During this time there are very few interactions with the mother. In fact, often the only contact the infant has with a caregiver is during medical procedures.

Research by DiVitto and Goldberg (1995) suggests that mothers of premature babies behave differently towards their infants than do mothers of full-term babies. Whilst there is less interaction in the hospital nursery, when at last in the home setting, mothers of preterm babies become more actively involved with their children than do mothers of full-term babies. Some researchers have noted that the interactions are excessive to the point of being intrusive and over-stimulating for the infant.

BLISS work hard to support premature babies.

Given that early infant–caregiver contact is generally considered important for attachment development, it seems likely that these early experiences are going to have some effect on the infant–caregiver relationship. It would not be surprising to find that the attachment patterns of preterm infants and their caregivers were different from those of full-term infants and their caregivers. Indeed, there is some support for this. For example, Plunkett et al (1988) found a higher percentage of insecure attachments than might be expected from a similar-age sample of full-term infants. Minde (1999) found that many preterm infants who had been assessed

as securely attached at 12 months were reassessed as type D (disorganised) at 4 years. Results of research into the attachment quality of preterm infants are often contradictory. Frodi and Thompson (1985) assessed forty 12 month-old infants (20 full-term infants, all born close to 40 weeks and 20 preterm infants born, on average, at 34 weeks) using the Strange Situation and found no significant differences in attachment classification.

There are important methodological issues arising from the study of preterm infant attachments and these might account for some of the inconsistencies in research findings. The age of an infant is taken from the time of birth. However, preterm babies are born at an earlier stage in their development. This means that they will lag behind full-term infants in important ways which might affect their attachment classification. For example, their motor skills may be delayed. In practical terms, the age of preterm infants should be considered as their chronological age plus the

> **ASK AN EXAMINER**
>
> *"When you're evaluating this bit and are stuck for criticisms to make, think back to research methods. We've made the point here that there may be problems of grouping all preterm infants into a single group as they differ from one another in many ways. This casts doubt on the validity of the findings."*

number of days they are premature. Another factor which might confuse matters is the nature of the prematurity. Infants are born prematurely for many different reasons and after birth they show a wide range of different medical complications, including neurological problems. All of this is going to have an impact on an infant's behaviour and experience. Clearly, it is unwise to think of preterm infants as a single homogeneous group.

Despite these contradictions, a general picture is emerging from research where age has been corrected for prematurity. Goldberg (2000) suggests that the over-attentive maternal behaviour observed in mothers of prematurely born infants is mostly seen early on after reunion and is a form of compensation for the earlier difficulties in the caregiver–infant relationship. By 12 to 18 months of age preterm infants tend to show no differences when compared to full-term infants in their attachment classifications, and there is no convincing evidence of any long-term problems.

FAILURE TO FORM ATTACHMENT

According to Rutter, to use the term 'deprivation' suggests that there has been an attachment but that it has been broken. However, some children never have the opportunity to form a close attachment in the first place. He called this *privation*. This distinction is important, since privation and deprivation are likely to have different effects on a child's development. For example, the consequences of privation could be seen as more serious since deprivation can be graded, i.e. it can be short-term or long-term with degrees of consequence. Privation, on the other hand, is simply a lack of an attachment bond.

Most attachment research has focused on deprivation since instances of privation are actually quite rare. Unfortunately, cases of privation do occur. One approach has been to study cases of children who experienced extreme maltreatment and radical changes in caregiving at a young age. One well known example is the study by Koluchova (1976). She described the case of twin boys who, for five and a half years until they were discovered aged 7, had experienced extreme physical and psychological cruelty. Care was restricted largely to being fed. Other than when they were locked in a cellar – they lived together almost permanently in a very small room. There were no toys other than some building bricks and they lived in relative isolation. When discovered they were malnourished and had a great deal of scarring from beatings. They could not talk,

their intelligence was too low to be measured and they were constantly suspicious and fearful of others. They were eventually fostered into a warm and caring environment where they flourished. Their physical condition rapidly improved and their intelligence reached average levels by the time they were 14. Studies such as this seem to suggest that extreme early experiences do not necessarily have either long-term or permanent effects on social and emotional development. It could be argued, however, that this is not an example of privation since the twins could have formed an emotional bond with each other. The outcome would have been much more severe if either twin was reared in solitary confinement. It might even be that social isolation is more important than maternal privation, i.e. it is the lack of quality contact with any other human being which leads to major long-term effects. Cases of extreme child abuse such as this, whilst they tell us a great deal about human nature and the resilience of children, are not carefully planned psychological investigations, and we have to be careful about how we interpret the outcomes of these studies.

The effects of institutionalisation

It has been suggested that group day care, or 'institutionalised' care, is the type of out-of-home care most likely to cause problems with social and emotional development.

Institutions that do not meet the basic needs rarely provide either adequate stimulation or consistent and sensitive caregiving. This is the most difficult need to satisfy, even in institutions that are well managed with low staff–child ratios, and which provide a stimulating and enriching environment. The necessity for staff changes during the day and weekend, and these absences create an environment which undermines any sense of stability in the child–caregiver relationship.

LEVELS OF PRIVATION

According to Gunnar et al (2000), children may encounter three levels of privation in an institution:

1 At the most basic level, there are needs for adequate nutrition, proper hygiene and suitable medical care.

2 The next level involves a child's needs for environmental stimulation in order to support physical, cognitive and social development. This is more than just providing toys and painted walls – there must also be social stimulation, where the child has the opportunity to interact with others.

3 Finally, the child needs stable interpersonal relationships and the opportunity to develop an attachment to a consistent caregiver.

There is a long history of research into the effects of institutionalised care. For example, Goldfarb (1943) compared one group of children who had experienced institutional care for the first three years of life before being fostered, with another group of children who had been fostered straight away. He found that the early fostered group were much more socially skilled and scored higher on intelligence tests that the institutionalised children. Studies like Goldfarb's however were generally poorly controlled and conducted, and were largely descriptive, so we must be very careful about the conclusions we draw from these findings.

The first longitudinal study on the effects of institutionalisation to be conducted as a natural experiment (see Study Outline) was by Tizard and Hodges (1978).

The Tizard and Hodges study however does have its flaws. For example, it is not known whether or not those children who were adopted and those who stayed in institutionalised care differed in some important respects. Neither were there any independent checks on the reliability or validity of the interviews and questionnaires used by the researchers to gather information.

Many children institutionalised in Romanian orphanages experienced severe privation.

STUDY IN FOCUS

Early global privation and cognitive competence O'Connor et al (2000)

What were they doing and why? The English and Romanian Adoptees (ERA) study follows the development of 165 Romanian children adopted between February 1990 and September 1992. All had experienced severe privation whilst in institutional care before their adoption. This study was a follow-up to a previous study which investigated the effects of early experience on cognitive development at age 4.

How did they do it? This was a natural experiment. That is, different groups of participants are chosen – some that have been exposed to privation and some that have not.

The sample was as follows.

WHEN WERE THEY ADOPTED?	NUMBER OF CHILDREN	WHERE WERE THEY FROM?
Between 0 and 6 months	58	Romania
Between 7 and 24 months	59	Romania
Between 24 and 42 months	48	Romania
Between 0 and 6 months	52	UK

Most of the children were originally from **Romania** and had experienced privation in their early development. The group of children from the **UK** was a comparison group. The children in this group had differing backgrounds but none had experienced privation.

Assessment at age 4
A semi-structured interview was carried out, with the adoptive parents, about attachment signs and behavioural problems and children themselves were assessed for intellectual functioning.

Assessment at age 6
The interviews with adoptive parents were repeated and the children given further tests for intellectual functioning.

STUDY IN FOCUS

What did they find? Cognitive performance at 4 and 6 years was related to the amount of time the children had spent in institutions before their adoption.

Children adopted before 6 months scored similarly to UK adoptees.

Children aged between 6 and 24 months at adoption had slightly below average scores.

Children aged over 24 months at adoption showed the greatest impairment.

● There was also a strong relationship at both 4 and 6 years between the **duration of institutional care** and **attachment quality**. It seems that the later the adoption (or in other words the longer the institutional care) the greater was the risk of insecure attachment and attachment disorder.

● Romanian children aged less than 24 months at adoption had 'caught up' with the UK comparison group in terms of cognitive ability by the age of 4 years but showed little evidence of further gain between 4 and 6 years. Where there was catch-up this was most evident in children who were particularly impaired at 4 years of age.

● Recovery in physical development was very strong and nearly complete in most of the Romanian children, with a few persistent problems. There was no clear evidence that physical deprivation was related to cognitive performance.

● Many of the Romanian children demonstrated an inattention/overactivity behavioural disorder.

Take a closer look ● Because the ERA study is a natural experiment, the families adopting from Romania and from the UK could not be closely matched. Whilst the families resembled one another in terms of their socio-economic background, there were differences. For instance, the Romanian adoptees were on average older and a greater proportion of Romanian adoptee families already had biological children. It is not known how these family factors might have influenced the findings. Similarly, adoptee families do not resemble the general population as a whole. For example, they are generally middle class and better educated.

● Because natural experiments are not planned as such, they are not constructed to answer all research questions that might arise. Because of this there may well be issues, surrounding the effects of early experience, which this longitudinal study is not going to be able to answer. For instance there may be issues of individual differences. Some may be more sensitive to the effects of privation that others, but this study is not able to address this issue.

● It has been suggested that the study lacks an adequate or appropriate comparison group. Rather than a sample of UK adoptive children, it would have been better to have used a comparison group of native Romanian children who had never been institutionalised. If this had been done, one of the variables that may influence the effects of privation (cultural differences) would have been controlled.

● Despite shortcomings, the ERA study may be one of the most informative studies yet of the effects of early privation, using a reasonably representative sample whose experience of early privation was limited to the first months or years of life.

STUDY OUTLINE

Effects of long-term institutional care

Tizard and Hodges (1978)

Tizard and Hodges studied the long-term effects on children who were reared in institutions for the first two to four years of life. Whilst in the institutions the children received good physical care and received a fair amount of attention from adults. However, they could not form lasting attachments to specific people because of high staff turnover (for example, the institutions were used to train student nurses). They compared the development of four groups of children: a group who remained in the institution; a group who were adopted between 2 and 4 years of age; a group who were returned to their biological families between 2 and 4 years of age; and a non-institutionalised comparison group. On measures of cognitive, behavioural and social development, the adopted group had the most favourable outcomes, with the institutionalised group faring least well. However, problems persisted in the institutionalised children's social relationships, such as an inability to form close relationships, indiscriminate friendliness towards strangers, attention-seeking behaviour, poor peer relationships, attention deficits and disciplinary problems.

More recently, studies have been conducted using children adopted from Romanian institutions. In the 1990s, the leading source of international adoptions for many Western countries, including the US, Canada and the UK was Romania, an Eastern European country which was revealed, during a time of political change, to have severe problems in its treatment of institutionalised children. Although conditions varied across Romanian institutions, for most children the ratio of child to caregiver was as high as 20 to 1. Children were rarely held and would spend almost all their time in cribs in overcrowded rooms with drab walls and unsanitary conditions.

At the time of adoption, most children were severely physically, behaviourally and cognitively delayed. O'Connor et al (2000) studied the progress of 165 of these Romanian orphans adopted into UK families. They found that, once placed in families, these children do remarkably well given the very poor circumstances of their early life. It seems that cognitive functioning can rapidly recover – many infants who were a year or more behind normal age levels at adoption were functioning at normal or superior levels within a few years. This is also the case for language, even though the Romanian children had the extra challenge of having to learn the language of their adoptive English families. In line with the findings of other studies of institutionalised children, attachment disturbances were observed, as were behavioural disturbances such as inattention and overactivity. There was a strong relationship between the presence and severity of problems and the duration of institutionalisation before adoption. Rutter et al (2007) report further findings of the same group of adopted Romanian children, now at 11 years of age. Results suggest that the effects of early institutional care continue to persist, especially in those children who had been adopted between the ages of 6 and 42 months, i.e. those who experienced the greatest amount of institutionalised care. This is despite having spent at least seven and a half years with their adoptive families in caring and stimulating environments.

"Thinking about evaluating? As ever, research methods to the rescue. Think about methods and research design issues when you are working out how to evaluate these and other studies. A little knowledge of research methods goes a long way."

EVALUATION OF RESEARCH INTO INSTITUTIONALISED CARE

1 It is almost impossible to know for sure the extent of privation experienced prior to adoption. Children are likely to experience different degrees of privation even within the same institution. For example, Ames (1997) points out that institutions often have 'favourites', children who receive special care and attention by staff. It may be that this explains some of the differences in speed and degree of recovery in children following adoption.

2 Whilst many of the problems were due to privation, it is not clear whether prematurity, parental alcohol exposure (which is a major problem in Eastern Europe) low birth weight or some pre-existing developmental disorder, such as autism, could have contributed to the effects.

Indeed, it has been suggested that the reason many of the children were institutionalised to start with is that they had some pre-existing problem and were consequently rejected by their parents.

3 It has been suggested that the tests used to assess development in adopted children are not sufficiently sensitive to reveal subtle problems such as in cognitive functioning. For example it has been pointed out that, despite appearing to have adequate language abilities, post-institutionalised children tend not to use language effectively for such things as emotional expression and abstract thought. This suggests that linguistic skills may not be as developed as the psychological tests suggest and remain affected in subtle ways by the early adverse experience.

Attachment in Everyday Life

Day care can be a rewarding experience for children.

Studying attachment can be both interesting and practical. We can apply the knowledge we have learned to real life. Where to send a child to day care is an extremely important decision. Not only is it often very expensive, but it may have a very significant influence on their development.

DAY CARE

Many mothers of young children work outside the home and have to make decisions about what to do with their children during the time that they are away from them. There are many care options available to mothers, both full-time and part-time, for example in day nurseries, with childminders, or with relatives and friends.

In the past, such decisions have been influenced more by psychological theory than by information provided by scientific research. For example, Bowlby's maternal deprivation hypothesis had a great impact on a mother's decision whether or not to work at all. After all, it stated that it is not good for a child's development for it to be separated from its mother before the age of 3.

> "It is a fact that more and more people are using childcare and preschool services for their young children. Nine out of every ten children in England have been in non-parental care of some sort before starting school.... More mothers have jobs today than at any other time since the end of the Second World War. By 1991, nearly half of all mothers with a child under 5 were in paid work."
>
> Mooney and Munton, 1997

During the last few decades however psychologists have started to directly investigate the benefits or otherwise of day care as opposed to more traditional care in the home. Much of this research has focused on the effects of day care on social development. Childhood presents many opportunities to interact with others, and it is from these experiences that a child develops its social behaviours, from being shy or insecure to being self-confident and assertive, socially skilful or aggressive.

THE IMPACT OF DIFFERENT TYPES OF DAY CARE ON SOCIAL DEVELOPMENT

When comparing the impact of different forms of day care on children's social development, Clarke-Stewart et al (1994) found that it was important to consider both the quality and quantity of care experienced by the child. They conducted a study comparing the experiences of children in home care; for instance those looked after during the day by a parent or childminder, and centre care – those looked after in a nursery or pre-school centre.

The most socially competent children had some experience of good quality day care. One aspect of better quality centre care was children being given some independence by the caregiver. These children were left to play

free of caregiver interaction; they had less direct contact and guidance in activities. Children who attended day care centres like this interacted more with their peers and this was possibly the factor that helped develop their social competence.

Better quality home care, on the other hand, was defined by children as being given *more attention* by the caregiver with more playing, direct contact and talking. This may be because, as social contact with peers is less available, children gain some benefit from interaction with caregivers, otherwise there would be little or no social interaction at all.

Clarke-Stewart et al also found that social competence was related to the *quantity* of day care experienced. For children in home care, the more day care they had the greater the development of social competence. For children in centre day care, the opposite relationship was found, with children spending the most time (measured in hours a week and number of months) showing the poorest development of social competence.

It appears that being around a variety of other children, especially older ones, results in more positive social interactions with friends outside of day care, such as playing, cooperating, showing affection. They also showed less aggression. However, Clarke-Stewart et al found that this mainly applied to children who were in part-time day care. One possible reason for this is that by being part-time, children had increased opportunity to both engage with, and therefore benefit from, day care activities *as well as* play with friends afterwards.

For Clarke-Stewart et al (1994) then, an important factor in determining social competence in young children seems to be the quality of their environment. Regardless of whether time is spent in day or in home care, aspects of poor social development, including

" Yet another chance to show us what you know about research methods! The Vandell et al (1988) research is a longitudinal observational study which involved correlational analysis. So much you can say about that lot! Check back to the Research Methods section to remind yourself of how these methods are applied and of the problems associated with them."

poorer relationships with peers and higher levels of aggression, are linked to unstructured and unstimulating environments. This is supported by Phillips et al (1987). They studied the experience of children in day centres that varied widely in quality. Children attending high quality centres were rated as more cooperative, sociable and confident, less dependent, and engaged in less negative play than children attending low quality centres. For Phillips too, whether or not day care has a positive or negative effect on peer relations seems to depend on the quality of day care that they receive.

Vandell et al (1988) supported this finding but also showed that children who attended good quality day care centres at 4 years of age showed greater social competence as 8 year olds than children who experienced poor quality day care. They defined good day care centres as having better trained teachers, having lower enrolments, having small adult–child ratios and having more plentiful materials available. Children who had attended good day centres were observed to have more friendly interactions with peers (for example less argument and conflict), be more socially competent (for example more cooperative, less shy) and generally happier. One very important finding was that children who were most socially competent experienced more time interacting positively with adults. Moreover, this was found to be the case with both good and poor quality day care centres. Vandell et al suggest that the main benefit of good quality day care was that children are likely to spend more time with adult carers, which in turn reduces the amount of time that they spend aimlessly wandering.

Since high quality day care appears to have such positive benefits for children then it might be supposed that the more care of this kind a child receives then the more a child should benefit. Andersson (1989) followed 119 Swedish children from their first year of life up until the age of 8, at which time they were tested for social and personal development. He found that children who started day care before the age of 1 (and had spent at least 25 hours a week in day care) were rated by teachers as having greater social competence (for example, interacting and cooperating with others) than children who began later or who did not experience day care.

For Field (1991), whilst any amount of high quality day care is better than poor quality day care, the benefits are best when there is both high quality and quantity. They found that receiving high quality full-time day care was positively related to better social relationships during the early teens. It was observed that teens who had received *full-time* day care were rated more attractive and popular, having higher self-esteem, showed less aggression, and greater leadership and assertiveness skills. Furthermore, those teens who had received the most day care tended to be rated most highly. For Field, more experience with other children in good quality controlled day care settings leads to the development of greater social skills, e.g. social competence and confidence, and therefore greater popularity.

Although these and other studies have shown positive benefits of attending day care, other studies suggest that day care can actually have negative effects. For example, Violata and Russell (1994) found that day care had a negative effect on social development, with the effect being most noticeable in those children experiencing over 20 hours of day care a week.

In an observational study, Vlietstra (1981) compared the behaviours of children aged between 2½ and 4½ years attending full day pre-school day dare with those attending half day pre-school day care. It was found that teachers judged those that were in full day care not only less able to get on with their peers but also more aggressive. It seems from this that the quantity of day care is an important factor influencing the development of social behaviour in children. This is supported by Belsky et al (2001).They found that the more time children spent in day care, the more likely they were to

STUDY IN FOCUS

Experiences of day care– A longitudinal study
Vandell et al (1988)

What were they doing and why? The researchers were interested in the long-term impact of day care experiences of varying quality. Are the effects of poor quality day care short lived, or does this kind of early experience have any long-term impact in the child's development?

How did they do it? This was **longitudinal** research. An **observational** method was used with 4-year-olds at day care centres and again when the same children were 8 years old during play sessions. The data gathered for behaviour at 4 years of age were part of a previous (1983) study by Vandell and Powers.

● *Observations at 4 years of age (from Vandell and Powers, 1983)*

A total of 20 children (ten boys and ten girls) were observed in a random order during a free play period at their day care centres at 20 second intervals for 16 minutes. The behavioural categories used in the observation were as follows:

- positive/negative interaction with peers
- positive/negative interaction with adults
- solitary play and unoccupied behaviour

● *Observations at 8 years (new observations)*

Children were videotaped through one-way glass for 45 minutes whilst engaged in prearranged triadic (i.e. three-child) play. The play was designed by the researchers to encourage social behaviour. Whilst the children were playing, the mothers completed a questionnaire about family circumstances and the child's day care history.

A behavioural checklist was completed for each child using the following behavioural categories:

● **Friendly** interactions (positive or neutral exchanges between two or more children)

● **Unfriendly** interactions (negative behaviours including sarcasm, negative actions, etc.)

● **Solitary** play (child plays alone with objects without communicating with peers, and not doing what another child is doing at the same time)

STUDY IN FOCUS

The child play observations were coded separately to the videotapes: A single-blind technique for controlling investigator effects was adopted, so that different observers and videotape coders were used and neither was aware of the children's day care history.

The reliability of the observations and behavioural checklist were checked by having different observers code a random selection of 35% of the children.

What did they find?
Correlational analysis of the data showed that:

Compared to children from poorer quality day care, children from better quality day care had **more friendly interactions** and **fewer unfriendly interactions** with peers, and were rated as more socially competent and happier.

There was a relationship between the 4-year-olds' behaviours in the day care centres and the children's functioning at 8 years:

● There was a positive correlation between positive interactions of 4-year-olds with adults and ratings of empathy, social competence and peer acceptance at 8 years.

● There was a negative correlation between unoccupied (i.e. aimless) behaviour at 4 years and ratings of empathy, conflict resolution and social competence at 8 years.

Take a closer look
● There is a lack of control, in this study, of family factors that might affect the results. For example, there might be a different quality of parent–child interaction between parents who select good quality day care and parents who select poor quality day care. These interactions might account for some or all of the results.

● The life experiences of children in the four years between observations were not taken into consideration. It might have been that some of the children experienced periods of great unrest during this time which might have affected their behaviour and hence the results.

● The sample size is very small (only 20 children) and therefore only limited conclusions can be drawn. It might be that with a larger sample more subtle differences are revealed in the behaviour of children attending different types of day care. More research, involving more children, would help us draw more confident conclusions.

show aggressive behaviours during the early primary school years. Belsky et al asked teachers, mothers and other carers to rate the behaviour of the children in their sample. Of those children who spent more than 30 hours a week in day care 17% were rated as being aggressive towards their peers. Of the children who spent less than ten hours a week in day care only 6% were considered as aggressive.

For Haskins (1985), the age at which a child enters day care is also an important factor. He studied the behaviour of children during the first two primary school years and found that children who began centre-based day care during their first year of life showed greater levels of aggression than children who began day care after their first year. He noted that the early start children:

1 Were more likely to engage in behaviours such as arguing, threatening and swearing.

2 Were more likely to use aggressive acts such as kicking, pushing and hitting other children.

3 Showed aggressive behaviours in several school settings, such as the playground, dining room and school corridors.

4 Were more likely to be recognised by their teachers as having behavioural problems related to their aggressiveness.

5 Were less able to diffuse situations which might lead to aggression, for example by discussion or walking away.

This is supported by Bates et al (1994) who found that children who spent time earlier in life in child care were more aggressive and less popular with peers at school. However, what is important here was the total amount of time spent in day care at a young age, rather than the age of children when in day care. They also point out however that many other factors affect levels of aggression in children, including parental discipline and the child's temperament.

There is also evidence to indicate that long hours spent in day care can have long-term consequences. Belsky et al (2007) suggest that the effects of day care are not necessarily immediate or short term but might emerge later in life. They found that negative effects of day care persisted over time and, in their study, were still showing in the behaviours of young people in their early teens. They suggest that whilst quality parenting is the most important early influence on the social development of children, the quantity of day care experienced consistently emerges as a factor influencing later problem behaviour. Findings of their study indicated that problem behaviours such as aggression and disobedience are most evident in 12 to 13-year-olds who had experienced the most day care. Also, care being provided by a day care centre is a more important factor in later behaviour than whether or not pre-school care is provided by relatives or non-relatives.

A number of studies then seem to suggest that children who spend long hours in day care from an early age are at risk of developing behaviour problems. For Kopp (1982) it is the effect that day care has on *cognitive development*, for example language and thinking skills, which is a key to understanding this influence of day care. He suggests that day care has an effect on a child's ability to *regulate* their own behaviour. Self-regulation is an aspect of a child's cognitive ability and it is this which is disrupted by the experience of day care. Thus, children who experience high quantity and low quality day care are less able than children without this experience to either control aggressive behaviours or initiate adequate alternative responses.

It has been suggested that research has focused too much on factors within day care that might influence peer relations and aggressive behaviour at the expense of broader social factors. For example, Borge et al (2004) did not find any major increases in aggressive behaviour that could be clearly attributed to attending day care. They gave questionnaires to 3,431 mothers of 2 to 3-year-old children who were either in group day care or cared for at home, measuring:

(a) levels of physical aggression in their children if they were attending day care

(b) levels of physical aggression in their children if they were looked after at home

(c) the social and economic family circumstances

They found that, in general, aggression was much more common in children who were looked after by their own mothers than in children experiencing day care. In particular however, aggression was most strongly linked to home care provided by families rated as 'high risk'. A family labelled 'high risk' was one where the mother was poorly educated, work was low-paid/unskilled, there was a larger than average family and poor family functioning. For Borge et al, child care effects are different for different subgroups in society so that when home circumstances are poor, good quality day care is preferable and might even offer opportunities to compensate for family adversity. This is supported by Bradley and Vandell (2007). They found that whilst behavioural problems were more likely in children who began child care early in life and were in care for more than 30 hours a week, there were still real advantages to be had from day care. This was especially the case when high quality care was provided for children from disadvantaged backgrounds. For Bradley and Vandell, "child care experiences interact with experiences at home and the child's own characteristics".

There appears to be conflicting evidence regarding whether or not day care is responsible for increases in aggressive behaviour. One explanation for differences in research findings according to Arsenio (2004) is that the various studies are using different *operational* definitions of aggression with some of the behaviours recorded as aggressive in one study not being seen as aggression in another. Clarke-Stewart (1989) points out for example that one benefit of day care might be to give a child a greater sense of independence and assertiveness. In some circumstances these behaviours could be interpreted as being aggressive, whereas in reality the children could in fact be demonstrating a *benefit* of day care.

EVALUATION OF DAY CARE RESEARCH

There is a vast amount of research into the effects of home or day care on children's social development. It seems however that there are many contradictory findings and relatively little progress has been made in determining the exact influence of day care. There are many possible reasons for this.

1 Howes (1990) points out that most studies of day care are conducted in day care centres attended by children from relatively wealthy families that are able to provide excellent facilities and care. Most parents however do not have the income to be able to get access to such high quality day care. It is this population of children, enrolled in lower quality care, whose social development may be most affected by their non-parental care experiences.

Whether an increase in aggressive behaviour is due to day care is not clear.

2 One problem with researching day care is that it is not open to true experimentation – random assignment of children to different child care conditions is neither practical nor ethical. Researchers instead rely on inferring causal relationships from the methods that they are able to use – usually observation and correlational analysis. However, causation is only one possible explanation, with so many extraneous variables to control (and indeed, many not controlled) it is almost impossible to rule out the likelihood that there is more than one possible explanation for a research finding.

3 Most day care research is conducted with relatively small groups of children that have been followed at most for just a few years. This means that we cannot be too certain about the long-term effects of day care, or be sure to what extent we can generalise the findings of this small scale research to the much greater wider population of children in day care. Even when there has been longitudinal research, there are so many methodological problems that drawing the conclusion that it is early day care that is responsible for the problems is very difficult indeed.

4 It has been pointed out that the effects of day care might to some degree be a reflection of the personality of the principle parental figure, usually the mother. For example, more social (extroverted) mothers might enter their children earlier and for longer, ensure that their children participate in lots of activities, encourage larger friendship groups, encourage more assertive behaviour in their children, etc.

5 According to Arsenio (2004) methodological issues might account for some of these differences in findings and conclusions. For instance, studies tend to adopt different methods of rating children's behaviour. Some studies use only mothers to do the observing and rating, others use a combination of mother, caregiver and teacher. It could be that teachers, because they see more children than mothers do, are better at assessing behaviours. On the other hand it could be that mothers, because they see a lot of their own infant, have more opportunity to observe aggression or they may be biased to see less undesirable behaviours in their own children.

6 Children attending day care are exposed to a range of experiences. Day care environments vary considerably, differing for example in the physical environment, the materials available to children, group sizes, the quality of caregiver and the nature of the interactions between carers and children. Day care is clearly not a single 'thing', often rendering comparisons of findings virtually meaningless.

IMPLICATIONS OF RESEARCH INTO ATTACHMENT AND DAY CARE FOR CHILD CARE PRACTICES

There has been considerable debate about the effects of children being cared for outside the home. There are some researchers who support the view that it is bad for a child to be looked after by anyone other than parents and close relatives – that is, anyone that they have not already developed an attachment to. Alternative research findings suggest that a child may receive care outside of their immediate social circle as long as the care is of good quality.

It is generally agreed that the quality of attachment has a major influence on later social and emotional development, and that the most important factor influencing

IN HOME CARE, MORE SOCIALLY COMPETENT CHILDREN...	IN DAY CARE, MORE SOCIALLY COMPETENT CHILDREN WERE FOUND IN CENTRES WHERE...
...were in more child-orientated physical settings (e.g. fewer hazards and less mess, more toys and less adult decoration)	...there were lower adult–child ratios
...were with fewer younger children	...they interacted with fewer peers who were older
...were offered more school-like activities and individual attention	...they spent more time watching and listening to older children
...had caregivers who were less controlling and demanding	...they spent more time in group activities with older children
...spent less time interacting with other children in the home setting	...they received more individual attention and discipline from the caregiver

Table 5: showing factors which indicate good quality child care.   Source: Clarke-Stewart et al (1994)

attachment is the responsiveness and sensitivity of the caregiver. Any kind of child care which reduces parental availability, especially early in life when attachments are forming, might affect attachment quality.

Some studies seem to confirm that daily separations due to child care can harm the development of a secure attachment. For example, Belsky and Rovine (1988) compared the reunion behaviour and attachment security of infants with and without day care in the first year of life. They found that children who spent more than 20 hours a week in day care were more likely to be insecurely attached.

However, more recent research suggests that this need not be the case. A National Institute of Child Health and Human Development (NICHD) study in 2003 found that factors such as quality, amount, age of entry and type of day care had no significant effects on attachment quality. One possible reason for this difference in findings is that since the 1980s there have been general improvements to the quality of non-parental care.

The importance of quality of care a child receives outside the home was highlighted by Vandell and Powers (1983). They found that children attending high quality centres were more likely to interact positively with others. Good quality day care centres had well trained teachers, spacious accommodation, lower enrolments, lower adult–child ratios and plentiful materials. Poor quality day care centres on the other hand had carers who received less training, had cramped or crowded accommodation, higher enrolments, higher adult–child ratios and less materials.

Clarke-Stewart et al (1994) suggest that whether or not child care is provided in the home or non-parentally, for example in day care centres, quality was of crucial importance in the development of socially competent children. They identified a number of factors which indicate good quality child care and these can be seen in Table 5.

Howes et al (1992) distinguish between structural and functional factors in child care.

Structural factors include the number of children present, the number of children per carer (the child–carer ratio), the training received by the carers and the furniture and toys available.

Functional factors include the motivation of the carers, their sensitivity and warmth towards the child, the caregivers, abilities to adjust to the child and the child–caregiver attachment relationship.

Structural factors influence functional factors which in turn influence the child. This research highlights the need for child care outside the home not only to provide the right physical environment for children but also to respond to a child's emotional needs in providing adequate substitute care.

Further research by Howes (1999) highlights the complexity of the attachment relationship. It may be that the child has a primary attachment to the mother that influences all other experiences the child has. This means that whatever non-parental care the child receives it is always going to be less important than the relationship with the primary caregiver.

Alternatively, the child may be able to develop multiple attachments of equal importance. In this case good quality child care could serve a very important purpose as it suggests that children who have inadequate care at home could benefit from high quality care outside of the home. This would go some way towards compensating for their poor quality home care.

Research in the US has shown that disadvantaged children seem to benefit the most from compensatory child care. Children who attend pre-school programmes such as Head Start are more likely to succeed in school and less likely to be placed in special education. The long-term benefits of Head Start are small or non-existent for middle class children. One reason for this may be because Head Start provides a good quality experience including more caregiver attention and educational activities. Middle class children usually get these experiences at home, while many disadvantaged children do not.

Whilst quality of non-parental child care is influential, family factors are even more important in their impact on the child. A National Institute of Child Health and Development study in 1997 found that the quality of parental care is more important than the quality of non-parental care. It compared the importance of quality in parental care and non-parental care and found that family factors had a greater impact on child outcomes than non-parental factors. So although compensatory programmes can only benefit disadvantaged children there is no evidence to suggest that they can undo the harm caused by poor quality home care.

For Belsky et al (2007) however, whilst timing, amount and quality of child care are important factors influencing a child's experience, it is that children receive non-parental child care of any kind which is of crucial importance. Whilst high quality child care can have positive benefits for some skills such as language, it can result in a range of behaviour problems being exhibited later in life. They found that the more time children spent in non-parental care from birth to pre-school, the more problem behaviours were observed in early adolescence, such as arguing, disobedience and aggression. Whilst Belsky et al accept that these negative effects are modest, they suggest that the vast numbers of children in non-parental care, and potential problems being created, makes them very significant indeed.

WANT TO KNOW MORE?

If you'd like to read more about Developmental Psychology you should find these books interesting.

Bee, H. (2006) *The Developing Child*, Allyn and Bacon

Meggitt, C. (2006) *Child Development: An Illustrated Guide (2nd Edition)*, Heinemann Educational Publishers

Smith P., Cowie H. and Blades, M. (2003) *Understanding Children's Development*, Blackwell Publishing

Section 4

Biological Psychology – Stress

WHAT YOU WILL LEARN ABOUT

The biological basis of behaviour focuses on the interaction between a person's body and their behaviour. Biological psychologists are interested in the influence of evolution, genetics and other aspects of our physiology such as the nervous system. The topic you will learn about in this section is stress, a common behaviour with important consequences. It can affect our enjoyment of life, and can also lead to psychosomatic illness, that is, illnesses that are partially caused by psychological factors.

WHAT YOU NEED TO KNOW

Biological Psychology is in Unit 2 of the specification. You are expected to develop your knowledge and understanding of Biological Psychology, including concepts, theories and studies. This includes a knowledge and understanding of research methods and ethical issues as they relate to this area of psychology. You also need to develop the skills of analysis, evaluation and application. Rather than just recall and reproduce information, you are expected to be able to apply your knowledge and understanding. The subject content is split into two parts:

Stress as a bodily response

- The body's response to stress, including the pituitary-adrenal system and the sympathomedullary pathway
- Stress-related illness and the immune system

Stress in everyday life

- Life changes and daily hassles
- Stress and work
- Stress and personality, including Type A behaviour
- Emotion-focused and problem-focused approaches to coping with stress
- Stress management, including psychological methods (cognitive behavioural therapy) and physiological methods (drugs)

Stress as a Bodily Response

Stress is a part of life.

What is stress and how do we and others deal with it? People often describe themselves as 'stressed out' or 'under a lot of stress' and it is this negative view of stress that we will be concentrating on in this section. We begin by describing how our bodies respond when we are stressed.

THE BODY'S RESPONSE TO STRESS

The quickening of the heart or the bursts of energy or excitement we feel in times of stress are there to help us deal with the situation in hand. The body's response to stress is very important in preparing us for action. We may feel more alert and have a burst of energy, which is just want we need to confront the thing making us stressed (fight) or run away from it (flight). Either way, the body responds to help us cope. We will begin this section with some definitions.

Stress can be defined in a number of different ways. It can be a response to something in our environment or it can be a perceived mismatch between the demands of a situation and your ability to cope with it.

A *stressor* is the stimulus that brings about the stress-response. If scared of flying, airports might be a stressor for you; if scared of the dentist, the sound of a drill might bring on a stress-response. Later on in the section we will see that different aspects of our lives can bring about a stress response, such as a death in the family, and even Christmas. We'll see later that different aspects of a job may be regarded as stressors, such as a perceived lack of control over our activities or a large workload.

How does the body respond to stress? Imagine that your day is perfectly normal. The usual things happen, you see the usual people and do the usual things, until the middle of the afternoon. You are minding your own business, reading a passage in a book when the door opens, a man in a police uniform walks over to you, takes your arm and leads you to the door where another policeman is waiting with handcuffs. Imagine now how your body might be reacting. Your heart will be thumping hard and fast, your legs will be shaking, your hands may feel a little sweaty. Your stomach feels tight, your mouth feels dry and you are on heightened alert, looking all around you at your friends and colleagues watching what is happening. Your body is reacting to the event.

In your normal life you may have experienced these feelings before. You may have sung in front of people or played an instrument in a band or orchestra. You may have competed in sports and anticipated catching a ball or the crack of a starter's pistol before you began your race.

These feelings are not unusual – they are part of the normal reaction of the body to a stressor. This stress response begins in the brain, in an area called the *hypothalamus*. This is the point at which the perception of stress by higher brain centres (where functions like thinking are controlled) begins a major physiological change in the body. The hypothalamus causes this change by triggering two biological mechanisms: the *pituitary-adrenal system* and the *sympathomedullary pathway*.

THE NERVOUS SYSTEM

The nervous system consists of billions of specialised cells called *neurons*. Neurons pass information to each other using electrical and chemical communication. The chemicals they use are called *neurotransmitters*. The nervous system is divided into two major parts: the *central nervous system* (CNS) and the *peripheral nervous system* (PNS). The CNS consists of all the neurons in the brain and spinal cord, and it is their activity that is the basis for all our thoughts and behaviours. The PNS consists of all the neurons that lie outside the brain and spinal cord. It includes sensory and motor neurons that bring information to and from the CNS about such things as pain, touch, temperature and muscle movement. Some of the neurons in the PNS make up what is called the *autonomic nervous system* (ANS). This system connects the body's organs to the brain via the spinal cord. It operates automatically with very little voluntary control. One of its important functions is to arouse the body in an emergency, such as the type of sudden shock you might experience when narrowly missed by a car when crossing the road. The *sympathetic* branch of the ANS performs this activity. When the emergency has passed and the body no longer needs high arousal levels, the *parasympathetic branch* of the ANS returns the body to normal.

The pituitary-adrenal system

When we sense a stressor, the higher brain centres send signals to a part of the brain called the hypothalamus telling it to ready the body for action. This is part of the 'fight or flight' response. The hypothalamus does this by communicating with another part of the brain called the pituitary gland, causing it to release adrenocorticotrophic hormone (ACTH). ACTH is detected in the bloodstream by the adrenal cortex, and in response it releases further hormones into the bloodstream called corticosteroids. There are a number of corticosteroids, each having specific effects on the body. For example, one kind of corticosteroid causes the liver to release glucose, fatty acids and cholesterol for the extra energy needed during stress. Other kinds of corticosteroids change the water and salt balance of the body. Another still ensures faster coagulation (clotting) of the blood in case of injury. When the corticosteroids are detected by the brain it has the effect of switching off the stress response (that is, as long as the stressor has gone away – if it hasn't the hypothalamus will continue to receive signals from the higher brain centres to continue the stress response). This system, also known as the hypothalamic pituitary adrenal (HPA) system is chemical based and

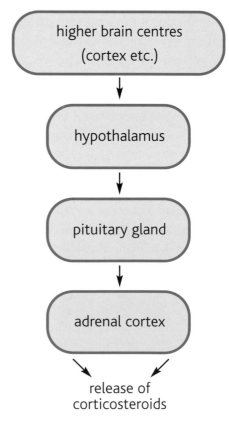

Figure 7: The pituitary-adrenal system.

"The diagrams for the pituitary-adrenal system and the sympathomedullary pathway look a little complicated but they're not really. Learning to draw them is a brilliant way to visualise what happens in the different systems and it will really help you remember the differences between the two."

because of this, whilst still fast, the communication is slower than the sympathomedullary pathway. It can be thought of as the mechanism that prolongs the stress response. Hormones are released into the bloodstream and because these chemicals take a while to break down and disappear their effects will be felt for some time after the original stressor has passed.

THE ENDOCRINE SYSTEM

The *endocrine system* is a system of glands that control many biological functions and affect a wide range of behaviours. They do this by releasing chemicals into the bloodstream called *hormones*. These hormones travel rapidly through the bloodstream to all parts of the body where they either influence a specific organ or gland, or have some general effect on the body. There are a number of endocrine glands in the body, and they vary in terms of the hormones they produce and the function they serve. For example, a part of the *adrenal gland*, called the *adrenal medulla*, is triggered by the sympathetic branch of the autonomic nervous system (ANS) to produce adrenaline, a chemical which contributes to physiological arousal. Another part of the adrenal gland called the adrenal cortex releases a range of hormones called *corticosteroids*, which are essential for such things as sodium (salt) and glucose (sugar) levels in the body. One gland which exerts an influence over all others in the endocrine system is called the *pituitary gland* (it is sometimes called the 'master gland'). This is located at the base of the brain, just under the *hypothalamus*. It is this close association with the hypothalamus which connects the fast-acting nervous system to slower-acting endocrine system.

This is why, when someone makes us jump with shock (they stress us), we are fast to react but slower to recover. Depending on the severity of the shock we can be jittery for quite some time afterwards!

The sympathomedullary pathway

The hypothalamus activates the sympathetic nervous system, a part of the autonomic nervous system involved in arousing the body. The sympathetic nervous system stimulates a

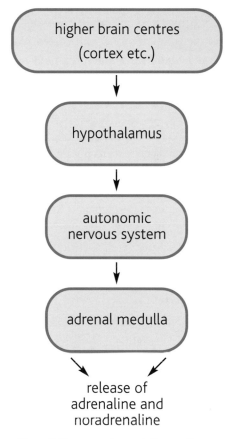

Figure 8: The sympathomedullary pathway.

gland in the body called the adrenal medulla to release two hormones called adrenaline and noradrenaline into the bloodstream. These hormones have wide-ranging effects, but principally serve to increase blood pressure and heart rate. Because the sympathomedullary pathway is a system that uses electrical communication it is very fast acting. For example, there appears to be very little delay between someone giving us a fright and us jumping in response.

Stress-related illness

The stress response is said to be adaptive, that is, it evolves to serve a useful purpose. Essentially, it developed to allow us to either deal directly with the stressor, or to escape it (the stress reaction is sometimes called the 'fight or flight' response). This fight or flight response evolved to deal with quite different stressors to those which modern life exposes us. Whilst originally it was needed to respond to attack, threat and starvation, the world we live in now is much more complicated. We now have a tendency to interpret many more events around us as stressors. Research has found that repeated exposure to mild stressors, as well as long-lasting exposure to more severe stressors, can seriously affect our healthy functioning and can lead to physical and psychological exhaustion and illness.

In the 1940s, Han Selye developed a theory which has helped us understand why and how stress leads to illness. He subjected animals to a variety of stressors, such as injection, poison or extreme temperature, and found that, regardless of the nature of the stress, a similar pattern of physical responses could be observed. He called this the general adaptation syndrome (GAS). Whilst Selye's model has many limitations (e.g. it tends to underestimate the importance of our thinking in how we respond to stressors) it is still a very useful way to think about stress and illness.

Stage 1: *The alarm stage*
In this stage, various physical responses designed to deal with the stressor are activated, such as the pituitary-adrenal system and the sympathomedullary pathway. We can see and feel our body changing, so for example heart rate, blood pressure, breathing and energy levels increase. Our bodies are now ready to deal with the threat; we are tense, alert and ready to fight or flee.

Stage 2: *The resistance stage*
If the stressor persists then the body must adapt and maintain a more stable and long-term level of arousal. Whilst sympathomedullary pathway activity decreases, reducing the initial sense of 'shock' caused by the stressor, output from the pituitary-adrenal system is maintained or even increased. Since we have a limited resource of hormones, there is less available for each new stressor that appears, eventually causing the body's resistance to be lowered.

Stage 3: *The exhaustion stage*
The strategies that we have for resisting stress will see us through most stressful experiences. However, if the stress persists then the exhaustion stage is reached. The body now has fewer resources to expend on stress and the body's response systems begin to break down. This stage is characterised by symptoms such as fatigue, illness, anxiety, depression, impaired physical and mental abilities, etc. If ways to manage stress are not found then in extreme cases death may eventually occur, but more usually stress-related illnesses appear.

Stress and heart disease
There has been an increasing body of evidence supporting a relationship between long-term stress and cardiovascular disease, such that nowadays a link between the two is hardly disputed. The cardiovascular system comprises the heart and blood vessels, their

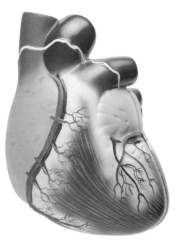

"A bit later on in the section we talk about the types of people that suffer with heart problems. Linking issues covered in different places in the book can really help when you are learning and preparing for exams. Your memory for the information becomes stronger and more detailed when you make this sort of link. Try to do it when you revise if you can."

purpose being to force blood to various tissues and organs in order to keep us alive. It is obviously a very important system and anything which affects its proper functioning is life threatening.

One of the biggest risk factors for cardiovascular disease is high blood pressure, or *hypertension*. Raised pressure produces greater wear and tear on blood vessels. A number of mechanisms control blood pressure, and most of these are affected by stress. One of the main consequences of activating the sympathomedullary pathway is the constriction, or narrowing, of blood vessels. The heart must now work harder to force blood to all parts of the body – this is the increased blood pressure. Blood pressure is also affected by water and sodium (salt) regulation. Too much of these increase blood volume, further increasing blood pressure.

Some of the hormones released during stress have direct effects on the regulation of water and salt. Short-term changes in blood pressure due to stress are quite normal, and there are mechanisms in the body that work to return normal levels as quickly as possible. Research suggests that long-term raised blood pressure, perhaps caused by prolonged stress, can cause small blood vessels to become permanently constricted.

The second major risk factor for cardiovascular disease is coronary heart disease (CHD). There are two main types of CHD: *angina pectoris* is a severe chest pain brought on by a temporary reduction of oxygen to the heart; *myocardial infarction* is a much more serious disorder, since a severe lack of oxygen has caused heart muscles to die. The disease that causes CHD is *coronary atherosclerosis*, whereby blood vessels carrying blood to the heart become narrowed by a fatty substance known as 'plaque'. Whilst there are many risk factors associated with CHD, for example smoking, poor diet and lack of exercise, there is strong evidence linking CHD directly to the stress response. Some of the hormones released by the body when stressed cause the increase of fatty acids in the bloodstream, clogging up vessels. This, on top

IMMUNE SYSTEM

The immune system is the mechanism that provides a defence against infectious organisms that invade our body and cause disease. Without some kind of defence against these 'invaders' (or *antigens*) we would quickly become very ill and possibly die. The cells that make up this defence are white blood cells called leukocytes. There are two type of leukocyte (phagocytes and lymphocytes) which together hunt down and destroy antigens. Phagocytes provide the first line of defence, providing a general barrier against antigens. Lymphocytes provide a more specialist 'seek and destroy response', since these are able to recognise previously encountered antigens. There are two types of lymphocyte, T lymphocytes (T-cells) and B lymphocytes (B-cells). T-cells attack and destroy anything in the body which may carry disease. B-cells are designed to eliminate a particular antigen. If the antigen is present, the B-cells produce antibodies that will hopefully destroy it. A reduction in the effectiveness of the immune system is called *immunosuppression* and this can occur in several ways. Probably the most common cause is stress. It is not entirely clear how stress reduces immune system function. It is thought however that some of the hormones, such as cortisol (a hormone released by the adrenal cortex during stress), causes the immune system to produce fewer lymphocytes.

of constriction already caused by other parts of the stress response, means that stress leads to a greater risk of CHD.

Rosengren et al (1991) studied the health of several thousand men over a number of years, none of whom had experienced myocardial infarction. It was found that those who assessed themselves as experiencing the highest levels of stress at the start of the study were more likely to have had myocardial infarction after an average of 11.8 years. Even controlling for risk factors such as age and lifestyle, it seems that this study is demonstrating a clear link between stress and cardiovascular disease.

Stress and the immune system

Research on a wide variety of stressors has shown that stress can reduce the effectiveness of the immune system. The purpose of the immune system is to protect us from infection and disease. It recognises 'foreign invaders' such as bacteria and destroys them, thus protecting us from their potentially harmful effects. It is widely recognised that during times of stress people show increased rates of infectious disease, including colds, herpes and glandular fever.

A range of stressful situations have been linked to lowered immune system functioning. Arnetz et al (1991) studied a group of manual labourers for several years and found that reduced lymphocyte activity was associated with experiences of unemployment. Several studies have also linked bereavement with immune system functioning. For example, Irwin et al (1987) found that the immune systems of women whose husbands had recently died were functioning at a much lower level than age-matched women who had not experienced this stressful life event. Immune system functioning has even been linked to examination stress. It is not uncommon to see major increases in such things as coughs and colds in students at the time of

Short-term stressful experiences can sometimes be quite positive.

STUDY IN FOCUS

Stress and the immune system
Kiecolt-Glaser et al (1984)

What were they doing and why?
The researchers wanted to see if the immune system was influenced by the external stress of important examinations such as medical examinations at university.

How did they do it? Blood samples were taken from 75 medical students on two different occasions. First, blood was taken a month before their examinations, a relatively low stress time. Second, blood was taken during the examinations (a high stress time).

Each of the participants completed a questionnaire to assess them for things like loneliness, unhappiness and stressful life events. The researchers looked at each of the blood samples to calculate the NK (Natural Killer) cell content. NK cells are like T-cells (see page 151). The more NK cells, the more efficient the immune system.

What did they find? The results were very clear. The blood samples taken during the examinations were much lower in NK cells than the samples taken a month earlier. This suggests that the body had fewer natural defences during the stressful time, so during the examinations the participants were more vulnerable to illness. When the researchers looked at the questionnaires they found that those who were experiencing stressful events in their lives were those with the lowest NK cell activity. They concluded that the immune system is suppressed by the stress of exams. They also concluded that if we have a stressful life we become more vulnerable to the effects of stressors that happen occasionally, like examinations.

Take a closer look

- The research is correlational. We discussed the problems of correlational research in the Research Methods section and this is a good example of the causality problem. We cannot infer that the stress caused the reduction in the immune system, only that the two events are related in some way.

- There may be a sampling bias. As with much research, the participants were students. It is possible that they may respond to stress differently than some other types of people. For instance, what if there is a relationship between IQ (intelligence level) and 'susceptibility to stress'? If there was such a relationship, the researchers did not control for it in their research. You can never be sure with correlational research what actually caused the relationship between the two variables, so be careful.

- Being a natural experiment this study has high validity and there are likely to be few or no demand characteristics. However, like all natural experiments, control of variables was not possible, and it was very difficult to identify all the extraneous variables which might have influenced the results.

important examinations. Kiecolt-Glaser et al (1984) found reduced levels of lymphocytes in university medical students after their final exams compared to levels measured before examinations began. This suggests that examination stress reduces immune function making students more vulnerable to illness.

"It can be daunting sometimes when you come to revise this stuff. Remembering names and dates often causes people real anxiety and problems. If you're clever, you can turn it to your advantage. Use the name to help you organise your revision. Remembering the order that names come in your revision can be a brilliant memory cue to what you want to say in an answer if you prepare carefully."

Prolonged periods of stress are not necessary for changes in immune system functioning to take place. Research suggests that the response of the immune system to stressors can be quite rapid, thus making individuals vulnerable to illness within a very short time following a stressful experience. In an experiment by Weisse et al (1990) it was found that within a couple of hours of being stressed by loud noise and electric shock, the lymphocyte count in their participants had significantly reduced.

Stress can be brought on by such things as social and life changes such as the loss of a job or the change of financial circumstances. The experience itself of being ill, for example with a life-threatening illness or pain and discomfort, can itself bring on stress. One study which investigated the effects of stress during illness was by McGuire et al (2006). They found that patients experiencing the greatest stressful pain following stomach surgery took the longest to heal a small deliberate wound. They concluded that the illness-induced stress was resulting in an immune system taking longer to heal the wound, and suggested that the stress of

hospital admission is a key factor influencing recovery after surgery.

The evidence then seems to suggest that an immune system which is not functioning as well as it should because of stress gives people a greater vulnerability to infection and illness. The relationship between stress, immune system and illness is not a straightforward one, however. According to Dhabhar et al (2000) the effect of stress on the immune system depends on whether or not the stress is *chronic* or *acute*. Acute stress is short-term and is often positive, such as with an exciting roller coaster ride.

There is even evidence that acute stressors lead to an *increase* in immune functioning. On the other hand, chronic stress is negative stress which continues for a longer period of time, such as with bereavement or illness. This is the kind of stress that tends to lead to impaired immune system functioning and stress-related illness.

> ## STUDY OUTLINE
>
> ### Fighting illnesses by reducing stress
> ### Fawzey et al (1993)
>
> There is evidence to suggest that supporting the body's immune system during times of illness-induced stress can have positive benefits for individuals suffering often very serious illnesses. Fawzey et al (1993), for example, studied the progress of 56 patients with skin cancer. 38 of these patients received six weekly one-and-a-half hour stress management sessions. All patients received the usual medical care for their illnesses. Six months after treatment they found that immune system functioning was higher in those patients who had received stress management than those who had not. In a follow-up study five to six years later, it was found that those who had not received stress management tended to have more reoccurrence of cancer and were more likely to have died. This is not saying of course that the stress management cured cancer. As well as fighting infectious illnesses it seems that the immune system can to some extent control cancerous cells and slow down the growth of tumours. Thus, by reducing the stress of having an illness, the immune system is better able to defend the body against attack by the disease.

Stress in Everyday Life

People deal with stress in lots of different ways.

There are many ways of dealing with stress. Some meditate, some play sport, it depends largely on what sort of person you are. In this section we will introduce the idea of personality. We all have one, and we'd all agree that some people have a more agreeable personality than others. The things that make our personalities different, such as 'sensation-seeking' or 'risk-taking' as well as 'shyness' and 'calmness' can also influence how much stress influences us. Here we describe different personality types, and how they deal with stress. You may not be surprised to hear that some people are better at dealing with stress than others.

PERSONALITY FACTORS

Personality is one thing that makes us different from others. We display certain characteristics, which may be called 'traits'. We all know people who are quiet and perhaps a little shy – people who keep themselves to themselves. We also know people who are completely opposite to this. These people are outgoing, perhaps a little exciting, maybe even a little dangerous! In much the same way, some people are helpful and kind, some less generous in their help. These things, or 'traits', make up our personalities, and they also influence how we react to stress.

In personality research we refer to 'personality types'. A 'type' of personality is one characterised by certain 'traits' and patterns of behaviour. Each type differs from the other in the kinds of characteristics that are used to describe it.

PERSONALITY TYPES

Type A behaviour is characterised by competitiveness, impatience and hostility. People like this appear driven to do well and struggle to achieve more. They also become hostile and angry when challenged. An alternative (Type B) behaviour pattern on the other hand is characterised by the relative absence of these traits. According to Friedman and Ulmer (1984) Type A behaviour can be described as a reaction to, and a method of coping with, insecurity. This insecurity develops as a result of early childhood experience, particularly a lack of trust in other significant people and experiences of being harshly criticised resulting in a fear of failure.

Crucially in terms of stress, Type A people display *stronger and more frequent stress reactions* – it could be said that they are more prone to having their 'fight or flight' response triggered by the things that they experience in their environment than other personality types. It has been found that, when faced with stressors, Type A personality types are prone to greater increases in blood pressure, have more circulating stress hormones and higher blood pressure. This excessive activity of their stress systems and the resultant effects on the body over the course of years probably make a significant contribution to the development of coronary heart disease (CHD). Indeed, it appears that Type As are more than twice as likely to develop CHD as Type Bs. This connection was supported by a very influential study called the Western Collaborative Group Study (Rosenman et al 1975). This study followed several thousand initially healthy men for a period of years and found that those displaying Type A behaviour patterns at the beginning of the study were

PERSONALITY TYPES

People with a Type A personality are quite different from those with a Type B personality. The table below describes a number of ways in which they differ. These personality characteristics were described in 1959 by Friedman and Rosenman as part of their research into personality and coronary heart disease, and later in the Western Collaborative Group Study (Rosenman et al, 1975).

TYPE A	TYPE B
● excessive competitive drive	● less competitive
● impatient and hostile	● less hostile and more patient
● fast movements	● easygoing and tolerant
● rapid speech	● slower speech
● very 'intense'	● slower movements
● more likely to suffer from coronary heart disease	● less likely to suffer from coronary heart disease

ASK AN EXAMINER

"This is a really useful thing to try and remember. Very often you'll come across a piece of research that you want to provide an evaluation for. One thing to look out for is whether the work has considered 'personality types'. For instance, work on stress and illness should really consider whether the person has a Type A or Type B personality. Knowing that personality type can influence whether we suffer from some kinds of illness can be a simple and useful way to gain marks in the exam."

more than twice as likely to develop CHD as people with the Type B pattern.

EVALUATION

Despite the wide acceptance and use of the Type A personality concept, it does have some problems.

1 It is quite difficult to assess someone accurately as Type A. A range of structured interviews and questionnaires have been developed to do this, but none of these consistently agree with one another. There are many reasons why this should be the case, but high on the list is the notion that dividing the world into a few categories is just too simplistic. For example, people may have a mixture of Type A and Type B characteristics, or people might have only some of the characteristics of Type A but not all of them. In other words, a 'purely' Type A or Type B person is actually very hard to find.

2 Type A is a collection of characteristics, and research has suggested that some components are more likely than others to be closely related to stress and stress-related illness. For example, a growing body of evidence suggests that the most important aspect of Type A in this regard is *hostility*. Using data from the Western Collaborative Group Study, Hecker et al (1988) related each individual component of Type A behaviour separately to CHD risk and found that hostility was the best predictor of later CHD. Their study also suggested that some components of the Type A pattern appear quite benign in that they did not appear to be related to CHD at all. Another important Type A factor appears to be anger. Ironson et al (1992) exposed their participants to various psychological stressors and found that those related to anger had a greater effect on the ability of the heart to pump blood. Anger had a greater effect even than physical exercise.

3 There is good evidence to suggest that the Type A behaviour pattern is only, or at least largely, found in Western cultures. For example,

Cohen and Reed (1985) found that Type A behaviour is much less prevalent in Japanese men compared to males in the United States (18.7% compared to 50%).

4 Some research has not supported a clear link between Type A behaviour and CHD. For example, Ragland and Brand (1988) suggest that although people with Type B were less likely than those with Type A personalities to have heart problems, they were more likely to die from them. The survival rate for those with Type A personalities was higher, suggesting that something about the Type A personality pattern is important in the recovery from heart attack, which is lacking in Type B.

The hardy personality

Some people appear to live with high levels of stress and do not seem to obviously suffer as a consequence. According to Funk (1992) such

---

STUDY OUTLINE

THIS MAKES ME SO CROSS! – Anger and the Type A personality Ironson et al (1992)

Lots of things influence how our hearts behave. Lots of things make it pump a little faster: the thought of those we love, running for the bus, watching one of those awful penalty shoot-outs our football teams are usually so terrible at winning! It seems that another emotion that makes our heart beat quicker is anger. Ironson et al (1992) looked at many aspects of the Type A personality and found that anger was the most effective of all in affecting the way in which the heart pumped. Looking at anger management and ways of dealing with angry thoughts or actions might be a very good way of helping the Type A person reduce the chance of CHD.

STUDY IN FOCUS

The Western Collaborative Group Study (WCGS)
Rosenman et al (1975)

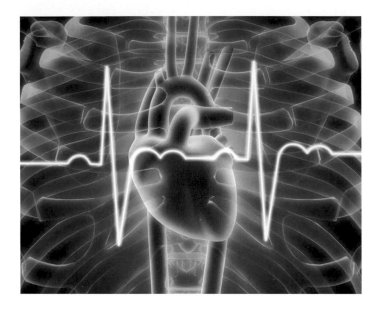

What were they doing and why? Following on from earlier reports (Friedman and Rosenman, 1975) that suggested that Type A personalities were more prone to coronary heart disease (CHD), the WCGS embarked on a study to see what was really going on.

How did they do it? Their study investigated 3,154 healthy Californian men. They chose a longitudinal study, which means they followed the men over a long period of time, eight years in fact. They used structured interviews to decide whether the men were Type A, Type B or something else, which can be described as Type X – a mixture of the two. They then looked at their health records over the eight year period of the study. This allowed them to control for lifestyle choices, such as whether the men were smokers or whether they were overweight. This control allowed them to investigate whether only personality type influenced the number that suffered with CHD.

What did they find? The findings were astonishing. CHD was twice as prevalent in the Type A men than the Type B men. 70% of those that developed CHD (256 in total) were Type A men. They concluded that a behaviour pattern that matches a Type A personality makes us more vulnerable to CHD. It follows that if we can help change the personality type, by looking carefully at helping people change their behaviour, then we can also help people reduce the risk of CHD.

Take a closer look
- The research is correlational. We discussed the problems of correlational research in the Research Methods section and this is a good example of the causality problem. We cannot say that the stress caused the cardiovascular disorder, only that the two things are related in some way.

- The researchers did attempt to control as many variables as possible in this study, but there are likely to be many more aspects of lifestyle contributing to cardiovascular disorder that the researchers were not aware of or could not control.

people have fewer illnesses, have healthier habits, feel less threatened by stressful events and create less stress for themselves in their daily life. He suggests that such people, when faced with stress, are demonstrating the personality trait of *hardiness*. Kobassa (1979) argues that possessing certain aspects of personality can make some resistant to the effects of stress. The three characteristics of a hardy personality are:

Commitment

Hardy individuals have a sense of purpose in life. They do not go through the motions but tackle tasks head on, as though they want to rather than have to. For example, faced with an exam, they are organised and give themselves plenty of time to prepare.

Control

Hardy individuals see themselves as being in charge of their lives. If they do not have the skills to succeed at a task then they will acquire them. When faced with an exam, for example, they will acquire the knowledge and skills in order to do well.

Challenge

Problems are seen as a challenge rather than an obstacle. Because of this, they are willing to devote the necessary time and energy. When it comes to something like an exam, it is seen as a challenge, an opportunity to demonstrate their abilities.

For Kobassa, this psychological hardiness is acting as a kind of 'buffer', or protection, against the negative effects of stressors. This theory is supported in a study by Weiss (2002). She found that parents of children

" These three aspects of the hardy personality are called the 'three C's'. It's a useful way of remembering what the hardy personality is. Just remember Commitment, Control and Challenge – the 3-C's."

with autism experience more negative effects of stress than parents of children with other psychological disorders or parents of children who are developing 'normally'. However, those parents who demonstrated greatest hardiness (as measured by a scale called the Hardiness Test) showed the least stress-related symptoms, such as depression and anxiety. Weiss says that these findings demonstrate the importance of hardiness as a buffer against stress and that having hardiness increases resistance to stressful situations.

EVALUATION

1 The concept of a hardy personality has had positive consequences in that it has led to the development of a successful stress management technique called Hardiness Training. Kobassa (1979) argued that if having the three C's makes an individual hardy to the effects of stress, then these factors can be increased in the less hardy (those without the 'three C's').

2 Whilst there is ample evidence to support the importance of control in stress, there is much less evidence to show that challenge and commitment are important. In fact, Funk (1992) says that being 'negative' and hardiness are actually the same thing, and the effects of stress really come about from this 'negativity'.

3 Maddi et al (1998) showed that hardiness training was more effective in reducing stress than other methods (e.g. relaxation and meditation). However, the work was done with the business community, with participants drawn from the middle classes. This makes generalising the findings to the rest of the population very difficult.

4 There have been relatively few studies which have investigated whether or not personal hardiness is consistent over time within the same population. Most studies investigate hardiness at one point in time and assume that it is a stable aspect of personality, that is to say, our hardiness level stays the same over time. Although Kobassa suggests that the hardiness is stable, some research suggests that whether or not this is found to be the case depends to some extent on the method used to measure hardiness. For example, Greene and Nowack (1995) found that over a three year period scores on the Cognitive Hardiness Scale successfully predicted work-related illness in their participants, but other measures of hardiness used in their study did not.

> **ASK AN EXAMINER**
>
> *"Lots of the research done into personality has used self-report techniques, like questionnaires and scales like the Hardiness Test. There are some problems with measures like this. For instance, how do you know the person is telling the truth? This is a really good example of how you can apply your knowledge of psychological research methods to gain marks."*

Stress reaction style

'Hardiness' is a psychological *trait*. Traits are aspects of personality which consistently affect how we feel, think and behave. The influence of these traits will be apparent regardless of the presence or absence of stressors. For example, people with Type A personalities are said to be competitive, impatient and time conscious whether or not they are actually experiencing stress. However, knowing that someone is a Type A tells us nothing about how they are going to respond to and cope with a stressor when it arises. It is certain that there are going to be significant individual differences in how Type A people react to stressors. The same logic applies to the hardy personality, or indeed any approach which categorises or classifies people in this way.

According to Guenole et al (2008) research has tended to focus on assessing stress after it has happened – on things in the environment that cause stress and the consequences of stress for different types of people. They argue that it would be much more useful to be able to make *predictions* about how people are likely to react

to stressors should they arise. To this end, they developed a method of measuring a person's *stress reaction style*, that is, a way of assessing how individuals might react to future stressful events. Their measure of stress reaction style is a questionnaire requiring respondents to indicate how they anticipate they would respond emotionally, behaviourally and physically to future stressful events. Thus, stress reaction style measures the symptoms, or reactions, that individuals are likely to experience when faced with an environmental stressor.

EVALUATION

1 This approach is likely to have a number of important real world applications:

● *Job selection* – the scale could be used to select those likely to demonstrate less extreme stress reactions in high pressure jobs, such as police and military work.

● *Organisational stress management* – occupational stress costs business many millions of pounds a year, so therefore knowing how employees are likely to react to job stressors would allow a company to be proactive and plan for this, for example with appropriate stress management training.

● *Self-awareness* – individuals who are aware of their own likely reactions to future stressors might be encouraged to seek appropriate employment and develop effective coping strategies.

2 The idea of measuring *stress reaction style* is new and has yet to be supported by further research. For example, the measure indicates likely reactions to future stress but it is not yet clear how accurate this prediction is. According to Guenole et al (2008), "the reaction style construct would therefore benefit from longitudinal research to show that anticipated symptoms are the symptoms that are subsequently experienced."

WORKPLACE STRESS

Work is a very important part of everyday life. Adults are often asked what they do for a living, and students what they intend to do for a future career. Work not only provides us with the obvious things like income to enable a standard of living and a quality of life, but is an important part of people's self-concept. A great deal of what we are and who we are is derived from the relationship we have with our occupation. This might not be surprising given that, for most adults, work is where they spend the majority of their time.

Whilst work can be a great source of satisfaction and fulfilment, for many people it can be a very challenging environment. According to the United Kingdom Government, research shows that more than one in five people claim to suffer from stress caused by their work, with work-related stress accounting for more than a third of all new reports of ill-health to GPs. There clearly seems to be a cost to the individual in terms of ill-health, but there is also a significant economic cost. Each stress-related illness results in an average of 30 days off work, with a total of 12.8 million working days lost to stress in 2004/5. Work-related stress is said to cost the UK over £3.7 billion every year.

Stress then, can be very costly, for firms which have to bear both the costs of lost employees and lost production, and to individuals who have to suffer the ill effects of having to work. Not surprisingly perhaps, a lot of psychological research has focused on the effects of stress in the workplace, and various factors within work have been found to make a significant contribution to our levels of stress.

The work environment

The place in which we work can significantly affect us. If we work in an open office, where people are constantly moving into the space, talking or having meetings, then concentrating may be very difficult. Beaman and Holt (2007) suggest that noise could be an important factor. They found that different types of noise influenced memory, and this in turn may lead to increased arousal and frustration. Halpern (1995) has also shown that the temperature of the environment also influences our behaviour, with aggression levels rising in hotter surroundings, all of which may lead to increased stress.

Workload

Our workload can sometimes be very light, but it can sometimes be very heavy indeed. Work overload means having more work to do than the time given to do it. Two kinds of

STUDY IN FOCUS

Stress in the workplace – control
Johansson et al (1978)

What were they doing and why? The workplace is a stressful place, but what makes it like this? Even if people dearly love what they do, some things can be stressful. Bills must be payed, accounts done on time, customers satisfied and staff paid. All of these things may be stressful. What if the ability to carry out these tasks was governed by something else? If the person giving you the information for the accounts does not do their job, then you cannot do yours. This is out of your control. Johansson et al (1975) looked at the role control plays in workplace stress.

How did they do it? They found a Swedish sawmill whose business was taking trees and turning them into finished timber. The last stage of the process is called 'finishing'. The speed that the 'finishers' work depends on how fast the machines that provide the wood to the final stage are running. The work is 'machine-paced'. Finishing requires great skill. The amount of finished wood produced determined the wages for everyone working at the factory. Johansson et al compared 14 finishers with ten cleaners, whose job was described as 'low risk' and was not paced by a machine, but could be done at their own speed. The rates of absenteeism and stress-related illness in each group were compared, as were the levels of adrenaline and noradrenaline (stress-related hormones) found in their saliva and urine both on work days and rest days.

What did they find? They discovered that the finishers had higher levels of stress hormones on work days than on rest days, and that these levels were higher than for the cleaners. Perhaps not surprisingly, the finishers also had higher levels of absenteeism than the cleaners and suffered with more stress-related illnesses. They concluded that the high responsibility level of the finishers, the repetitive nature of their work and also the lack of control over their workload all added up to increased levels of stress, illness and absenteeism. This allowed them to conclude that if employers want to avoid stress and absenteeism then workers should be given some control over their work, and the variety of work should be improved to avoid the repetitive nature of the job.

Take a closer look
- The personality type of the finishers and cleaners may have been a factor influencing their stress responses, or even general physical health, but this was not investigated. It is very difficult to be confident about the findings of studies like this which have not fully considered the impact of individual differences on the results.

- A number of factors influencing stress were identified, but it is not clear from the research which is the most important, or if the factors worked together (interacted) to form the stress response from the finishers. This is a problem with studies which are natural rather than laboratory experiments – a lack of control means that it is very difficult to separate out the effects of variables in this study like repetition and responsibility.

workload have been identified: *quantitative workload* refers to the amount of work required in a given task (an example might be having too much work to do resulting in long hours worked), whilst *qualitative workload* refers to the complexity of the task (an example might be being given a job to do which is too difficult to do under the conditions given to do it). One of the consequences of work overload is the problem it causes with balancing the demands of work with those of family life. People often complain about their partners being 'married to their jobs' and balancing work life and private life can be a major source of pressure on relationships. For example, Wallace (1999) found that both married male and female lawyers reported work overload as a factor influencing conflict at home. The way we work must be looked at in terms of work overload. For instance, traditionally women hold different types of jobs and do different types of work than men in society, although this is, of course a generalisation. Often women work outside the home but still handle domestic chores. Many women find themselves dealing with the challenges and stress that can accompany single parenthood, such as working multiple jobs to make ends meet. In addition, women may find themselves continuous caregivers sandwiched between generations — caring for their young children while also caring for sick and older family members. These kinds of stressors might make you vulnerable to illnesses that relate to stress, such as depression.

Lack of control

Research has consistently indicated that more stress is felt in situations where an individual feels they have little or no control. It is not unusual for people to work under these conditions. For example, people who use machines to produce goods usually have their pace of work dictated by the machines they

'operate'. Johansson et al (1978) studied people working in a Swedish sawmill. They found that those workers who had the most repetitive work, and work whose speed was governed by how fast the machines worked (machine-paced), showed the highest levels of stress-related hormones in their urine and had the highest stress-related illness and absenteeism rates.

Logan and Ganster (2005) looked to see whether increasing a sense of control in workers could *improve* job-related stress. They identified areas of lack of control in the jobs of area managers of a large trucking company in the United States. These areas of control were addressed in a series of training events. They found that those managers with supportive supervisors reported an increased sense of control and hence job satisfaction after four months. Individuals who have job control have the ability to influence the planning and execution of work tasks. For example, Jackson (1983) found that participation (attendance at staff meetings) had a negative effect on perceived job stress, and a positive effect on perceived influence. This, in turn, influenced perceived emotional strain, job satisfaction and absenteeism. In general, job control is the ability to have some influence over one's environment so that the environment becomes more rewarding and less threatening.

"You don't need to remember a long list of workplace stressors. You're better off knowing just a few in a little more detail, along with some research to support the points you are making. The Johansson et al study is a really good study to use here. Not only is it pretty simple and easy to remember, but it says quite a lot about factors in the workplace that cause stress. It can be used to support all three factors mentioned here!"

LIFE CHANGES AND DAILY HASSLES

Our lives change all the time. The major changes might include moving away from home, getting married or dealing with a death in the family. In order to accommodate these changes into our lives changes often need to be made, and these changes can be very stressful. It is not just these major events that can be stressful. We often find ourselves concerned with more 'everyday' worries and hassles, such as money worries and problems with our houses or social lives. This section is concerned with how life changes and daily hassles influence us.

LIFE CHANGES

Major changes in our lives can cause stress. The death of someone close to us, injury, relationship difficulties, starting a new school or college; these are all stressful experiences. These events cause change to our lives in some way: we may be prevented from achieving certain goals because of them, or we may have to adjust the way we think, feel and behave. These events

Airports can be very stressful places. Crowds, heat and delays all add up to a recipe for a very stressful day!

do not need to be obviously negative to cause stress – for example, most people would see a holiday as a positive event but many people experience considerable stress as a result of the preparation and travel involved!

One of the most famous studies on the effects of life events was conducted by Holmes and Rahe (1967). They were two doctors who noticed that many of their patients had suffered disruption to their lives during the previous year. They constructed a questionnaire to investigate the possible link between life events and physical ill-health.

They examined the medical records of over 5,000 patients, and from this compiled a list of 43 different 'life events'. These were rated in terms of the time it would take to readjust life back to normality following the event. 'Marriage' was given an arbitrary score of 500, then participants rated the other events in comparison to this. They averaged out the scores and divided them by 10, so in the final

STUDY IN FOCUS

Life changes and stress
Rahe et al (1970)

What were they doing and why? Rahe et al wanted to see whether the onset of an illness could be related to scores on the Holmes and Rahe Social Readjustment Rating Scale (SRRS).

How did they do it? They took an SRRS score from 2,500 male US sailors before they embarked on a six month tour of duty. During the six months medical records were kept which provided a detailed record of the health of each of the sailors. After six months the SRRS score was correlated with an 'illness score'.

What did they find? They found a significant positive correlation between SRRS score and illness scores. This means that as one went up, so did the other. Remember, this does not mean that one caused the other, just that there is a positive relationship between the two. They were able to conclude that experiencing unpleasant life-changing events increases our likelihood of suffering with illnesses, but experiencing stressful events does not guarantee that illness will result.

Take a closer look
- The research is correlational. We discussed the problems of correlational research in the Research Methods section and this is a good example of the causality problem. We cannot say that life changes cause the illness, only that the two things are related in some way.

- The strength of the coefficient here was very low; in fact it was only marginally significant. It is quite possible that if they repeated this study they would not replicate the findings.

- The sample of participants was very restricted – male US military personnel. We cannot be sure that the same results would be found in females or in people from other cultures.

scale 'marriage' has a score of 50. These scores were called Life Change Units (LCUs). The scale of events starts at 100 LCUs for 'death of a spouse, and ends with 11 LCUs for 'minor violation of the law'. People would add up the score for each life event and this would be their total LCU. They believed that a score of over 300 meant an 80% chance of developing a serious physical illness in the following year.

This relationship between life change, stress and illness was supported in research by Rahe et al (1970). They studied sailors aboard US Navy Cruisers and found a link between life changes and physical illness. The greater the SRRS score for the previous six months, the more likely they were to fall sick some time during their seven month tour of duty.

EVALUATION
Although many studies have been conducted using the SRRS, there are problems with this scale.

> ## STUDY OUTLINE
>
> ## The Holmes and Rahe Social Readjustment Rating Scale (SRRS)
>
> The Holmes and Rahe Social Readjustment Rating Scale (SRRS) identifies a number of items that are rated as stressful. Some of the items include things like 'death of a spouse' and 'divorce' so it isn't that much use to younger people! Insel and Roth (1985) developed a stress scale which focused on students and included items like 'number of missed classes', 'pregnancy' and 'death of a close friend'. It is important then, that the tool you are using to measure your variable (in this case stress) is the correct one for the job. If it is not then the conclusions you draw from the results may lack validity.

1 The life events listed in the scale will have different meanings to different people. In other words, there will be significant individual differences in the amount of disruption an event causes, which means that the impact in terms of LCUs is not the same for all people. For example, the effects of divorce varies enormously, depending on such things as length of marriage, family and financial ties, and the extent to which children are involved. Whilst divorce can certainly be a devastating experience for some people, others may derive a sense of relief from it.

2 Life events are *correlated* with stress and ill-health. This means that a rise in stress levels may be accompanied by a rise in ill-health. Correlations do not indicate cause. Any number of other factors could explain the relationship. For example, illness could precede divorce and be a factor in the separation rather than be a consequence of it. Also, even when research does suggest a link between life events and stress, the correlation tends to be rather weak.

3 As well as obvious negative life events, such as 'death of a spouse', the SRRS contains events which might be interpreted as positive, such taking a holiday. However, Martin (1989) could find no correlation between positive life events and ill-health.

The Life Experiences Survey (LES)

Because of the shortcomings of the SRRS it is rarely used in psychological research today.

However, the idea of life events being related to ill-health remains a valid one, and the SRRS inspired the development of a range of other, more relevant ways of assessing this relationship.

More recent research suggests that the relationship between change and stress is not so straightforward. Sarason et al (1978) argue that life changes do not cause as many unpleasant stress reactions as Holmes and Rahe would have us believe. Whilst all life changes cause disruption, it is the degree to which the events are perceived as positive or negative which is important in assessing their impact on us. Sarason and colleagues created an updated life experiences survey, addressing many of the problems of the SRRS. The Life Experiences Survey (LES) is a 57-item questionnaire which allows each event to be rated in terms of positive or negative impact. 47 of the events applied to everyone, and ten events only to students. For example, the survey includes events such as 'new baby' and 'lose job'. Each event is rated from +2 (very good) to -2 (extremely bad) which allows us to calculate a *positive* LES score and also a *negative* LES score. Also, the scores can be added together to give an overall LES score. The survey has certain benefits over the SRRS. For instance, positive and negative events are clearly separated from one another by whether a negative score or positive score is given. The scale is different for everybody, so it takes individual differences of opinion into consideration. It is a very useful tool in

Table 6

LIFE EXPERIENCES SURVEY (LES)
Health: Major illness or injury
Health: Major change in sleeping habits
Health: Major dental work
Work: Retirement from work
Work: Difficulty finding a job
Work: Troubles with co-workers
School: Beginning or leaving school
School: Problem in school
School: Change in career goals

Some examples from a Life Experiences Survey. Each statement is under a 'subheading' and we've included examples from **Health**, **Work** *and* **School** *here. Those completing the survey must identify each statement as 'good or bad' and then rate it on whether each has an effect on their lives (0 for 'no effect' to 3 for 'large effect').*

STUDY OUTLINE

Not everyone responds to social support in the same way

Sarason et al (1981)

Sarason et al used the LES as part of their 1981 study when they looked at how different people deal with different forms of social support.

She had participants complete the LES and then divided them up into groups who scored negatively and groups that scored positively. Next, she gave each a series of difficult problems to solve and provided members in each group with different forms of support or help. These included working alone or working in groups.

She found that those who scored negatively on the LES responded differently to different types of social support than did those who scored positively. More positive opinions of social support related to positive measures on the LES.

identifying people who rate events as bad or good. See the Study Outline for more on the LES, and Table 6 for some example statements from the survey.

These life experience surveys are very useful. Sarason's LES has been integrated into a number of measures that are being used in psychology at the moment. It is quite possible that you may be asked to rate events as part of a job interview or if you are unfortunate enough to fall ill with depression. If this does happen you may well be using a rating scale built on Sarason's important work.

DAILY HASSLES

Whilst major life changes can be stressful and have an impact on us, they are actually relatively rare things. Much of the stress of modern life arises from what might be described as 'non-events', such as being kept waiting for a bus. These are the annoyances and irritations of everyday life. Perhaps a better predictor of our physical and psychological well-being are these relatively minor everyday 'hassles' we all experience. Hassles are small-scale annoyances and irritations, such as being caught out in the rain, misplacing your keys, missing a bus or being late for the cinema. Whilst individual hassles are unlikely to trigger large-scale stress responses, according to Lazarus (1981) hassles tend to accumulate and the combined level of stress can cause problems.

STUDY OUTLINE

Life has its ups and downs: Hassles and uplifts – a combined scale DeLongis et al (1988)

DeLongis et al (1988) developed a combined hassles and uplifts scale. For each event, those completing the survey are asked to rate it twice: once as an 'uplift' (a positive event) and once as a 'hassle' (a negative event). The ratings are as follows:

0 - none at all, or not applicable
1 - somewhat
2 - quite a bit
3 - a great deal

Some of the items from the scale include:

- Your physical appearance
- Enough money for emergencies
- The weather
- Amount of free time
- Your workload

If you were wondering, the top hassle was 'worry about the future' and the top uplift was 'completing a task'. Clearly this will not be the same for absolutely everyone, so we must be careful when using scales – like knowing that if average measures are used, they may not be exactly what everyone thinks.

It is not the occurrence of a 'hassle' itself that is important, but it is the frequency (how often), duration (how long) and intensity (the size) of hassles that give them their impact. For example, misplacing your keys might be no more than an uneventful occurrence, soon forgotten. However, if it is the third time you have lost them, and this time you have been unable find them for an hour, and you really have to be somewhere else in a hurry, then this relatively minor hassle has now become something much more significant. Of course, not every event we encounter in a day is going to be negative – many things are actually going to be quite positive, for example having fun in the company of friends or enjoying sunny

weather. The effect of day-to-day hassles therefore has to be balanced to some degree against the effect of our day-to-day uplifts.

Kanner et al (1981) developed the 'hassles scale', a 117-item questionnaire used to examine the relationship between hassles and health. This was later developed by DeLongis et al (1988) into a combined hassles and uplifts scale.

DeLongis et al (1982) thought that the relative rarity of life events explained the weak correlation between life events and health. They set out to investigate whether or not daily hassles would be better predictors of later health than life events. For a period of a year their participants were required to complete monthly measures of hassles and uplifts, life events and health status. They found a significant positive correlation between intensity of hassles and health status – the greater the hassles experienced, the more likely there would be a health consequence. However, no relationship was found between health and uplifts, and no relationship between life events during the period of study and health. They concluded that daily hassles and uplifts may be a better way to predict health consequences of stress than the usual life events approach.

The relationship between daily hassles and health issues, such as increases in headaches, respiratory infections and the common cold has been confirmed elsewhere. DeLongis et al (1988) looked at married couples over a period of six months, assessing them 20 times in that time, and showed very clearly that negative life events were strongly correlated with illnesses of the type mentioned, as well

"Be careful not to mix up 'life events' with 'daily hassles'. We often see that sort of thing in exam papers. This is a serious mistake to make because questions may ask you to write about one or the other. Make sure you know the difference; it can mean the difference between full marks and no marks at all."

as backache. Their research did though indicate that whether stress influenced us psychologically might depend on the type of support we have around us. Even with relatively low levels of daily hassles, without social support we are still much more likely to suffer from psychological problems.

EVALUATION

1 Many of the problems of the SRRS are shared by the hassles scale. For example, because the relationship between hassles and ill-health is correlational, it is difficult to be certain about cause and effect. One possibility is that ill-health is magnifying the impact of a hassle which at other times might be insignificant.

2 Although there appears to be a link between major life changes and subsequent illness, research has shown that the association between recent hassles and illness is stronger, making measures of daily hassles a better and more useful predictor of day-to-day health than more distant life events.

3 There are likely to be significant individual differences in the ways that people interpret hassles, so that an event which is a hassle to one person might not be a hassle to another, like going to the dentist or being late for work. Also, whether or not an event is interpreted as a hassle will vary, so that it can be a hassle one time but not at another; for instance, paying bills may be less of a hassle when there is more money in the bank than after Christmas when many people are less well off.

4 Like the rating of life events, the rating of hassles is completed retrospectively, that is, people have to think about and evaluate past events. This relies on accurate recall. However, research suggests that recollections are affected by current state of mind. This is an important consideration here because the scale might involve someone rating past hassles when they may be currently experiencing ill-health. It is possible in this case that they will over-report negative events and under-report positive ones.

COPING WITH STRESS

Events within the family, work, school and social life, that is, daily living, naturally present us with a range of stressors which we must deal with as best we can. To experience some degree of stress is normal and in moderate amounts is good for us; it keeps us alert and responsive, activates us and since it actually improves performance, it keeps us productive.

When the experience of stress is positive and we are able to cope with the demands made on us the experience is called *eustress*. However, there can be too much stress (or, even too little, leading to boredom and apathy), in which case the experience is labelled *distress*. Successfully coping with stress involves both reducing the sense of distress whilst also making the experience of eustress more familiar and normal.

Stress is rarely a simple thing. The conditions producing stress, and our responses to them, are usually complex in terms of thoughts, emotions and life obstacles. It is therefore often difficult to find a single strategy for coping with stress, especially one which satisfies both the goals of successfully reducing distress whilst also increasing eustress.

Since stress has become a major social issue in recent years, many methods which claim to manage its negative effects have been developed. Some of these are commonly seen produced in glossy magazines and self-help books. A therapy industry has also developed, with stress managers, life coaches, etc. offering their services to both businesses and individuals. There are many ways of categorising these methods, but according to

Lazurus and Folkman (1984) one way is to make a distinction between *emotion-focused* and *problem-focused* methods of coping.

PROBLEM-FOCUSED METHODS OF COPING

These methods are also known as 'approach' methods of coping. As the name suggests, these techniques involve the person dealing with the stress by treating it as a problem to be solved, actively engaging with it. Relief from their symptoms comes by dealing with the stress using the following techniques:

Anticipatory coping

Stress and anxiety come with certain symptoms which might include physical responses, like a tightening of the stomach or shortness of breath. It might also be accompanied by psychological feelings of helplessness and paranoia. Our behaviour may change; for instance we may not be very sociable or we may become short-tempered. Anticipating these changes can help us deal with them. For example, if we anticipate a change, or we have a sensitivity to dealing with crowds, then we might change our plans to avoid crowds. Because of this our stress levels will not increase. Another example of this might be avoiding watching the news if you have a relative in the armed forces. Any news about troop movements or casualties may increase your anxiety levels, and controlling the flow of this news into your home helps you to cope. So, to improve our anticipation we need to gain information about what makes us stressed and develop a plan of action to help us deal with it once we have successfully anticipated it.

Seeking social support

Our friends and family can often be an invaluable source of help and support when we are experiencing stress. Discussing problems can often help us make sense of the problem we have, and cope with the stress more successfully

If we can identify events in the environment that are either causing or are likely to trigger stress, then we can take practical steps to either avoid it or better deal with it should it arise. For example, examinations can cause a great deal of stress, and one of the main reasons for this is that students are often insufficiently prepared for the emotional impact of important examinations. In this case, learning techniques to deal with exam stress might be very beneficial. Another thing to do would be adequately prepare for the exam! It can be seen with this example that problem-focused methods deal with the root cause of the problem. Engaging in a form of training is also useful. That way, when stress comes along people are better practiced and better able to cope with it.

Psychological methods of stress management – cognitive behavioural therapy

Stress inoculation training (SIT) is a form of cognitive behavioural therapy developed by Meichenbaum (1972). He argued that people could be made resistant to stress ('inoculated' against it) in much the same way that one could be against a virus. (If you were to travel to parts of the world where malaria is in evidence, then you would be inoculated against it before you went. This involves introducing a tiny amount of malaria into the body using an injection. The body learns to deal with the malaria, so experiencing it when travelling does not cause a problem because we have the biological 'ammunition' on board to look after us.) SIT deals with stress by restructuring how we think about events. It uses various techniques to change the way people think about their stressors so that when we encounter them we are better prepared.

SIT has three phases:

1 Conceptualisation

Here the client is encouraged to reappraise stress, that is, begin changing the way they think about it. The therapist discusses the nature of stress with the client and explores stressful experiences that the client has had in the past. This involves a consideration of what it was about the event that was stressful, what methods the client has used to cope and analysis of the success or otherwise of these coping strategies.

2 Skills training and rehearsal

In this phase of training the client is taught various ways of coping with stress. These can be quite specific and focused on actual stressors discussed during the conceptualisation stage, but will also include general strategies such as relaxation.

3 Application and follow through

In this final phase, clients are encouraged to apply their training to the real world. This might involve simulations at first, in order to develop confidence and skills. The stressors may be graded, gradually increasing in intensity. Follow-up sessions are provided if necessary, which could involve further training as well as feedback and discussion.

STUDY IN FOCUS

Exams!
Meichenbaum (1975)

What was he doing and why? Michenbaum wanted to investigate how effective his own 1972 stress inoculation therapy (SIT) was. Meichenbaum believes that anxiety arises as a result of negative internal monologues we hold with ourselves when faced with a stressful situation. It is this that then influences a negative outcome.

How did he do it? Meichenbaum studied anxious pre-exam college students. An independent measures quasi-experimental method was used. The three conditions were as follows:

Condition 1: eight weeks of stress inoculation therapy
Condition 2: eight weeks of systematic desensitisation
Condition 3: no therapy – students were told they were on a waiting list

Efficacy (the efficiency of SIT) was evaluated through exam performance and self-reports. Simply, if the students felt it had been successful, and they performed well in exams, SIT was judged to have worked.

What did he find? The SIT group gave the most positive self-reports, and outperformed the other students in their exams. The students on the waiting list remained just as anxious.

Stress inoculation therapy as a form of cognitive behavioural therapy (CBT) proved to be very successful in this case, and is often shown to help reduce anxiety in stressful situations. However, as an example of CBT, it only applies to anxiety and not depression.

Take a closer look
- The researchers used self-reports of whether they felt their treatment had been successful. These are not necessarily reliable. Just because a person feels that something has not worked does not mean that they will receive no benefit from it.

- SIT was found to be more successful following eight weeks of treatment. It could be that more systematic desensitisation would have helped the students even more. This study does not address 'optimum treatment period' so we cannot be sure which of the methods is best, only that SIT worked better than systematic desensitisation if a treatment period of eight weeks is used.

EVALUATION

1 SIT is flexible in that it can be tailored to individual needs. Because of this it can be used to inoculate against a wide range of potential stressors. For example, it has been used in the treatment of military combat stress, stress caused by medical and psychiatric illness, and stress caused by traumatic events like divorce. Meichenbaum (1975) found that SIT proved more effective than other methods in reducing the pre-exam stress felt by college students.

2 SIT is neither a quick, easy or cheap method of stress management. According to Meichenbaum (1996), "In most instances, SIT consists of some 8 to 15 sessions, plus booster and follow-up sessions, conducted over a 3-to-12-month period." Clients have to be sufficiently motivated to openly discuss their experiences, practise stress management techniques and confront the stressor (which was significant enough to cause them to seek therapy in the first place).

3 The time, effort and expense of SIT is still usually preferable to other physiological methods, such as drug treatments. Unlike drugs, the benefits of SIT can be long term: it deals directly with stressors and teaches ways of handling stressors which might appear in the future.

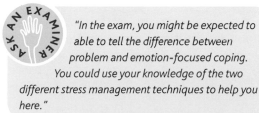

"In the exam, you might be expected to able to tell the difference between problem and emotion-focused coping. You could use your knowledge of the two different stress management techniques to help you here."

EMOTION-FOCUSED METHODS OF COPING WITH STRESS

Emotion-focused methods are also known as 'avoidant' methods of coping. Emotion-focused methods of dealing with stress are common, and they especially apply in circumstances where a person feels that there is nothing to be done to change the problem, i.e. the source of the stress. If the situation which causes the stress must be accepted, then methods are employed to regulate the emotional responses to the stressors. An 'emotion-focused' method of dealing with stress is one that provides the stressed person with relief from their symptoms by dealing with the stress using a range of possible techniques.

Defence mechanisms

The stressed person may put up psychological barriers to their stress to help them cope. A defence mechanism is a way of blocking out the stress. There are a number of defence mechanisms, one being *denial*. This is where the person refuses to believe that the stressful event is happening at all. They deny it. Another defence mechanism is *intellectualisation* where the person manages to explain away the stress to themselves – they 'intellectualise' it rather than accept it as a reality. Their reasoning may not seem rational or sensible to others, but to them they have managed to make sense of the stress, rather than deal with it as something that really is occurring.

Reappraisal of the situation

Here the stressed person may take another look at their stressful situation, and 'reappraise' it. By this we mean that they may simply change the way that they *feel* about the situation. If the person can reconsider a stressful situation and manage to regard it differently, for example by caring less about stressful events and their consequences, then their feeling of stress may no longer cause them as much concern.

Arousal reduction

When a person becomes stressed their senses become heightened, they become more aroused. Reducing this arousal reduces the symptoms of the stress and makes the person feel better. There are a number of ways that this can be achieved. One way of dealing with increased arousal is by taking physical exercise, perhaps in the gym or on the sports field. Certain chemicals released by the body during rigorous exercise have been found to have stress-reducing effects. Alternatively, a person may learn to meditate or learn other forms of relaxation training. Another way is to self-medicate, by taking illegal or recreational drugs, like alcohol. The most common emotion-focused therapy however is to take drugs prescribed by a doctor.

Physiological methods of stress management – drugs

Because stress is a physical and psychological reaction, it is often treated by trying to reduce these symptoms. The logic is simple: reduce the symptoms of stress and stress should no longer exist. The most widely used anxiolytic

drugs prescribed today are the benzodiazepines. (The word anxiolytic means that they reduce the physical feelings of anxiety.) Benzodiazepines lessen tension and nervousness and have an overall calming effect, and they can be used for both sudden severe stress and general tension.

Benzodiazepines work by affecting levels of naturally occurring brain chemicals (called neurotransmitters). Specifically, they increase

" Alcohol is a drug too, and some people use it to combat stress. It is called 'self medicating', or deciding for yourself whether to take drugs or not. By all means use this kind of information in your writing, but please read the question carefully! If asked to write about drugs, the best way to gain marks is to give the information we have given you here, particularly the section about benzodiazepines."

BETA-BLOCKERS

Benzodiazepines are not the only drug taken for stress, sometimes beta-blockers might be prescribed by some doctors. These have a direct effect – lowering heart rate and reducing blood pressure and may be useful in some cases of panic attacks. Beta-blockers block the effect of adrenaline and so stops the physical effects of a person's natural fight or flight response. Lau et al (1992) found beta-blockers reduce risk of death by about 20% in patients suffering from heart disease, so it is clear that they do have an action on how the heart works. People with suspected 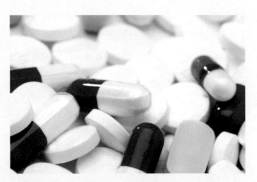 coronary heart disease, or those who have had a heart attack, are usually prescribed beta-blockers, because they reduce the strain on the heart.

Beta-blockers do serve a purpose. They start working relatively quickly – about an hour and half after taking them – so can used to directly combat a stressful situation. Beta-blockers have, for instance, been used successfully to reduce stress in musicians and public speakers before performances (Taylor, 1995). They reduce stress because people do not need to worry about public speaking events that may be coming up in the future – they know they can do it after the first event, supported with beta-blockers. This can have the effect of improving confidence for the next event, which may not need drug support. Even if the speaker does need drugs for the future events, they know that the beta-blockers can work for them, and so are not worried and stressed in the period between events. These are not in any way the perfect cure for stress though. Like other drugs such as benzodiazapines, beta-blockers are only a temporary fix. They do not address the causes of the stress, only the symptoms.

STUDY IN FOCUS

Emotional approach and problem-focused coping: A comparison of potentially adaptive strategies Baker and Barenbaum (2007)

What were they doing and why? This very recent piece of work set out to answer just the sort of question many people ask: which is best, an emotion-focused approach to coping with stress or a problem-focused approach?

How did they do it? 89 American psychology students volunteered as participants. Each was required to participate in a certain number of experiments each year as part of their psychology degree. The gender mix was approximately equal (44 females and 45 males). They were split into two groups. All participants identified a current stressful situation. One group wrote about their feelings for five minutes (emotion-focused – EF). One group wrote about how they might solve the stressful situation (problem-focused – PF). On top of this, all participants filled out a self-report questionnaire on how well they coped with stress after exercise during the week. All participants were then assessed for a number of things such as how well they communicated their feelings and their mood using a range of psychological assessments.

What did they find?
● Many individual differences were identified that played an important part in whether the EF or PF strategy was best. For instance, if the participant was not used to accessing their emotions, the EF strategy was useful to them as it helped them identify their emotions in a way they may not have considered.
● There was also a significant gender difference, with females engaging with more EF strategies than males.
● It also depended on what the stressful event was. If it was an interpersonal stressor, like a problem with a boyfriend or girlfriend, then people are more likely to engage in EF strategies. On the other hand, if it was an achievement stressor, like an examination or test of some kind, people are more likely to engage in PF strategies.

The researchers concluded that the best type of coping strategy depends partly on the thing you are coping with (the identity of the stressor) and partly on what type of person you are. For instance, those dealing with an achievement stressor using a PF strategy will not do very well because they will not have all the information on board to make the best decision. They found that hastily choosing a problem-solving strategy without help from the emotions was counterproductive, so they concluded that those that were more in touch with their emotions did better on the PF strategy.

Take a closer look
● Those participating in the study were American psychology students. This means that extending the findings to people outside this rather limited group may not be valid.

● The assessment was in part self-assessment. It may be that the participants' answers reflected a social desirability. For instance, the participants may have felt that saying that they would deal with the stressful situation by 'calmly taking five deep breaths, and talking it through with their friend' was more acceptable than saying that they would 'throw a rock through the nearest window' to relieve their stress.

● At the beginning of the study, participants were asked to identify a stressful situation and write about their feelings. Ethically this is might be regarded as unacceptable. The researchers were not to know of any stressful experiences these students may have recently had, and making them think about them and write down their feelings could have resulted in making the students feel a lot worse.

the levels of a neurotransmitter called GABA. GABA has an inhibitory effect on the brain, that is, it quietens down activity, and in particular it decreases the activity of another neurotransmitter called serotonin. As a result, physiological arousal is reduced and a person feels calmer and less anxious.

There are a number of different benzodiazepines (for example, diazepam and alprazolam), and these vary in how fast they work and how long they remain in the bloodstream. Because of this, the kind of drug used can be tailored to suit particular needs. For example, someone who is suffering from severe stress because of a phobia would benefit from being prescribed a drug that acts fast but also clears the bloodstream fairly quickly. This would limit the effects of the drug, such as a dimming of mental alertness, on other aspects of the patients life where this might cause a problem.

EVALUATION

1 Anxiolytic drugs such as benzodiazepines are quick acting and can offer speedy relief from unpleasant feelings of stress. For some people this gives them sufficient support to encourage them seek more permanent solutions to their problems.

2 It has been argued that drug therapies do not treat the cause of the problem, only the symptoms. The issues which caused the problems remain, it is only that their effects are being 'masked' by the drug. In this case, strictly speaking drug therapy is not really treating stress. Addressing those things in life that are causing the stress would be a longer term solution.

3 Benzodiazepines have side effects. They have a tranquilising effect, therefore physical movement and mental alertness is going to be slowed, perhaps to the degree whereby normal day-to-day activities are significantly affected. The side effects can be made much worse with alcohol. This could be putting people at at risk, for example people who take benzodiazepines are going to have their driving skills affected.

4 Prolonged use of benzodiazepines can cause *tolerance and addiction*. Tolerance means that, over time, larger and larger doses of the medication are going to be needed in order to produce the same effects. Addiction means that stopping them can cause withdrawal symptoms which resemble, and are frequently worse than, the symptoms which encouraged a person to seek medication in the first place. One consequence of this is that benzodiazepines are sometimes continued for longer than necessary in order to avoid such symptoms. After long-term use, suddenly stopping can cause severe side effects, like paranoia and depression. Because of the addictive qualities of benzodiazepines, doctors prefer to gradually reduce their strength and frequency over time, rather than to suddenly stop their prescription.

Which is best? Emotion-focused or problem-focused?

This is one of those questions that doesn't really have a very satisfying answer. It isn't the case that one is better than the other, each has it's strengths and weaknesses, and each works best in different situations. Problem-focused strategies aim to change or alter or even remove or eliminate the stressful problem. Emotion-focused solutions, however, aim to control or regulate the feelings a person is having, not remove the problem. It has even been noticed that there may be gender differences in coping strategies. According to Soderstrom et al (2000) women are more likely to report using avoidance or emotion-focused coping strategies. The situation with approach or problem-focused coping is less clear however. Whilst some studies show that more men report using this form of coping, others have found the opposite, with more problem-focused coping in women.

To conclude then, emotion-focused methods of coping with stress are often fast and easily available. Such methods allow people to carry on with their lives even though the stressful situation is still there. In the long term there may well be consequences, as in the case of long-term use of drugs causing addiction.

A problem-focused approach does indeed aim to help the person deal with the stressful situation in its entirety, possibly even eliminating it. However, the methods involve other people willing to invest of their time and energy in helping the stressed person. This kind of help and loyalty is often hard to find. A professional version of this kind of social support can be found in a counsellor or therapist, but these are often expensive and have long waiting lists. A course of cognitive behaviour therapy can be time-consuming, and can require significant amounts of psychological stamina and determination from the stressed person, as well as the funds to pay for the therapy.

Basically, whichever strategy is chosen can depend on a number of things, including the type of event causing stress, the availability of people to help, the kind of person needing help, whether the stressed person is male or female and even the size of the bank balance!

WANT TO KNOW MORE?

If you'd like to read a little more about the areas covered in this section, and related areas, you should be able to find more information in these books.

Green, S. (1994) *Principles of Biopsychology* Psychology Press

Kalat, J. (2003) *Biological Psychology* (8th Edition) Wadsworth Publishing Co. Inc.

Section 5

Social Psychology
– Social Influence

WHAT YOU WILL LEARN ABOUT

Social psychology is a branch of psychology that looks at how social situations influence how we feel, think and behave. Human beings are very social animals. We depend on others for information about ourselves and the world. Indeed, time alone can quickly give an individual a sense of loneliness and isolation, and it can be a very unpleasant experience. In this section we will be looking at what social psychology has to tell us about the power of the presence of other people on behaviour.

WHAT YOU NEED TO KNOW

Social Psychology is in Unit 2 of the specification. As you learn you are expected to develop your knowledge and understanding of Social Psychology, including concepts, theories and studies. This also includes a knowledge and understanding of research methods and ethical issues as they relate to this area of psychology. You also need to develop the skills of analysis, evaluation and application. Rather than just recall and reproduce information, you are expected to be able to apply your knowledge and understanding. The subject content is split into two parts:

Social influence

- Conformity, including internalisation and compliance
- Explanations for conformity, including informational and normative social influence
- Obedience
- Explanations for obedience

Social influence in everyday life

- Explanations for independent behaviour, including resistance to conformity and obedience
- Individual differences and independent behaviour, including locus of control
- Implications for social change of research into social influence

Social Influence

Protesters getting their message across.

This part of psychology, more than any other, has a great deal to tell us about how people in society behave. In this section we will be focusing on social influence. Whenever we watch the news, we hear of war and conflict, and political unrest. We hear of people trying to change their society, sometimes successfully. How can we influence society around us? Is it possible to resist a viewpoint held by the majority? Why is it that some people appear to exert control over others? Social psychology gives us an extremely useful perspective on issues such as these.

CONFORMITY

Larger groups in society tend to exert a great influence over smaller groups.

In other words, the majority influence the minority. You may have experienced something like this without even noticing it. Peer pressure may be regarded as an example of majority influence. When all your friends are drinking alcohol at a party, it is quite difficult to resist joining in. It can be more subtle than this though and in the following section we'll see why people conform to certain patterns of behaviour and go along with the behaviour of others.

Conformity occurs when people alter their behaviour to match more closely the behaviour of a majority of others. According to Aronson (1976) conformity is 'yielding to group pressure'. This pressure to 'give in' and do as others do, might be real (perhaps a group of friends encouraging a person to join in with their smoking) or it might be unspoken or imagined. For instance, you might see it as expected by society to behave in a certain kind of way. These expectations are seldom written down, we just 'know' how to behave, and often feel a pressure to 'conform'.

We live in complex societies with many rules governing our behaviour. These rules are called *social norms* – these are standards of behaviour that are expected of us in certain situations, suggesting how we 'ought' to behave. For example, when we enter a shop we are expected to behave in a certain kind of way. Throwing food about or opening packs of sandwiches and taking bites out of them before putting them back on the shelf is unacceptable. Similarly, the shop worker is also expected to act in a particular way. Shouting at customers is generally regarded as

unacceptable. As long as both people go along with, or *conform* to, these 'rules' then the result should be a predictable and, therefore, comfortable experience for both parties.

Conformity is part of the 'glue' holding society together and can be seen as highly functional – if we did not conform to social norms then around us would be chaos – we would not be able to predict how others are going to behave and this would result in a high degree of uncertainty. So conformity is not necessarily a bad thing – any cost of conformity is ultimately small given the important benefits to the social group. To conform is not necessarily a sign of weakness – rather, it can be seen as a sign of trust, of relying on others for information and support.

According to Kellman (1958) there are three types of conformity:

Compliance
This involves going along with the group without a change in attitude. For example, we might behave as others in a group are behaving but we don't necessarily agree with or believe in the group behaviour. This is not

necessarily a long lasting change in behaviour – basically, it lasts for as long as the group pressure is exerted. We may feel pressured to smoke for instance while in school. We may be forced or bullied until we do so.

Identification

This is where conformity occurs because we want to be like the primary influence. The more attractive the influence, the more long lasting the conforming behaviour. In effect, we see others in a group as role models and try to be like them. We may want to be liked or accepted by a particular group who dress in a certain way, and so we too may begin to dress accordingly.

Internalisation

This is the most permanent form of conformity. The group opinion or behaviour is accepted as a belief by the individual and becomes part of their own thinking. Here, conformity occurs without any particular conscious effort. Religious belief could be described in terms of internalisation. The opinion of those in a person's family may be taken on board and internalised. Their views are accepted and are integrated into the person's own thinking and the person conforms.

Research into conformity

The autokinetic effect – Sherif (1936)

One of the first studies to demonstrate conformity was conducted by Sherif (1936). He used an optical illusion called the *autokinetic effect* (if you stare at a spot of light in a darkened room it will *appear* to move). His participants were first required to estimate how far they thought the light moved, then following this, to estimate again but this time in small groups. Sherif found that individuals tended to change their views and give estimates which resembled those of the group. It appears that individuals were *conforming* to a majority view. It is likely that the participants were demonstrating *internalisation* here – since

the ambiguous task would have given them no confidence in their opinion, the participants could readily have believed the group answer was the correct one.

The Asch studies

A problem with the Sherif study is that there is *no correct answer to the autokinetic effect* – it is an illusion which produces unique responses from individuals. The distance you think the spot moves will probably be different from the distance your friends think it moves. In other words, it is an *ambiguous* task where participants are asked to give an *opinion*. Asch (1951) argued that because of this Sherif was not demonstrating conformity at all. In his experiments, Asch carried out a series of studies to demonstrate conformity when the task was *unambiguous*, that is it required judgements of fact. Asch made each participant in his study work with several others in a line-length judgement task. Each person in the group called out, in turn, their judgement on the length of a line. The participant was always next to last and, unknown to him, the others in the group were confederates of the experimenter and were instructed to occasionally give false judgements (see Study in Focus). Despite the fact that these judgements were obviously wrong, Asch found that nearly one third of his participants called out the same wrong answers! 75% of his participants conformed at least once. The participants appeared to be displaying *compliance*, i.e. although they went along with the majority view they still *believed* that they were correct.

EVALUATION OF ASCH'S EXPERIMENTS

1 *Social climate*

It has been argued that the high levels of conformity found in the Asch studies reflects the norms of American society at the time. The 1950s was a time of high conformity in the US. For example, the Cold War with the Soviet Union was just beginning and activities regarded as 'un-American' were frowned upon and even actively discouraged. People were very concerned about stepping out of line and appearing to be different. Using an Asch-type set-up Perrin and Spencer (1981) found virtually *no conformity* in British university students, suggesting that the changed social climate of the 1980s did less to encourage conformity than the 1950s in the US. It should be noted though that the Perrin and Spencer study has itself been criticised on the grounds that it used engineering students as

STUDY IN FOCUS

Majority influence – Asch (1956)

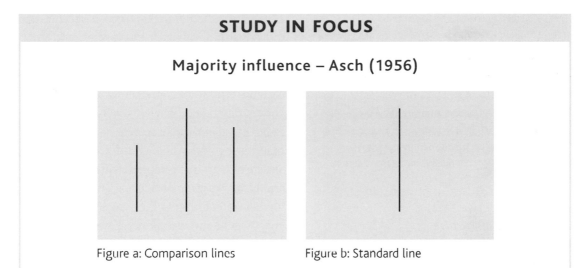

Figure a: Comparison lines   Figure b: Standard line

What was he doing and why? Asch wanted to see what people would do if they were put in a similar situation to that of Sherif's participants (see earlier), but with a task that was clearly unambiguous. He wanted to find out whether the opinions of participants could be influenced by a majority view.

What did he do? Each of his 123 student participants was tested on the task. The participant was seated at a table, with a number of others. The others were all *confederates*, that is, they were instructed by Asch to respond in a certain way and make the *wrong* choice in the task. In this way the participant experienced those sitting around the table making a clearly incorrect decision. The people at the table were shown three lines (Fig. a), then finally a fourth line (Fig. b), which Asch described as the 'standard'. Everyone was required to say which of the first three lines the standard matched. All but one of the confederates answered in turn, then the participant and finally the last confederate.

What did he find? 75% of the participants gave the wrong answer at least once. This means that they conformed on at least one occasion even though the correct answer was very clear. However, Asch also found that on 63.2% of all trials, where an unambiguous difference existed, participants did not conform.

Asch concluded that people show a tendency to conform even though in doing so they are compromising what they know to be true. He also concluded that there is still a resistance to this tendency to conform, as shown in the number of trials where a non-conforming answer was given.

Take a closer look
- Asch's participants were not fully informed about the procedure so there are ethical concerns about the research. The participants may also have found the procedure stressful which should also be considered unethical.

- Asch's procedure was very artificial and does not resemble the type of conditions in real life where we are likely to have to conform. This means that the findings may lack validity.

participants – people who are inclined to make exact measurements and so less susceptible to social influence in these circumstances.

> *"Psychology students often absolutely hate the fact that there is always something wrong with an experiment. You can always find something to criticise. It's a brilliant way of showing that you know what was done and why. If you can evaluate properly you really are on the way to being a top-class student. Take the Perrin and Spencer study in point 1 of the Asch evaluation in this section. We use it here twice. First we use it to show that social climate might be an issue in the study, but we then go on to provide a criticism of the Perrin and Spencer study itself. If you can do this sort of thing it shows real depth of understanding."*

2 *The nature of the task*

Crutchfield (1955) thought that the degree of conformity found in the Asch studies was a result of the procedures used. That is, the closeness to others in the line decision task exaggerated the degree of conformity. Take a look at the Study Outline for more information. He found lower levels of conformity than Asch did.

Allen and Levine (1968) suggest that conformity varies according to whether participants are required to respond to *objective* or *subjective* stimuli. For example, using the type of apparatus used by Crutchfield they found that participants were *far less affected* by the majority when the task involved expressing a political opinion (which is subjective) as opposed to line judgement (which is objective). It has been pointed out however that the artificial experimental setting of Crutchfield-type studies, rather than the style of question, might contribute in some way to variations in conformity.

3 *Culture*

Given that social norms vary from culture to culture it might be expected that the value placed on conformity might also vary according to culture. Smith and Bond (1996) compared 133 Asch-type conformity studies conducted in 17 countries. They found that, although conformity was, on average, lower than in the Asch studies, rates of conformity were not significantly different. They also suggested that variations in conformity between cultures depend on whether the culture is collectivist or individualist. Individualistic cultures tend to emphasise individual success and achievement and the pursuit of personal goals. Collectivist societies tend to be more family and community-based, where the actions of each individual member are seen as less important than those of the whole group. Collectivist societies occur most frequently in Asia, Africa and Latin America. The strong group identification found in these societies encourages a more conformist attitude.

4 *Ethics*

Although the participants were not actually physically harmed in any way, it is possible that their participation did leave them feeling a little misled, and this may have annoyed or upset them. In addition to this, the participants may have felt pressured to respond in a certain way. It is possible then, that they may have had an argument for being psychologically harmed in some way. This is not as unlikely as it may sound. Bogdonoff et al (1961) show raised blood pressure and increased heart rate in participants involved in a study using an Asch-like procedure. In addition to this, the Asch procedure necessarily involved a level of *deception*. Because of this, participants were unable to give informed consent.

> *"This is a perfect example of why you need to have a good understanding of research methods and ethical considerations. These things crop up all over the place, in all sorts of areas in the book. Take some time and make sure you know your ethics and methods."*

Investigating conformity: It all depends on how you do it Crutchfield (1956)

Crutchfield thought that the results Asch found may have had something to do with the procedures he used. Read over the Asch Study in Focus to refresh your memory of the task. He tested this idea by requiring the participants in his study to engage in Asch-type tasks whilst sitting in separate booths. Participants were required to respond to stimulus material, presented on a screen, by flicking one of five switches representing possible answers. Conformity was encouraged by giving participants what they thought were the responses of participants in other booths – in reality, all participants received the exactly the same information it was not related to the responses in other booths at all. Using this method Crutchfield found lower levels of conformity than those found by Asch. Most participants did not conform to the responses they thought were given by fellow participants in other booths.

EXPLANATIONS OF WHY PEOPLE CONFORM

Why people yield to the will of a majority has been a matter of debate in psychology for many years. There is general agreement however that there are two main reasons for conformity: *normative* and *informational* influence. This has also been called the *dual-process model of conformity*.

Informational social influence

Some individuals lack sufficient information about how to act. Think of your first experience of a nightclub for instance. In unfamiliar situations like this we need information about the right thing to do and we look to others for this. Where to stand, where to sit and how to behave so as not to look too stupid!

New or unusual places can often seem daunting.

The behaviour of others can often provide us with very persuasive information. The Sherif study on the autokinetic effect (page 184) is a good example of this – there was no right or wrong answer with the autokinetic effect so the participants looked to what others were doing to guide their own responses. They agreed with the behaviour of others and a group norm readily emerged. This idea is supported by studies which show that conformity varies according to the ambiguity of the task that participants are given. For example, Asch (1956) found that conformity increased when he made his line comparison task more difficult by reducing the differences between the lengths of the lines. It appears that the more uncertain people are, because of a lack of information, then the more likely they are to conform.

Normative social influence

Normative influence occurs because of the basic need we have to be accepted as a member of a group. Interestingly, this group does not have to be meaningful to us in any way. For example, it could be a random group of people who might never meet each other again. The important thing is the need for acceptance and approval from this group, which encourages agreement with the norm, or central view, of the group. It isn't necessarily important to agree with the group, as long as there is the appearance of agreement or harmony. This is the likely explanation for conformity in the original Asch studies – even though the right answer in the line judgement task was clear (so informational influence could not be operating) people went along with the majority by giving the wrong answer in order to 'belong'.

The power of social roles

Social roles are behaviours that are expected of us in certain circumstances. These roles carry with them *expectations* – people *expect* you to behave in a way consistent with your role. They exert pressure on people's thoughts, emotions and behaviours. Roles are powerful and their influences are often subtle – we usually do not know how our behaviour is being influenced by the role we occupy. For example, there are social roles associated with being a student or a teacher, though we are rarely aware of the pressures on us to conform to the expectations of these roles. Teachers are expected to behave in a certain way, as are students. The issue of social roles is raised later in the chapter where we describe research by Zimbardo.

Social impact theory

Latane (1981) developed social impact theory (SIT). It helps to explain obedience in a number of ways. SIT says that the amount of influence a person has in a social situation depends on:

● The number of people there. The larger the social group, the less impact the views of any individual will be.

● The perceived strength of the individual exerting the influence. The more powerful, the higher the status or expertise, then the stronger the influence.

● The immediacy of the person exerting the influence. The nearer the person is physically, and also in time, the more influence they will have.

We can apply social impact theory to studies we have already encountered in this section. Asch showed that as the *number* in the group goes up so to does conformity. Crutchfield showed that *immediacy* in the form of the nearness, or proximity, of others, also influenced conformity. The nearer people were, the higher the level of conformity.

Mullen et al (1990) investigated jaywalking behaviour (crossing roads without using an official crossing). They found that if you include people in the environment who do not jaywalk, then the jaywalking behaviour of others is reduced. Importantly, if the people you include are perceived as being of *high status* (*strength*) then jaywalking is reduced even further.

OBEDIENCE

Some social influences, can appear subtle and indirect. However, social influence can also be straightforward and direct. For example, a teacher instructs her students to do a particular piece of work and they do as they are told; or a parent tells a child to behave and it does so. In both these cases the instructions from the authority figure (teacher or parent) are likely to be seen as somehow reasonable and in everyone's interests. These are examples of obedience – people are acting in direct response to an authority figure.

Obedience can be seen as beneficial. However, sometimes people are urged by an authority figure to do things which are actually or morally wrong. Imagine being a policeman and being told by a senior officer to 'turn a blind eye' to something. It is easy to see then how obedience could be a destructive influence. Indeed, history gives us many examples of the effects of such destructive obedience. It was the example of apparent blind obedience by Nazis, such as Eichmann, and concentration camp guards who used the defence that they were 'only following orders' during the second world war to justify or excuse their terrible actions, which influenced Stanley Milgram to design a series of experiments in the early 1960s (see Study in Focus).

Milgram's participants were asked to act as teachers in a memory task. If the learner made a mistake then the teacher was required to punish him by administering an electric shock. The voltage level of the shock would increase gradually with each mistake, from a mild to severe shock (which would probably mean death to the learner). In reality, the learner was a confederate of the experimenter and there was no electric shock. As the memory trials progressed the experimenter acted as the authority figure by urging the participants to continue when they protested. Prior to the experiment it had been estimated that only 3% would go to the maximum level of shock but, as you can see in the Study in Focus box, this figure was very wrong. Milgram's obedience studies clearly demonstrate how much impact a situation can have on our behaviour, and how destructive blind obedience can be.

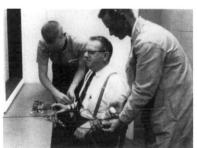

Receiving a sample 'shock' from Milgram's apparatus.

ASK AN EXAMINER

"Look at how many ways you could evaluate Milgram's obedience study using what you already know from research methods, particularly in terms of ethics and validity. It's really important that you remember that psychology isn't all about learning facts. To get the best marks, you've got to show us that you can apply your knowledge."

STUDY IN FOCUS

Obedience to authority – Milgram (1963)

The apparatus used in Milgram's famous experiments.

What was he doing and why? Milgram was interested in investigating whether people would obey a legitimate authority figure even if they were asked to do something which was clearly morally wrong – injure another person.

How did he do it? Milgram recruited his participants by advertising for volunteers to take part in a study to see how punishment influenced learning. They would be paid for their time and they were told that even if they quit the study they would still receive the money. The procedure was relatively simple. Milgram employed two confederates whom he called an 'experimenter' (dressed in a lab coat) and a 'learner' who looked like a perfectly normal individual. The learner was wired to an 'electric shock machine' . The participant (teacher) sat, in an adjacent room, beside the controls for the machine. The participant (who would be administering the shocks) was required to give shocks of increasing voltage to the 'learner' each time he (the learner) got a question wrong. Of course, the shocks were fake; the fake 'learner' would receive no shock at all, but the participant would believe that he had administered a real voltage. Milgram had instructed the 'learner' to give wrong answers, and to remain silent while the fake shocks were received, until the 'level' of the shock given by the participant (teacher) reached 300 volts. At this level the 'learner' acted as follows:

● At 300 volts the learner banged on the wall between himself and the participant. No response was given to the next question.

● At 315 volts he did exactly the same thing.

Above this level, the participant (teacher) often asked to stop. The fake 'experimenter' now stepped in, encouraging the participant by telling them 'you have no choice' or 'you must go on' and 'it is essential that you go on'.

What did he find? The results were surprising and can be seen in Figure 10. There was a line marked 'Danger: Severe shock' on the apparatus. Voltages past this line were clearly dangerous. 65% went to the maximum voltage the machine would 'give' – 450 volts, way past the danger line. A tiny proportion (12.5%) – that's just five of Milgram's 40 participants – stopped at the 300 volt level, where the 'learner' had begun to object.

STUDY IN FOCUS

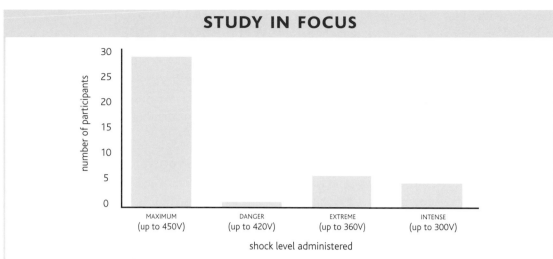

Figure 10: The results of Milgram's 1963 study of obedience.

Milgram concluded that if a figure has legitimate authority, ordinary people would obey their demands to do extraordinary things even though these demands were clearly morally wrong. Milgram went on to conclude that acts of evil were not necessarily carried out by evil people, but the acts were, at least in part, due to the **situation** in which they took place. Even though a person's **disposition** may drive them to make a particular decision, their actions depend on whether an authority figure has given them what they believe to be a legitimate order. These situational *and* dispositional factors are both important factors in whether people obey.

Take a closer look
● There is some evidence that the kind of obedience Milgram found does occur in other cultures. However, because the different research used slightly different methods we cannot be sure that the results are comparable.

● It is not really possible to extend Milgram's findings to other time-periods. Milgram's work was done in the 1960s and work like this stopped with the introduction of ethical guidelines in the 1970s. It is not clear whether his findings would apply today.

EVALUATION OF MILGRAM'S EXPERIMENTS

1 The way that Milgram designed his study has attracted many criticisms. For example, it has been claimed that the teachers (i.e. the real participants) did not really believe that the learner was receiving electric shocks. Orne and Holland (1968) called this a 'pact of ignorance'. On the face of it, this criticism seems reasonable. For example, how could an employee of Yale University, a prestigious university, allow such harm to be inflicted? Or why was the 'teacher' needed at all? A researcher could easily have conducted the memory test and administered the shocks without the need for an intermediary. However, films made of some of the studies

and post-experimental interviews show participants under extreme stress highlighting the reality of the situation for participants.

2 It has been claimed that the very fact that Milgram's obedience studies were laboratory experiments means that the behaviour was artificial, and this gave rise to the extreme levels of obedience observed. This puts into question the validity of the findings. More realistic field studies have tended to support Milgram's general findings. For instance, in research with nurses (see Study Outline) Hoffling found that the majority of nurses would give a high dose of an unfamiliar drug to a patient if ordered to do so by what they believed to be an authority figure even though they knew the dose was wrong, as it was indicated on the bottle. However, Rank and Jacobson (1977) carried out a similar study, where nurses were ordered to give a high dose of the familiar drug Valium; 89% refused the order. This shows that situational factors can really influence obedience levels.

3 Evidence in support of Milgram comes from Slater et al (2006). Their research was a version of the original Milgram study, but instead of using a real 'human' learner they used a 'virtual' learner in the form of a human female, a film of a woman as seen through a window. As in the Milgram task, when the 'woman' made an error on a task, participants administered a 'shock', with each participant's heart rate recorded throughout the research. The results showed that even though participants were clearly aware of the 'virtual' nature of the learner, their physiology and behaviour responded as if she were real.

4 There are a number of ethical considerations with Milgram's study. These are reviewed on page 193.

EXPLANATIONS OF WHY PEOPLE OBEY

Why do people obey others? As with most things in social psychology the answer is not straightforward. We have to take a number of issues into consideration.

Personal responsibility

During his experiment, many of Milgram's participants raised the issue of *responsibility* – if any harm should come to the learner, who would be responsible? Advising participants that the experimenter was responsible was enough to encourage many participants to continue with their electric shocks. Milgram points out that in many real-life instances where obedience has led to harm the perpetrators have used this lack of responsibility to justify their actions. It follows then that those people who feel they have relinquished personal responsibility for their actions, because of an authority figure assuming it, are more likely to obey.

In the same vein, disobedience is more likely when personal responsibility is

STUDY OUTLINE

Doctors and nurses: Obedience in real life
Hoffling et al (1966)

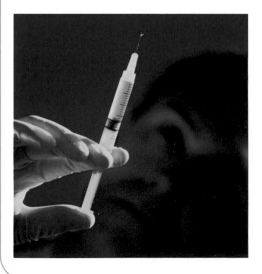

Hoffling et al set out to address the issue of whether the levels of obedience observed by Milgram can really be related to a real-life situation. Their participants were nurses who were not aware that they were taking part in a study. The nurses were telephoned by a fictitious 'doctor' and instructed to administer a potentially dangerous medication. Despite the fact that the telephone instruction clearly broke hospital rules it was found that 95% of the nurses were willing to carry out the order. These findings show that obedience can and does occur in real-life settings. The **validity** of the Milgram study is supported, showing that the findings can be related to other situations.

ETHICAL ISSUES IN MILGRAM'S STUDY OF OBEDIENCE

In the Research Methods section, we discussed issues that need to be considered in the design of a study if it is to be regarded as ethically sound. Before you read this section, look over the details of Milgram's experiment to refresh your memory. Most participants said afterwards that they were glad to have taken part in the study but, despite this, it raises many ethical issues

Psychological harm

Milgram's study is likely to have caused severe stress to the participants. Films of the procedure show participants in distress as they gave the shocks and as they listened to the complaints and screams of the confederate 'learner'. It is clear that the majority really believed that they were **causing pain** by giving severe electric shocks. This would surely have resulted in **damage to their self-esteem** and other potential long-term damage caused by the **stress**.

The right to withdraw

Milgram made it very clear to the participants (when he recruited them) that they would still be paid if they were to withdraw from the experiment without completing it. However, the regular encouragement from the confederate experimenter to continue with the shocks would have made it terribly difficult for many to withdraw when they wanted to. The results clearly show that this was the case, with very few removing themselves from the procedure at an early stage.

Deception

Milgram did not tell the participants exactly what was going to happen. He **deceived** them. He could not tell them as this would have ruined his procedure. If participants were aware that the 'learner' and the 'experimenter' were confederates, and that the 'electric shock machine' was not providing real shocks it advertised, then their behaviour may well have been rather different.

Informed consent

Without the correct information about the procedure and aims of the experiment, participants were unable to provide **informed consent**. If they were not told of the true nature of the procedure, how could they possibly have made a decision as to whether they wanted to be involved or not?

Milgram's defence

Milgram defended himself by saying that he could not possibly have known what was going to happen, and no one could have predicted the levels of stress actually experienced by the participants. He pointed out that the vast majority of those interviewed later (over 80%) felt pleased to have taken part and over 70% said that they had learned something about themselves and gained some kind of personal development from the experience. He goes on to say that it is not the experiment itself that people find offensive, but the conclusions that indicate that we are all capable of such awful behaviour in the appropriate circumstances.

Baumarind (1964) was very critical of Milgram's work because of the ethical concerns. It is often the case that people try to find reasons to justify their actions, and it is not enough to say 'I learned something from my involvement in the study'. The fact remains that people really did assume that they were giving the learner electric shocks and Milgram's critics maintain that the resulting stress that this generated is not justified by the results of the experiment increased. For example, Hamilton (1978) suggests that obedience levels drop dramatically when participants are told that they are responsible for their own actions. It is also likely that some people refuse to relinquish personal responsibility even when another person is willing to assume responsibility for their actions. Why some people are more willing than others to do this is not entirely clear, but it has been suggested that individual differences in morality are important, as are other personality characteristics.

Milgram's agency theory

Milgram developed his own theory to explain the obedience levels he found in his experiments. He proposed that individual social consciousness can operate in two ways:

The autonomous state is when individuals assume responsibility for their actions. Because an individual's own values and beliefs are guiding their behaviour they are more likely to behave in moral and pro-social ways.

Police have legitimate authority in our society. This is encouraged, at least in part, by the recognisable uniform.

The agentic state is when individuals feel that they have diminished responsibility because they are the 'agents' of others, i.e. they act on someone else's behalf. In this state of mind they are likely to feel less conscience and guilt about the consequences of their own actions, and are more likely to engage in antisocial acts.

These states have evolved because they serve useful social functions. For example, an agentic state allows us to live successfully in hierarchical societies, where we give up control over aspects of our lives to other legitimate authorities, such as teachers or police. The agentic state is something which develops early in life; for example, parents encourage their children to obey, follow rules and respect others' authority. As we grow up we are encouraged to take more responsibility for ourselves, thus to be autonomous. In the context of obedience studies, people who are obeying the authority figure, the experimenter, are in an agentic state – they are agents of an external authority. Those who remain independent and thus *disobedient* are thus expressing autonomy rather than agency.

Legitimate authority

Research shows that participants are most obedient when the authority figure is considered credible and legitimate. For example, when Milgram situated one of his studies in a non-university location, the levels of obedience reduced; that is *disobedience* increased. Presumably this had something to do with the authority figure having reduced legitimacy outside the esteemed university setting. This was further demonstrated by having another participant give the orders, rather than an experimenter in a white coat. Again, there was a dramatic increase in disobedience, where fewer participants obeyed the 'authority' figure.

Social impact theory and obedience

As well as explaining majority influence, Latane's social impact theory can also be used to explain why people obeyed in Milgram's studies.

For example, in Milgram's study, the experimenter had an impact on the participant – there was *immediacy* because of their close proximity. This is supported by the findings from *variations* in the study; for example, when Milgram had the experimenter give instructions over the phone (low immediacy) obedience dropped substantially. When the immediacy was increased by, for example, having the experimenter in the same room as the participant, obedience levels increased. Immediacy might also explain why obedience levels dropped when, in another variation, the learner was brought into close proximity by having the participant and learner in the same room and the participant held the hand of the learner onto the shock plate – the extreme touch proximity condition. The impact of an experimenter (someone with prestige or status) on the participant might also have contributed to high levels of obedience. Indeed, with a later version where the experiment was moved to a run-down setting (such as a shabby office – thus reducing the perceived strength and prestige of the experimenter) obedience levels dropped. Reductions in a combination of immediacy, strength and number of people present, all factors in social impact theory are all likely to be important factors underlying *disobedience*.

> "Social impact theory is quite a simple theory to learn, but it is so helpful. You can use it to explain conformity and obedience. Two answers for the price of one bit of learning!"

Social Influence in Everyday Life

Some people resist the pressure to conform.

Research has told us a lot about how social influence causes people to behave the way they do. Often, people resist these pressures and behave independently. Understanding these processes has implications for our understanding of social change.

INDEPENDENT BEHAVIOUR

Social influence is not an all-or-nothing effect. Social situations and thus the pressures to conform and obey vary enormously. Whether or not someone is obedient, whether they conform or whether they behave individually, is also likely to be affected by dispositional factors – that is, what mood a person is in or what kind of personality someone has.

How do people resist group pressure? How do they resist the influence of the largest group in society? Some people are obedient and do not rebel. Whether someone is obedient, whether they conform or whether they resist, both obedience and conformity may depend on a number of factors.

RESISTANCE TO CONFORMITY

It is often all too easy to allow much of our behaviour to be shaped and structured by the majority. Fashions and trends are good examples of this. Dressing in socially acceptable if not necessarily 'up to the minute' fashion means that we avoid conflict and having to explain ourselves to others. In other situations, such as areas of political debate or social unrest, resisting conformity is often even harder. What is it that influences people's decisions not to conform?

Exposure to dissent

Imagine a society where everyone held exactly the same opinions. Perhaps even a society where people were given their opinions by their governments. How might people find the strength or desire to resist? One way is by seeing people resisting.

If we experience a minority view, we may assume that the opinion held is wrong, simply because the view is held by a minority.

STUDY OUTLINE

Resisting conformity: Exposure to dissent
Nemeth (1986)

If we are exposed to a minority view then we are more likely to think about the issue. Later in the section we give some examples of minority views, including those held by the Campaign for Nuclear Disarmament and the movement for women's suffrage in the 1920s. Nemeth says that being aware that people hold a different viewpoint makes us more aware of the issue in hand – it makes us think about it. Another example used later is that of Darwin's theory of evolution. At the time this was a radically new viewpoint in science, with the majority believing that we did not evolve, and preferring explanations of our existence provided by their religious teachings. However, a consistent argument, fostering thought and further investigation helped people to think differently.

However, as time goes on and we remain exposed to the minority view, people may begin to regard the minority view as a real alternative. They are encouraged to question their beliefs and opinions about the issue. It is the minority's 'divergence' from the majority view that encourages thought.

Asch (1956) showed that people can often change their opinion when exposed to a majority view for only a few minutes. However, taking on a minority decision requires more exposure. Once someone has decided to take on a majority viewpoint it takes quite a lot to change his or her mind!

Reactance

Reactance is where we change our views to a position opposite to that expected. It may be that the general view held in society is being forced on us in some way and people 'react' against this, either by changing their opinion away from the majority viewpoint or by actively not accepting it. Some people are classed as having 'high reactance' and some as 'low reactance'. This means that some people are more likely to react (take an opposite view) than others. The Study Outline from Bushman and Stack (1996) describes how these people's behaviour may differ.

If you saw a sign telling you not to write graffiti on a toilet wall what would you do? Pennerbaker and Saunders (1976) showed that it depended at least in part on how authoritative the sign was. If the notice was signed by the 'chief of security' people were more likely to ignore it and write graffiti than if the notice was

---

STUDY OUTLINE

Forbidden fruit
Bushman and Stack (1996)

Labels like 'Contains scenes of nudity' or 'WARNING: Obscene Lyrics' can have quite an effect on sales of DVDs or CDs. **Reactance theory** says that when a person's freedom to take part in something (be it listening to a CD or watching a film) is threatened in some way, then they feel the pressure of having this freedom removed. One way to reinstate the freedom is to actively take part in the behaviour that has been  limited. In other words, a CD with a warning may result in higher sales simply because people are actively seeking to buy it. This is called a 'boomerang effect'.

Bushman and Stack (1996) describe these restricted items as 'forbidden fruit'. They carried out psychological tests on people to determine whether they often showed reactance (high reactance individuals) or whether reactance was not a regular part of their personality (low reactance individuals). They showed these individuals information labels about films and also various warning labels, and found that the warning label was more likely to influence a judgement of whether to watch the film or not. The more aggressive the warning, the more likely the 'high reactance' individuals were to want to watch the film. With 'low reactance' individuals the aggressiveness of the warning did not influence their desire to see the film nearly as much. It seems then, that a warning label can do wonders for music or film sales; the content does not, in the short run, seem to matter quite so much.

signed by a 'grounds committeeman'. Also, an aggressive authoritative notice ('DO NOT write on the walls') was more likely to be ignored than a polite notice ('Please do not write on the walls'). Reactance then is more likely if the perceived restriction on freedom is given by an authority figure, in this case a chief of security, and if it is 'requested' aggressively.

Psychosocial identity

Mugny (1980) says that we are more likely to resist conformity if the minority group is one that we see ourselves belonging to in some way. If we feel that we share a 'psychosocial identity' with members of the alternative group then it is much easier for us to agree with their non-conformist attitudes or join in with their non-conformist behaviour. Mugny says that although joining the minority and not conforming may be viewed as socially unacceptable, people see themselves as sharing traits and attributes with the minority. It follows that that person may feel more comfortable holding a non-conformist view if they see themselves as belonging to the minority group in some way.

Group size

According to Stang (1976) the rates of conformity do not rise inevitably as the group size increases. Group conformity is at its greatest when the majority number between three and five people. After that, increasing the size of the majority has little effect. However, this might not always be the case. Research suggests that when there is a correct answer, especially one which an individual cares about, then conformity does occur, as Stang suggests. On the other hand, group size has a different effect in circumstances of *informational social influence* (when there is no objectively correct answer). In these circumstances, conformity will increase as group size grows. It appears then that the kind of judgement asked of group members, as well as the size of the group, are important.

It follows that, in these circumstances, the smaller the group size the more likely people are to be able to resist conformity and act more individually.

Group unanimity

Research suggests that conformity will be significantly reduced (independent behaviour becomes more likely) if the majority is not seen to be unanimous in its opinion. To put it another way, if the people making up the majority do not seem to hold the same view, if their opinions and ideas are split, then it is easier for individuals in the minority to resist. It does not seem to matter *how* the unanimity of the majority is broken. Asch (1956) found that just one other group member agreeing with the judgement of the true participant was enough to greatly reduce conformity (from 33% down to 5.5%). However, group dissent does not have to be *supportive* for conformity to be reduced. For example, an incorrect but different view from a group member reduces conformity, as does a dithering response to questioning. Even when the competence of the 'supporter' is questioned (for example, by being visually impaired) conformity is still reduced. As soon as the unanimity of the majority group is weakened, or even put into question, non-conformity or dissent is more likely to be seen, by other individuals, as an appropriate response. It is, then, easier to resist group pressure if the members of the majority group do not hold a consistently unanimous view. You could relate this to politics. If the government in power (with more voters and supporters) can be made, by the opposition

"You could be asked in an exam to explain resistance to conformity or resistance to obedience. Learning the factors listed here, and being able to say something about each one, will help you get lots of marks easily. As a bonus, if you are asked to explain independent behaviour, then you can use this same learning to answer that question too!"

party, to seem to be split in its opinions, then people will find it easier to split from the majority party and vote for the opposition. You see it all the time in British politics – one party regularly trying to identify points where the other party has problems with unanimity.

Gender

Research suggests that females are more likely than males to conform. It has been suggested that these differences emerge because females are either being exposed to male-oriented tasks or because females respond differently to males in face-to-face situations. Research suggests that this conclusion might be a little too simplistic. Eagly and Charvala (1986) found that whilst there were no sex differences in conformity among their younger participants (under 19 years), older females were more conforming than older males (over 19 years) and this increased when they thought their opinions were observed by the others. It seems that age, task, concerns about personal status and a range of other factors influence sex differences in conformity.

Personality

The finding that conformity is not necessarily predictable has led many researchers to believe that aspects of personality affect whether or not an individual conforms. It has been suggested that a range of characteristics associated with personality influences whether or not a person conforms. Some personality characteristics that might be associated with conformity include: nervousness, feelings of inferiority, need for approval from others, insecurity and self-blame. In general, however, efforts to identify aspects of personality that might allow us to predict who is most likely to conform have not been successful. It seems that whatever personality characteristics there might be are being significantly influenced by *situational factors* – for example, the kind of task employed, the make-up of the group and the importance of the decision.

RESISTING OBEDIENCE

The pressures to conform are closely related to the pressures to obey others. Personality, for instance, plays important roles in whether someone is more likely to be obedient or not. Related to personality is the idea of *locus of control* – whether people think they are in control or whether they think that others have control over them. This is a difference between individuals and we will describe it here.

Gender

Milgram found *no difference at all* between the obedience levels of males and females. However, Bandura et al (1996) say that whether a person feels able to make a moral decision or not may depend, at least partly, on whether they are male or female. It may be that the role of gender, as something that influences whether a person is obedient or not, may have something to do with what they are being asked to be obedient *about*.

Personality

People's personalities differ in all sorts of ways. We all know people who are more likely than others to be obedient, take instruction and follow orders. Aspects of a personality that influence obedience level are called *dispositional* factors. Personality describes a person's *disposition*. Milgram (1974) identified the *authoritarian personality* as one most likely to obey orders and give the largest shocks. An authoritarian personality is one who is intolerant of others, has a solid personal belief structure but is obedient and submissive to those they see as being in authority.

Locus of control

Locus means *place* (location). So locus of control refers to where an individual perceives the 'control' to be. Are *they themselves* in control or are they *being* controlled? The locus of control influences how individuals respond.

TECHNIQUE	EXPLANATION
Take responsibility	Disobedience becomes more likely as people begin to take responsibility for their actions
Become more autonomous	Moving from an 'agentic' state to a more 'autonomous' state means that we are operating more autonomously, not as 'agents' of others. This means we can behave more disobediently
Remove legitimate authority	If legitimate authority figures, such as the police or even the army, are removed it becomes easier for people to disobey as they become self-regulated
Consider immediacy, strength and number	Immediacy, strength and number are the three factors influencing obedience as described by social impact theory. Separating ourselves from those who may try and make us obey, and surrounding ourselves with lots of like-minded disobedient people who we do not see as authority figures will improve a person's ability to disobey

Table 7: Techniques for increasing the resistance to obedience.

If the person feels that they are in control of their own circumstances, we say the locus of control is *internal*, that is to say, within the individual. These individuals are described as *internals* and this identifies certain aspects of their personality. People with an internal locus of control have a certain confidence and security, a positive outlook and no real need for external approval.

On the other hand, the individual may see things as beyond their control. In this case we say that the locus of control is *external*, that is to say, outside the control of the individual. These individuals are described as *externals* and they bear the opposite personality characteristics from those of internals. They will be less confident, more nervous and more insecure.

Those with a high internal locus of control are often the *risk-takers* in society. They are less likely to conform and less likely to be obedient. Those willing to take risks can have a huge influence on the world around them. Great and powerful businesses are not the result of timid behaviour. Bravery and risk–taking is part of being a business leader, and whole communities can be changed by prosperity and employment that originates from the actions of an entrepreneur. We can relate this closely to the ideas of conformity and obedience; for instance, someone with an external locus of control is much more likely to conform and be less likely to take risks. Similarly, someone with an internal locus of control is less likely to be obedient and more likely to take risks.

"Watch out! It is well worth learning about locus of control and how this influences independent behaviour – you could be asked a question specifically on this! Make sure you remember what locus means, and how being internal or external influences conformity and obedience."

SOCIAL CHANGE

Sometimes the actions of a small number of people, or even a single individual, can have an enormous influence on society. In 1955, Rosa Parks refused to give up her bus seat to another passenger. The passenger was white, and she was a black woman. In Montgomery, Alabama, at that time, she was obliged to make way for the white passenger. Her refusal began a campaign of civil disobedience. The action of this single woman lit a fuse in the black community.

Rosa Parks' minority action, and her refusal to obey, led to the rise in prominence of one Martin Luther King. The Civil Rights Movement gathered steam, the rights of those in the black community were finally regarded as important and nine years later segregation was banned across the United States.

Conformity and justice

The research into social change has very important implications for how part of our legal system works. Nemeth (1986) says that when people make decisions about whether or not to conform, they often take the easiest route. If it is easy to conform, and there is little reason not to, or if it is *hard* not to conform, then people are more likely to show conformist behaviour. Nemeth says that in these situations people do not listen properly to arguments, or look carefully at evidence that might change their minds. This means that an important decision, such as one a jury must take, may not be given enough thought if a minority does not voice its opinions.

Conformity, creativity and problem solving

In business you may hear the phrase 'think outside the box'. What this means is that people are encouraged to think along new and often unusual lines. Earlier on we described how *locus of control* can often be something that influences obedience, and how *entrepreneurs* often have a high internal locus of control, making them willing to take risks and 'think outside the box'. These people are also often less likely to conform. Research into conformity shows us that conformist people do not consider alternatives to their opinions, and because of this they may miss valuable and useful problem solving methods and opportunities. The non-conformist shows independent thinking and so may provide a creative solution where a problem needs to be solved. The implication is that those with problems to solve should be encouraged to think creatively, and not to conform to the usual methods which are often too easy to adopt. Martin and Hewston (2003) say that this sort of innovative thinking is an extremely important aspect of the behaviour and importance of the minority.

Majority influence: maintaining order

Maintaining the 'status quo', or the 'stable order' of things, particularly socially and politically, is often one of the major goals of a majority. A government in power can bring about change carefully, but maintenance of order is a very important part of looking after a community.

Sometimes it is hard to see how research that has been done in laboratories or other controlled environments might be of use to us. It can sometimes be difficult to see what the implications of this research might be. With some research, however, the implications for social change are much clearer. The implications of the work of Philip Zimbardo and colleagues are relatively straightforward to see, and we will turn to that now.

Zimbardo et al (1973) were interested in the power of social roles in influencing conformity. Zimbardo's research is of interest not only because it tells us something important about conformity, but also because it a useful method for thinking about how *research into social influence has implications for social change*.

Zimbardo's prison simulation study (see Study in Focus) became one of the most controversial in psychology. He constructed a mock prison in the basement of the Stanford University psychology building. Participants

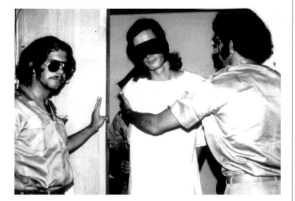

The Stanford prison experiment.

were randomly assigned to one of two roles: prisoner or guard. It was found that prisoners quickly became passive and depressed, whilst the guards became harsh and were frequently brutal. It seems that the roles of prisoner and guard, emphasised by appropriate clothing and realistic environment, were very powerful. Zimbardo's participants readily conformed to their new social roles

EVALUATION OF ZIMBARDO'S STUDY

1 The prison study has been criticised for not being realistic. For example, unlike real prison guards, the participants in this study were not given a code of conduct which real prison guards would have. Without these rules, the 'guards' were not limited and they could behave in more extreme ways. Similarly, they knew they were taking part in a study and allowed the researchers to take responsibility for their actions instead of themselves – an 'if I'm not being stopped I can't be doing anything *that* bad' mentality began to emerge. It was almost as if the lack of interference amounted to approval of the behaviour by the researchers.

2 In 2002 the BBC broadcast a TV series called *The Experiment* which could be described as a partial replication of the prison simulation study. Their results tended to contradict Zimbardo's. For example, Zimbardo concluded from his study that it is natural for certain situations to cause the kind of brutal behaviour seen in his study. Psychologists Haslam and Reicher, who led the TV series, disagree with this conclusion. They argue that it is not inevitable that situations like the simulated prison will cause misconduct. They point out that, whilst the situation is important, other factors must be taken into consideration, such as politics and group behaviour. Sometimes brutality in prisons is focused on particular groups. For example, not all POWs were abused by their German captors during the second world war, something which would be expected if the situation was the only factor.

STUDY IN FOCUS

The Stanford prison experiment
Zimbardo et al (1973)

What were they doing and why? The researchers wanted to know how we conform to different social roles. The motivation for the work was a feeling of unrest which resulted in riots within prisons in the United States in the 1960s. They wanted to know whether it was the personality of the individual (the **disposition**) that influenced their behaviour when given a role, or whether it was the **situation** in which they were placed, the role itself.

What did they do? 24 men were recruited from the student population, and paid $15 a day. Each was checked carefully for both physical and psychological well-being. Each was assigned randomly to the role of prisoner or guard. There were two reserves and during the experiment one dropped out. In the final stages then, there were 11 guards and 10 prisoners. 'Prisoners' were 'arrested' and taken from their homes to the 'prison' that had been set up in rooms at the psychology department. They were subjected to all the things a real prisoner would be, with 'delousing' to ensure cleanliness, searching and removal of their own possessions including their clothes. They were given a uniform to wear which consisted of a stocking cap and a smock-like item. Their uniform bore their prison number and they were 'chained' together at the ankle. 'Guards' were given mirror sunglasses and official-looking khaki coloured uniforms. They had whistles and clubs. This was all part of the **deindividuation** process where the individuals lost their own identities and became more of a member of a group than an individual. Both the prisoners and the guards had aspects of their own personality removed by the process. They became deindividuated and more conformist. The guards and the prisoners experienced life in these roles for 24 hours a day in the 'prison'. The prisoners were confined to cells for a large part of the day, with only three supervised toilet trips allowed each day.

What did they find? The guards' behaviour became more and more tyrannical. Their treatment of the prisoners became more and more sadistic, if not physically, then certainly psychologically. Some guards even took part 'out of hours', when they were not required to be there, simply because they enjoyed it. Zimbardo allowed one prisoner to leave during the experiment because he feared for the participant's psychological well-being. The experiment was timetabled to run for two weeks. It was stopped before it got too out of hand after only six days. The behaviour of the guards towards the prisoners surprised everyone involved. It was concluded that people do indeed conform to social roles. It was clear that it was the **situational** factors (where they were) that influenced the behaviour more than the **disposition** of the participants (what kind of person they were), with very ordinary, otherwise good-natured and highly intelligent students behaving in a very unexpected way once given a role to play. The researchers identified two very important issues that may have influenced the behaviour. These were **deindividuation**, which meant that the participants' feeling of individuality was reduced or removed, encouraging the others to treat them as less of an individual person. The other was **learned helplessness**. This is the feeling that nothing you do will have any effect at all, so what is the point of trying to change things or resist authority.

Take a closer look
● There are various different forms of social influence at play in the Stanford prison experiment. It is very difficult to disentangle the effects of conformity and obedience in the study.

● Zimbardo's involvement in the study both as a prison governor and as the principal researcher means that he might not have been as objective as he could have been. This is an example of an investigator effect.

Also, Haslam and Reicher argue that people don't react mindlessly to situations; they often think and reflect before acting. This can result in resistance rather than oppression. However, it was also the case that the participants in *The Experiment* knew about the original experiment and this may well have influenced their behaviour.

3 Making some participants 'prisoners' and some 'guards' introduced *demand characteristics*. The participants knew how they were supposed to behave, so the observed behaviour may have been more to do with this expectation, this demand characteristic, than their real behaviour. This puts the *validity* of the experiment into question. The findings are not necessarily related to the researcher's careful design, but more to do with this expectation of how the participants should behave. Also, Zimbardo himself was closely involved in the experiment, playing the part of prison warden. He was not, perhaps, ideally placed to be impartial in decisions relating to the conduct of participants in the study. He could not be said to be truly impartial.

4 The ethical issues surrounding the prison study are clear to see. The 'prisoners' experienced *psychological harm* and were clearly *distressed*. It seems likely that the experiment will also have caused the 'guards' distress. In his defence, Zimbardo could not possibly have foreseen the extremely unusual result. He also followed up on the participants over the years that followed and found no long-term effects. In addition to harm and distress, all participants were *deceived*. These issues are covered in detail in the Research Methods section of the book.

5 The implications of Zimbardo's prison study are wide ranging. The study was performed over 35 years ago, yet it still raises important issues that are just as important today. At the end of the Iraq war, images of American soldiers were broadcast on news channels all over the world. They showed dreadful and disrespectful abuse of Iraqi prisoners by their American army guards. The similarity to the prison experiment was all too obvious.

Zimbardo's view on the Abu Ghraib images is that they were inexcusable but not inexplicable.

Zimbardo says that although the images were inexcusable, they were not inexplicable. His Stanford prison experiment findings go a long way to describing the dangerous and often explosive situation the army guards and Iraqi prisoners were in.

Zimbardo (2007) says that when dreadful things like those seen in his prison experiment, and more recently at the Abu Ghraib prison, occur it is all too easy to blame the soldiers and guards. He says it is not the bad apple in the barrel that you need to look for, but rather a bad barrel. By this he means it is not the individuals who are to blame in the first instance, but *the system* that the individuals are part of. Zimbardo's research has implications for society and social change. If it is the society to which the abusive guards belong that encourages them to behave the way they do then his research has implications for all of us, as members of that society. We have a responsibility to look carefully at what it is that makes people behave in this evil way.

What is it that makes people evil? Zimbardo's very latest work investigates this, and he calls it the 'Lucifer Effect'. We must be very careful, and know that the kind of evil behaviour shown by the guards in the prison experiment and also those at Abu Ghraib is actually human nature. If you put people in a certain situation, without careful thought as to the possible consequences, the results might not be very desirable.

Making your voice heard: Can a minority bring about social change?

The research that we have presented on minority influence describes, collectively, how views held by the few can often influence those held by the many. The implications of this work to social change are quite clear. A single juror can work, carefully and consistently, to influence the opinion of many others on a jury to ensure that justice is done properly. The role of pressure groups in our society is also terribly important in raising awareness, of the actions of a government perhaps, or the research being done in a university on animals. Research in this area describes how a small group should behave to maximise its chances of influencing the majority group.

Between April and June 1989, the Chinese authorities killed or injured 200–800 civilians. The actual number is unknown. The picture below became world famous. If the actions of an individual can stop tanks, what else is a minority capable of?

Given the pressures to conform, can a majority ever be persuaded by a minority?

The bravery of a single individual. His actions halt a column of tanks in Tiananmen Square, Beijing, in 1989.

Consider terrorism. This form of behaviour is employed by people with a very weak social position – in a small minority – to attempt to force a change in society or at the very least put forward their opinion. In a democratic society, where the views of the people are considered and changes made on the basis of debate and agreement, terrorism has no place. The success of society and its democratic systems depends to some degree on having smaller groups of people – minorities – holding often unpopular views and attempting to exert some influence on the majority, but not violently.

The Campaign for Nuclear Disarmament – CND.

It has been shown that non-violent behaviour by a minority can encourage social change. Small groups in society that can hold radical views are often referred to as 'pressure groups'. The Campaign for Nuclear Disarmament (CND) for instance has been extremely active in the past, and worked tirelessly against the tide to raise awareness and influence governments to reduce the chances of them using or increasing their stock of nuclear weapons.

Another frequently cited example, demonstrating the importance of minority influence in social change, is the suffragette movement of the 1920s. *Suffrage* means the right to vote, and the *suffragettes* campaigned, against all odds, to bring the vote to women in the majority of Britain during the 1920s, gaining the same suffrage rights as men in 1928. Women like Emmeline Pankhurst carried out extraordinary acts of bravery that excluded them socially. Women at that time were not expected to be politically active in

Emmeline Pankhurst, a driving force in the women's suffrage movement of the 1920s.

this way, and the majority felt that their behaviour was not becoming of their gender – the actions of the minority in this case influencing the opinion of the majority. We might also think of Charles Darwin and his theory of evolution as an example of minority influence. Darwin's ideas about natural selection as a mechanism for the development of new species and the origin of man (humans and apes share a common ancestor) were, when first proposed, significantly at odds with the majority opinion that humans had been created in the image of God and were not animals. They caused quite a controversy. Over time this opinion has changed, and now most people accept the theory of evolution.

Darwin's research into the origin of man, his resulting theories and his expression of the idea of evolution had enormous implications for social change. His views were almost universally unpopular, but over time they became more acceptable to the majority, and evolution is now the dominant scientific theory to explain the great diversity of life forms on Earth. There are implications of this research for social change, particularly in terms of the beliefs of many in society about the origin of man. The research raises difficult questions about aspects of religion and still manages to cause a great deal of controversy.

The importance of any minority group is *not* necessarily about the view that they hold.

The important thing is that minority groups, such as CND and the movement for women's suffrage, exist. They raise awareness, make others feel that it is OK to hold a minority view, and make people question things and opinions held in their society.

Social change: minority and majority influence

Whether one group influences another to bring about some kind of social change can depend on a number of factors. Different pressures are present and different types of actions are required to bring each about.

Charles Darwin

● Social change can occur when a majority influences a minority because normative and informative influences produce *compliance*. The process is relatively *passive*. This means that social change just happens. It is not something that is actively sought out.
● Social change can occur where a minority influences a majority. It is a slower process, which requires people to undergo a change of thinking that is much greater – moving from one position to an often very different one might require a radical change of opinion. The opinion might need explaining to others but, more importantly, you need to be *able* to explain it to others, and so must clearly understand the opinion yourself. This is much more like *internalisation*; Moscovici et al (1969) called this kind of social change an *attitude conversion*.

How does minority influence occur?

A number of characteristics appear to make the influence a minority may have more effective. What appears most important is how a minority goes about its task of influencing the majority. Moscovici called this the behavioural style. There are a number of *behavioural styles*:

Consistency

Consistency is the most important behavioural style – a minority must be *consistent* in its position. Not only must individuals in a minority maintain their belief or attitude over time, but there must also be consistency between members of a minority group. This will give the majority a signal that the minority is *committed* to its position. Any dissent is likely to weaken the minority position, in that members of the majority are likely to exploit this inconsistency as a demonstration of the doubtfulness of the position. By being consistent, a minority is harder for the majority to ignore and sends a message that an alternative view to that of the majority is available.

Confidence

Confidence in a minority opinion sends a message to the majority that the position is a serious one which is not going to go away. This means that the minority view will demand attention and respect from the majority. With attention and respect comes a greater possibility of having an influence.

Persuasiveness

A minority should try to win over people from the majority, in other words it must be sufficiently *persuasive* to attract others over to its position. In politics these are often described as *defections* from one party to another. These defections would be seen as moral decisions by other majority members, as people could not possibly be joining the minority in order to gain popularity (by definition, a minority position is an unpopular one!).

Obedience, power and social change

Earlier on in this section we discussed obedience and the factors that influence it. These include a number of things, such as the presence of a legitimate authority figure, and whether people take responsibility for their own actions.

Turner (1991) says that for a group to function as a whole, individuals must give up responsibility and defer to others of higher status in the social hierarchy. *Legitimate authority* replaces a person's own self-regulation and they can become more obedient. This has implications for social change. A strong form of authority, that people agree is legitimate and has legitimate power, will encourage obedience. If the authority is not legitimate or people feel that they are not free to make their own decisions then there may be 'reactance' (see page 198), where decisions not to conform and to be less obedient may be taken. It follows that power,

---

STUDY OUTLINE

Name that colour
Moscovici et al (1969)

Moscovici et al (1969) attempted to experimentally investigate the effect of a minority on a majority opinion. In his study he asked participants in small groups to judge a colour – whether a slide projection showed blue or green. There were two confederates in each group who were instructed to consistently say that the colour was green, regardless of the actual colour. It was found that this minority opinion had some effect on the majority – for example, nearly a third of participants agreed with the minority opinion at least once. It seemed that if the two confederates *consistently* agreed with each other and were confident in their answers then they were able to persuade a majority (the other four participants) that blue colour slides were in fact green.

STUDY OUTLINE

How to become powerful in three easy steps!
Turner (2005)

Turner says that power can be described as a three-process idea. In other words, people and groups are not just naturally powerful. The traditional view is that a group gains control of the resources of a society or country, and this gives them power and influence over others.

● First a group of like-minded thinkers get together, and this group shares an 'identity' of some kind.

● Next the group begins to influence others around them by presenting their ideas and encouraging others to think, and perhaps join them (minority influence in action).

● Finally, through gaining authority and persuading others the group reaches a situation of power.

They can now exert their will and control the resources of the society. They are powerful and have achieved, potentially, legitimate authority.

and how it is applied, can have enormous implications for social change.

With legitimate authority comes power. All sorts of people have power over others. Heads of schools have power over lecturers and teachers, lecturers and teachers have power over pupils, and the police have power over all of us. How this power is applied can have very significant implications for social change. If we know what makes someone powerful then we can develop ideas and safeguards to make sure that we are all protected from change that could be damaging to our society. Research into obedience, including legitimate authority and the power that this brings, gives us insight into how society works in different conditions. The implications of this research are clear. If we can understand how people behave towards those with power, and how powerful figures and groups gain that power, then we can begin to make sure that that power is not abused, as it was in Abu Ghraib prison. The research has a lot to tell us about our role as social scientists and members of communities. We should not take things for granted. We can bring about change even as a minority and we must also be aware of the power we have and the power that others have over us.

WANT TO KNOW MORE?

If you'd like to read more about social psychology you will find more in these books.

Aronson, E. (2007) *The Social Animal*, W. H. Freeman and Co.

Baron, R. A., Byrne, D. and Branscombe N. R. (2005) *Social Psychology*, Pearson Education

Hogg, M. and Vaughan, G. (2007) *Social Psychology* (5th edition), Prentice Hall

"There's no way we can include every example of minority and majority influence in research into social change. Just because it's not here, doesn't mean you can't use it. Take a look at your school or college; how do the views of the majority get heard and acted on? How might the views of the minority make an impact? Feel free to use your own examples as long as they are clear."

Section 6

Individual Differences –
Psychopathology
(Abnormality)

WHAT YOU WILL LEARN ABOUT?

We all share similarities but we differ from one another in just as many important ways. These are what psychologists call individual differences – the study of why and how individuals differ from one another. The psychology of individual differences covers a broad scope. Some psychologists study personality to develop methods of measuring the individual differences. Other psychologists are interested in diagnosing and treating problems of mental health. It is this aspect of individual differences which you will study.

WHAT YOU NEED TO KNOW

Individual Differences is in Unit 2 of the specification. As you learn you are expected to develop your knowledge and understanding of Individual Difference, including concepts, theories and studies. This also includes a knowledge and understanding of research methods and ethical issues as they relate to this area of psychology. You also need to develop the skills of analysis, evaluation and application. Rather than just recall and reproduce information, you are expected to be able to apply your knowledge and understanding. The subject content is split into two parts:

Defining and explaining psychological abnormality

- Ways defining abnormality, together with their limitations:

  Deviation from social norms • Failure to function adequately • Deviation from ideal mental health

- Key features of the biological approach to psychopathology
- Key features of psychological approaches to psychopathology:

  Psychodynamic approach • Behavioural approach • Cognitive approach

Treating abnormality

- Biological therapies: *ECT • Drugs*
- Psychological therapies:

  Psychoanalysis • Systematic desensitisation • Cognitive behavioural therapy

Defining Psychological Abnormality

It's the fact that we are all so different that makes life interesting!

One in six people living in the UK will at some time seek help for a mental health problem. These problems range from relatively mild symptoms which a person can usually cope with to more severe symptoms which significantly disrupt the lives of the sufferer and those around them. 'Abnormal' simply means 'away from the norm' of acceptable behaviour. Sometimes, judging behaviour as unacceptable and therefore abnormal is a relatively straightforward matter. At other times distinguishing between normal and abnormal behaviour is very difficult. This is because 'normality' and 'abnormality' are relative terms; they change according to such things as who is deciding the 'norm' for acceptable behaviour, what the cultural values and expectations are, and when in history these norms are set.

WHAT IS ABNORMALITY?

In psychology the word 'abnormal' is used very carefully. This is because, whilst 'normal' is usually associated with good behaviour, 'abnormal' is usually equated with bad behaviour. Deciding that a person is abnormal can therefore be a value judgement rather than an objective assessment. Labels such as 'abnormal' carry with them all sorts of consequences, many of them negative for the person with the label. Someone might be regarded as 'abnormal' for a number of different reasons.

It could be that the person just doesn't seem to follow the unwritten rules that societies have and behaves in ways that particular societies find unacceptable. It could be that they are not able to engage with society in a way that most others can, for example, enjoying shopping trips and holidays, seeing friends or going to the cinema. It could even be that a person is just not as mentally healthy as they could or should be. The term 'abnormal' is used a great deal in everyday speech to describe someone who is behaving in an unusual or threatening way. The ways in which the word is used however vary enormously. In psychology, the word needs to be used rather carefully.

It seems that, in order to recognise whether or not someone is behaving in a psychologically abnormal way, we need a 'clear' *definition* of what exactly we mean by abnormal. The answer to this might be very simple, requiring no more than common sense: abnormality is the absence of normality. If we know what is 'normal' then anything outside this must therefore be abnormal. Unfortunately, defining normality presents us with much the same difficulty as defining abnormality!

There is no clear agreement about what constitutes either abnormality or normality. Whilst it is likely that no single definition will be acceptable to everyone, taken together the various attempts at defining abnormality have helped to clarify what exactly we mean when we label behaviour as abnormal.

Some may say this behaviour is abnormal. In most situations society says it is unacceptable to spray-paint walls and fences. In what situations might this person's behaviour be regarded as normal?

DEVIATION FROM SOCIAL NORMS

Norms are unwritten rules, created by society, to guide behaviour. They tell us which behaviours are expected and acceptable, and they provide us with some sense of 'order' in society. Generally speaking they are learned through early socialisation, that is, we pick them up from others around us during our childhood. Norms vary from society to society. Travel will cause us to encounter, and have to adjust to, the norms of other societies. For example, in France, it is considered perfectly normal for children to drink a little wine (albeit with water) with dinner. In this country it is not considered normal.

There are norms for just about every kind of social behaviour. Societies have age-based norms, for example, which tell us the kind of behaviours expected of different people at different ages – although we might not like what we see, we expect tantrums from a young child but do not expect to see the same kind of behaviour from someone in their thirties. Such behaviour might lead us to think that the adult is behaving abnormally.

Society also has gender-based norms. These reflect what is acceptable in clothing, activities and even professions.

Many mental disorders are seen to be clearly abnormal because the behaviours associated with them break norms. For example, some schizophrenics have difficulty controlling inappropriate emotions. They might cry when they hear a funny story or laugh at sad things, behaviour which would break rules of expected behaviour.

Is this type of tantrum-like behaviour appropriate for this woman?

This definition makes abnormality a *relative concept* – that is, what is abnormal depends on the tolerance of a culture for certain behaviours. For example, men of the Gururumba people of New Guinea occasionally enter into an emotional state known there as 'being a wild pig'. It is called this because, when in this state of mind, men behave just like wild pigs – running wild, stealing, being aggressive and generally being antisocial. The Gururumba people however are very tolerant of this behaviour – it is a cultural norm that 'being a wild pig' will occasionally happen to men aged between 25 and 35 and thus the behaviour, although unwelcome, is accepted.

LIMITATIONS

1 Societies change over time and so, therefore, do their norms. Because of this we cannot use opinions held in the past to judge a behaviour as *deviant* – it must be based on present day thinking. For example, as recently as the 1970s homosexuality was listed as a mental disorder in the Diagnostic and Statistical Manual (the DSM is the main classification and diagnosis system for mental illness used in the United States). Homosexuality between consenting adults over 18 years of age is now legal and would not be considered abnormal. It is widely portrayed in the media and within most Western countries and is now a behaviour falling within most social norms.

Another good example would be that of unmarried mothers. Before the 1970s this was considered abnormal – young women could be institutionalised in psychiatric institutions because of this. Now, things are much different. Homosexuality is more acceptable in society, and unmarried mothers are not at all an unusual part of our world.

2 Norms must be considered *in context*. Dress codes give us a good example of this. In the eighteenth century it would have been considered normal for men to wear quite elaborate wigs. By the twentieth century the habit had completely gone. A male wearing such a wig now would probably be considered abnormal. However, some kinds of eighteenth century style wigs are still worn ceremonially, for example, those worn by judges and barristers in court. In this context however it is not abnormal behaviour. Breaking a social norm does not necessarily make someone psychologically abnormal. Very often, it isn't just the breaking a norm which defines a behaviour as abnormal but the context in which the behaviour appears. Most people at some time in their lives either push against or break social norms.

3 It is important to be clear about who exactly is 'setting the norm'. In Western societies it is the behaviour of the majority white population that establishes a social norm. One must be cautious then about applying this Western white norm to all societies as a standard for behaviour. For example, whilst there are variations, in Europe the average age of consent is 16 years. An adult having sex with someone below this age would be considered to be having sexual relations with a child. This would clearly break social norms as well as several laws. In Indonesia however the age of consent is 19, whilst in Saudi Arabia extra-marital sex is illegal regardless of whether or not it is consensual. Clearly, what is considered abnormal or deviant varies considerably across cultures.

4 Breaking social norms is not necessarily a bad thing. In fact, it can be a good thing and can even stimulate positive social change. For example, slavery was once considered 'normal' in this society. It might even have been considered to be out of place, amongst the elite of society, not to have one or more slaves in their household. However, when some members of this social group broke norms and opposed slavery the eventual result was the abolition of slavery. There are other examples: voting rights for women, for instance, and rights for children.

FAILURE TO FUNCTION ADEQUATELY

An individual who is *failing to function adequately* is engaging in behaviours that are somehow 'not good for them'. That is, their behaviour is self-defeating in some way or, as psychologists phrase it, it is not adaptive or functional. For example, they might have difficulty maintaining close relationships, setting and achieving goals in life, engaging in social activities or living independent and fulfilling lives. Day-to-day living is difficult for these people. For instance, they may feel that they cannot bring themselves to go to the shops or attend a family gathering such as a wedding or a party of some kind.

A failure to function can be seen clearly in most abnormal behaviours. For example, *anorexia nervosa* is an eating disorder where there is an intense fear of becoming obese and a distorted body image. The efforts of an anorexic to get to what he or she considers to be his or her correct size and shape can cause significant disruption to their work, study and even their sleep. Many aspects of their personal life are seriously disrupted by anorexia, which can cause serious physical illness and even death. This is what psychologists call *maladaptive behaviour*. The person is not responding to the world, or to their environment, appropriately.

Not being able to get out of bed and face the world could be regarded as part of a failure to function adequately.

There are many ways of deciding whether or not someone is failing to function adequately. One of the most commonly used methods is the *Global Assessment of Functioning* (GAF) Scale, which is part of the DSM, mentioned earlier. With the GAF Scale, the highest level of functioning of an individual during the past year is assessed in terms of such things as family, interests and work. Each of these is given a score out of 100. This score is then compared to the individual's present level of functioning, which is assessed in the same way and is also given a score out of 100. For example, someone who is given a current GAF of 60 compared to a highest GAF for the past year of 75 is considered to be not functioning as well as they have done or could be. There are actually two different GAF Scales, one for adults and one for people under the age of 18, who are, for convenience, categorised as 'children'.

LIMITATIONS

1 The application of the failure to function approach relies heavily on personal judgement to inform decisions about the presence or absence of abnormality. For example, judgements have to be made about the presence or absence of *indicators of abnormality*, and then about the degree to which these are having an effect. For instance, if a person has very few friends, what influence does this have on him or her? By their nature, judgements are not objective (based on evidence); they are influenced by the personal opinion, emotions and background of the decision-maker. This kind of *subjectivity* increases the likelihood of a person being described as normal or abnormal by mistake. The process is made more difficult when you consider the fact that many abnormal behaviours are no more than exaggerations of normal behaviour. For example, it is normal to show grief at the loss of a loved one, but at what point does this distress become abnormal grief?

2 Using this definition, abnormality cannot be viewed in the same *context* in different cultures. What is *adequate* functioning in one culture might not be adequate in another. The grief example is entirely appropriate here also. Outpourings of grief in the UK are rather unusual. People tend to keep their emotions to themselves. In other cultures, very open displays of grief are common and not at all abnormal.

3 Most people would agree that someone who commits murder is abnormal. However, this behaviour, for the culprit, is not necessarily maladaptive. The person might be a satisfied murderer, the behaviour being rational and fulfilling in the context of their own lives. For example, there are many instances of people who make a living by killing and in all other respects lead normal lives. Hired killers and mercenaries are often paid to fight and kill in war zones around the world. These people are professional, privately funded soldiers, often called soldiers of fortune. Clearly, *maladaptive* does not necessarily mean *abnormal*.

GLOBAL ASSESSMENT OF FUNCTIONING (GAF)

GAF SCORE	EXPLANATION
91–100	Superior functioning in a wide range of activities. Problems never seem to get out of hand, is sought out by others because of his or her qualities. No symptoms.
81–91	Absent or minimal symptoms, good functioning in all areas, interested and involved in a wide range of activities, socially effective, generally satisfied with life, no more than everyday problems or concerns.
71–80	If symptoms are present they are transient reactions to psychosocial stresses which are to be expected; no more than slight impairment in ocial, occupational or school functioning.
61–70	Some mild symptoms OR some difficulty in social, occupational or school functioning, but generally functioning reasonably well; has some meaningful interpersonal relationships.
51–60	Moderate symptoms OR moderate difficulty in social, occupational or school functioning.
41–50	Serious symptoms OR serious impairment in social, occupational or school functioning.
31–40	Some impairment in reality testing or communication OR major impairment in several areas, such as work or school, family relations, judgement, thinking or mood.
21–30	Behaviour is considerably influenced by delusions or hallucinations OR serious impairment in communications or judgement OR inability to function in all areas.
11–20	Some danger of hurting self or others OR occasionally fails to maintain minimal personal hygiene OR gross impairment in communication.
1–10	Persistent danger of severely hurting self or others OR persistent inability to maintain minimum personal hygiene OR serious suicidal act with clear expectation of death.
0	Not enough information available to provide GAF.

Table 8: Global Assessment of Functioning Scale.

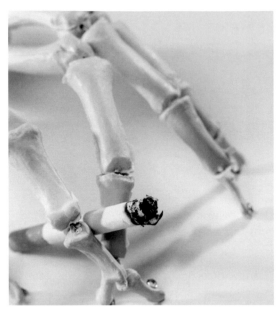

Even though they know their behaviour is risky some people continue to smoke.

Another example of this problem is smokers who have been told of the risk of cancer but continue to smoke. For them, the behaviour is maladaptive but not many people would label this behaviour as abnormal. Their decision to continue smoking is a risk they are willing to take, at least for the time being.

4 As with all forms of diagnosis, there is a danger with this definition of *labelling*. People who are labelled as failing to function, and therefore abnormal, may start to behave in ways that match the label. Once the label of 'criminal' has been applied it is rather hard to shift. If a person has been in prison, then it is often very difficult to find work from a mistrusting society. In these cases the person may return to crime because it is easier to behave according to their label rather than struggle against it.

DEVIATION FROM IDEAL MENTAL HEALTH

So far, definitions have focused on identifying abnormal behaviour. An alternative approach might be to consider what is normal – if we can decide on what normality is then anything not satisfying this condition must therefore represent abnormality. Jahoda (1958) talked about normality being a state of positive mental health. For Jahoda, several criteria have to be met in order to satisfy the conditions for what she called *optimal living* (or living life to the full).

1. Positive view of self
The person must have a feeling of self-worth, with a reasonable level of self-esteem.

2. Actualisation
The person must become the best that they possibly can.

3. Autonomy
The person must not have to rely on others for everything. They must show a level of independence in their behaviour.

4. Accurate view of reality
The person's view of the world around them must not be distorted in any way. They must not, for instance, think that everyone is untrustworthy and that everyone is watching their behaviour.

5. Environmental adaptability
The person must be able to change their behaviour to make it appropriate for different environments. For instance, a certain pattern of behaviour is expected at weddings, but not at funerals.

6. Resistance to stress
The person must be able to deal with the regular stresses and strains of life. They must be flexible in their ability to work through potentially difficult situations.

LIMITATIONS
1 This definition assumes that the absence of one of these categories implies abnormality. However, a number of the criteria are quite difficult to achieve. *Actualisation*, in

particular, is reached by few people in life, therefore if this definition is taken literally most people would be classified as abnormal! In reality, the criteria should be considered as a set of ideal standards which, if attained, would suggest optimal living rather than an absence of any of the elements representing abnormality.

2 It is not always clear what some of the criteria actually mean in practice. For example, it is not certain what an *accurate view of reality* is, given that 'reality' is a product of each individual's mind. Reality for a soldier in Afghanistan is somewhat different from that of an accountant in Manchester. Also, reality for someone living on benefits with three small children to care for is very different from the reality experienced by someone like the Prime Minister or a famous sportsperson like David Beckham. This means that the concepts are vague and difficult to measure, so that subjective judgements are needed in order to make the approach useful. *Positive view of self* is also open to interpretation. For example, a psychopath might be very happy and positive about himself, even though his behaviour is not seen in a positive way by others.

3 What is considered mentally healthy varies considerably across cultures. The categories of ideal mental health will not apply to all cultures – some of the criteria are culturally biased. They are based on Western ideas, which are not necessarily shared by all cultures. For example, in Jahoda's criteria there is an emphasis on personal and individual fulfilment. This is a particularly Westernised view which is not shared by all cultures. Some cultures place a great deal of emphasis on collective responsibility, where the welfare of the wider family is as important as that of the individual. The optimal living of one family member is going to be seen as less important than the welfare of the social group.

4 This system is positive in that it shifts the emphasis from *illness to health*. However, in its assumption that there is an ideal mental health it may be presenting a false goal. There may not be ideal mental health. What is ideal for one person may not be so for another. Similarly, if there really is an ideal mental health, then striving to reach this goal could be a problem in itself. If the person does not reach the ideal because it is unachievable then people are bound to fail and feel inadequate.

The Biological Approach to Explaining and Treating Abnormality

The biological approach regards abnormality as having a physical origin.

This approach is sometimes called the 'medical' or 'disease' model of abnormality and sees the outward symptoms of mental health problems, such as disordered behaviour and thought, as signs of disease affecting the functions of the nervous system. It is more concerned with identifying patterns of symptoms and classifying abnormal behaviour than it is in issues of defining abnormality. If abnormality is a disease, then like any other disease it is going to show symptoms that will lead to a diagnosis and recommendations for treatment. These treatments are physical in that they involve directly altering bodily states with drugs, surgery and electricity. As our knowledge of how the body works has advanced, so too has the effectiveness of physical treatments for mental health problems.

THE BIOLOGICAL APPROACH TO PSYCHOPATHOLOGY

The biological approach views mental health problems as illnesses, with identifiable symptoms, origins and treatments. This approach suggests abnormal behaviour can be traced back to biological factors, usually affecting the structure and functioning of the brain in some way. Although it is assumed that disorders have physical causes, sometimes this can't be identified precisely, in which case it is referred to as a 'functional' disorder. On the other hand, when the physical cause of the problem is identifiable, such as with a brain tumour or a biochemical imbalance, it is known as an 'organic' disorder.

Biology and behaviour are interdependent – changes in one produce changes in the other. *Damage* to certain parts of the brain can cause changes in behaviours such as memory, language and emotion, whilst alterations in brain chemicals (called *neurotransmitters*) can influence mood and perception. Changes in behaviour can also bring about changes in biology. Mood for example, can be improved by the simple act of physically smiling. Behaviours can also affect health. For example, Stone et al (1987) found that the body's immune system is affected by changes in mood – the immune system is less effective when people are in a negative mood.

This approach remains very popular despite the development of alternative non-biological approaches to mental illness. It is not uncommon in everyday speech, for example, to refer to behaviours like addiction and depression as 'diseases', despite a number of convincing psychological explanations for these behaviours.

"Think carefully about this section. When you are revising, make sure you know certain things about the 'approach' you are thinking about. First, make sure you know whether it is a biological or psychological approach, and second, make sure you know why your approach differs from other approaches. This information will be useful in different places in the exam so get it straight in your mind now!"

The biological approach considers a number of possible causes of mental illness.

Infection

This is the idea that *bacteria* and *viruses*, which invade the body, can cause mental illness. For example, although now a rare disorder, general paresis is a very serious condition where the sufferer experiences a gradual mental decline, often leading to death. It results from the bacteria that cause syphilis entering the nervous system and infecting (and thus damaging) the cerebral cortex of the brain. Other viruses have been known to cause brain damage. For example, the British musician, Clive Wearing, suffered an infection from the herpes simplex virus which damaged some areas of his brain. This left him with severe memory problems. He is unable to encode new memories, and, although still very much in love with his wife, believes that he has not seen her for a considerable time if she returns after having only recently left his room, to fetch a glass of water for instance.

Clive Wearing

Another example is EP, an 85-year-old Californian who suffers from loss of long-term and short-term memory after a virus infection (again, herpes simplex) damaged some areas of his brain.

More recently, research by Brown (2004) has found a link between schizophrenia and the influenza virus. It is claimed that women who have influenza during pregnancy run a greater risk of having children who develop schizophrenia later in life. This is because the virus may cause damage to the developing brain of the foetus.

If the abnormality is caused by infection the treatment might be a *drug therapy* whereby the infection itself is targeted by drugs, just as you might target a cold or throat infection.

Biochemistry

The brain has a number of important chemicals, called *neurotransmitters*, which brain cells use in their communication with each other. It has been suggested that an excess or deficiency in one or more of these are a possible cause of mental illness. Indeed, many kinds of disorder seem to be clearly linked to problems with brain chemistry. For example, schizophrenia is thought to be caused by an excess of a neurotransmitter called dopamine. Drugs are used to redress the balance of brain chemicals. This can be seen in the beneficial effects for some schizophrenics of medications which reduce dopamine levels in the brain. In some other conditions, dopamine levels may be too low, in which case a drug that encourages the production of dopamine, or the maintenance of dopamine in the system, may be used.

Brain damage

Some psychological problems result directly from damage to the brain. This is not a new idea – it was suggested as far back as the fourth century BC by Hippocrates, the Greek philosopher and 'father of medicine'. Common types of brain damage are those caused by injury (a blow to the head perhaps), tumours (abnormal growths in the brain) and strokes (loss of blood supply to parts of the brain). An enormous variety of behavioural changes can result as a consequence of brain damage – the

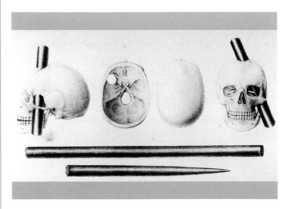

Drawings of the skull of Phineas Gage showing his injury and the tool with which he was hurt.

symptoms depend on which part of the brain is damaged. One of the earliest recorded and most famous cases of brain damage leading to abnormal behaviour is that of Phineas Gage who, as a result of a metal rod passing through his head, experienced a major change in behaviour, turning from someone who was reasonable and well-liked to a difficult and antisocial person. Where the brain has been damaged beyond repair, drugs may be used to help the brain deal with this damage. For instance, the brain may not be making enough of a particular neurotransmitter because of the damage, in which case drugs may be used.

Genetics

We know that all our physical characteristics are determined by the genes that we *inherit* from our parents. Some of these characteristics, such as mass (weight) and intelligence, are also influenced by the environment (nurture and nature working together). Genes code for brain chemicals and so they have a strong influence over our behaviour.

An example of genetic influence is PKU (phenylketonuria), a form of mental disease. It is caused by a defect in a single gene and is passed on to a child only when both parents are carriers of this gene. As a result of having this faulty gene, a child cannot convert a chemical called phenylalanine (commonly found in food) into another chemical called melanin. As a result, phenylalanine builds up in the body and causes irreversible brain damage. All newborn babies are tested within the first seven days of life (the Guthrie test) and those that test positive can be put on a special diet with very low amounts of phenylalanine. (You may have noticed on food labels a warning which goes something like 'contains a source of phenylalanine', which is a warning to phenylalanine-sensitive people to avoid these foods.)

Genes have been implicated in many mental disorders. For example, Holland et al (1988) suggest that closely related family members are

Identical twins are more likely to develop anorexia nervosa.

more likely to suffer from a particular eating disorder (see Study in Focus). They found that identical twins were much more likely than non-identical twins to both develop anorexia nervosa, suggesting a genetic component to the disorder.

"You could be asked to describe the biological approach to abnormality. Learning the four possible causes will really help you to explain how a problem can be caused, and it will really help you illustrate your answer."

BIOLOGICAL THERAPIES

For the biological approach, abnormal behaviour is a symptom of some underlying biological problem. For this reason, the biological therapies focus on altering the physical state of the body in order to bring about an improvement in symptoms. The most common way of doing this is to change the biochemistry of the brain in some way, either though administering drugs or by electroconvulsive therapy.

Drugs

It should be remembered that any medication can be either *curative* (that is, it cures the problem) or *palliative* (that is, the problem is still there but the symptoms are suppressed). All drugs prescribed for mental health problems are palliative – whilst on medication the symptoms reduce or disappear, but when

STUDY IN FOCUS

Genetics and anorexia
Holland et al (1988)

What were they doing and why? Holland et al carried out research into anorexia. They wanted to know whether the susceptibility to suffer with anorexia could be inherited – whether genes played a role.

How did they do it? The researchers found 45 pairs of twins where at least one twin had anorexia. 25 of them were identical pairs of twins (monozygotic – MZ), which means that they were born from a single egg. This means that the twins were identical, not just in the way they looked, but also genetically. The other 20 pairs of twins were non-identical (dizygotic – DZ) which means they were born of different eggs, and shared only half of their genes. If genes did play a role in the development of anorexia then the MZ, genetically identical twins, would be more likely to both suffer with the problem than the DZ twins.

What did they find? The results showed that 56% of the MZ twins both had anorexia, whereas only 5% of the DZ twins both suffered. This means that if the twins were identical, and one had anorexia, the other was much more likely to be anorexic than if the twins had been non-identical. This clearly indicates that the susceptibility to anorexia does have a significant genetic component.

Take a closer look: ● Although it is true that twins tend to be brought up together in the same environment irrespective of whether they are identical or not, it is also true that identical twins tend to be treated more similarly than non-identical twins. However, some of the twins in the study who both had the disorder were raised apart, in different countries. Each did not know that the other had the eating disorder, yet they still both suffered with anorexia, so factors other than genetics also influence whether someone becomes anorexic.

● Diagnosing anorexia is difficult, and it may be that those in the study diagnosed with anorexia may actually have been suffering with the related problem bulimia. Since we cannot be certain of the diagnosis, we cannot be certain of the conclusion that anorexia has a genetic basis, only that 'the susceptibility to suffer with an eating disorder' can be inherited.

● If anorexia was caused only by genetics, then 100% of the MZ twins should both have had anorexia. This was not the case, so other factors must have played a part in the development of the eating disorder.

the patient stops taking the drug there is a high risk of the symptoms returning. It is difficult to calculate the true figure, but it is estimated that the relapse rate may be as high as 80%. For many people then, drug therapy is a long-term response to mental health problems, where the symptoms are controlled and the experience for the sufferer is made more positive. Drug therapies fall into three broad categories, depending on why they are used.

Antipsychotic drugs are used to treat the more bizarre symptoms of psychotic disorders like schizophrenia, such as hallucinations and disturbed thinking (these are usually referred to as 'positive symptoms'). In the past, little could be done to control these symptoms, and the usual response was to institutionalise the sufferer. It is estimated that in the 1950s over half a million psychotic patients were in psychiatric hospitals. The development and use of antipsychotic drugs has revolutionised the treatment of people with psychoses, vastly reducing the need for hospitalisation and for many meaning a return to normal life. There are many different kinds of antipsychotic drug, though there is no evidence that any one is more effective overall than another – it depends on the patient and the severity of their illness. Most antipsychotic drug work in similar ways however, that is by reducing the effect of a neurotransmitter called dopamine. This results in a reduction in the intensity and frequency of positive symptoms. It is often the case that, once symptoms subside, patients continue to take medication in order to control the problem and ensure that it does not recur.

Antidepressants are used to treat mood disorders, especially depression. There are three types of antidepressant. *Tricyclic antidepressants* (TCAs) work by increasing levels of the neurotransmitter *noradrenaline*. About 70% of depressed patients taking TCAs show significant improvements. *Monoamine oxidase inhibitors* (MAO inhibitors) also increase levels of noradrenaline, although in a different way to TCAs. MAO inhibitors are not the first choice antidepressant however because of the severe side effects if taken with certain foods (for example, if combined with shellfish they can be fatal). The most widely prescribed antidepressants are the *selective serotonin re-uptake inhibitors* (SSRIs), such as *fluoxetine* (commonly known as *Prozac*). SSRIs increase levels of the neurotransmitter serotonin. They are particularly effective for milder forms of depression and successfully reduce symptoms in about 65% of patients. Whilst the success of the drug is not much different to TCAs and MAO inhibitors, the side effects are much less severe.

Anxiolytics are drugs that are used to reduce feelings of anxiety, for example in people suffering from phobias. The most widely used anti-anxiety drugs are the benzodiazepines, such as diazepam (known commonly as Valium) and alprazapam (known commonly as Xanax). These medications have an overall calming effect, achieved by reducing anxiety and nervousness, i.e. the physical experience of stress. More on the use of anxiolytics can be found in the section of the book dealing with physiological methods of stress management.

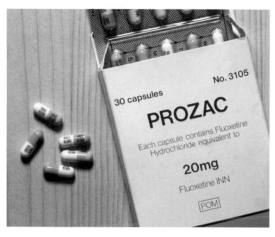

ECT

Electroconvulsive therapy (ECT) is a technique which induces convulsions by running an electrical current through the brain. A brief shock (less than a second) is delivered to the brain by electrodes placed on either or both sides of the head. A current to one side of the brain is called *unilateral*, and a current delivered to both sides of the brain is called *bilateral*. There is some debate about whether bilateral or unilateral treatments are best, but unilateral treatments are usually administered to the right side of the brain to minimise loss of language memory. (One possible side effect of treatment is short-term memory loss so shock is not given to the half of the brain which controls language). In order to make the procedure as safe and stress-free as possible, the patient is anaesthetised. The patient is also given a muscle relaxant. This is to ensure that the

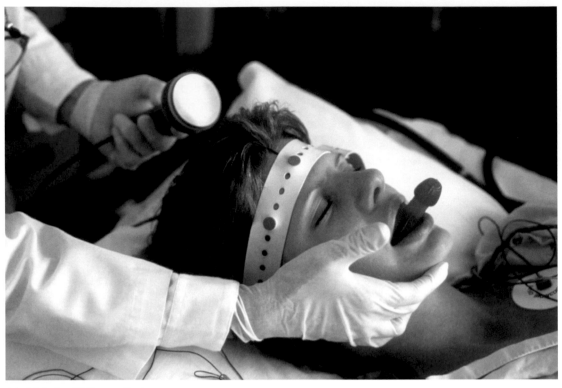

Administering ECT to a patient.

muscle contractions that occur during seizure do not break bones, tear muscle or dislocate limbs. Typically, the patient might receive about six treatments, with no more than two or three treatments in a week.

Whilst the use of ECT used to be quite common, it has reduced in popularity with the development of safer and more effective drug therapies. However, it is still used in some cases of severe depression which do not respond significantly to drug treatments. It is estimated that 50–70% of these patients benefit from ECT, although ECT does not eliminate the need for continued medical treatment. It is particularly useful for those patients with severe problems at risk of harming themselves. Rather than waiting three to six weeks to see if there is a response to drugs, ECT can offer a quick relief of these symptoms. Because of this, ECT has been credited with saving many lives.

It is not entirely clear how ECT works. ECT is thought to improve symptoms by affecting neurotransmitters in the brain, especially serotonin and noradrenaline. Traditionally, ECT has been criticised as a method which harms brain cells, and that this damage is the reason for the reduction of symptoms. There is however no convincing evidence that ECT causes damage to the brain. According to Reid (2005), recent research on rats indicates that ECT might actually *benefit* the survival of brain cells. It does this by stimulating the production of a protein in the brain which protects cells. This is an important finding, since very severe depression is associated with damage to brain cells in the frontal and temporal lobes. The implication is that ECT might stop or even reverse the damaging effects that some disorders have on the brain.

HOW EFFECTIVE ARE BIOLOGICAL THERAPIES?

Drugs are widely prescribed for a range of mental health problems, but do they work? Tamminga (1997) showed that drug therapies are successful in many cases of schizophrenia and do reduce symptoms and suffering, with patients experiencing fewer of the more extreme symptoms such as hallucination. However, many patients (up to 40%) did not feel any better in other ways, for example in terms of how withdrawn they felt from society, or how apathetic, or lacking in motivation they felt. So, in this regard, the success of this particular biological therapy is a little mixed. Antidepressants are a different type of drug, often prescribed to combat anxiety and depression. According to Lieberman (1998) antidepressant drugs reliably reduce symptoms of depression and anxiety, and have relatively mild side effects. These disorders occur in different forms however, and the effectiveness of drug treatments will depend on the type and severity of the problem. Disorders like schizophrenia and depression are not necessarily constant conditions – in some people they fluctuate, so that sufferers will have intermittent *episodes* of the disorder. Drug therapy sometimes serves the purpose of delaying or reducing the severity of the next episode rather than providing a cure. This provides welcome *relief* of symptoms for the sufferer, and for mental health workers it can make the problem more manageable. It can also provide an opportunity to introduce psychological therapies that might benefit the sufferer, such as *cognitive behavioural therapy*.

Electro convulsive therapy does seem to work in many cases, but not in others. The reason for this is not clear and the evidence from research is a little mixed. ECT seems to be of most use to severely depressed patients, particularly when there is a risk of entering a new period of depression. Rey and Walter (1997) say that up to 70% of patients with severe depression get relief with ECT. On the other hand, Schwartz (1995) says that 85% of those whom it helps often relapse into a depressive state, so the helpfulness of the treatment is often short lived. It has been suggested that any success of ECT is due to the damage caused by passing an electrical current through the brain. Coffey et al (1991) have shown that those who have been treated with ECT show no signs of brain damage at all. The therapy is deemed safe enough for the largest psychiatric association in the world (the American Psychiatric Association) to recommend it for those with severe depression who have not responded to other forms of treatment, including therapies. It seems that ECT remains a useful tool in a small number of cases.

The Psychological Approach to Explaining and Treating Abnormality

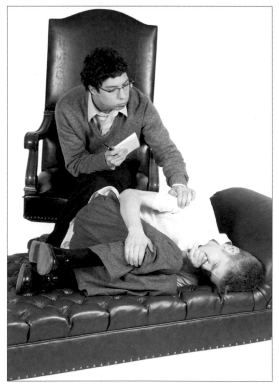

Psychotherapy – a psychological treatment.

How psychologists interpret abnormal behaviour depends on their perspective as to the causes of behaviour. Each perspective has its own assumption; some will focus on how abnormal behaviour is learned, whilst others will focus on how abnormal behaviours are a result of biases and errors in thinking. Each perspective makes recommendations about the best treatment of abnormal behaviour based on its own assumptions. In this section we will introduce the psychological approach to abnormality which includes psychodynamic, cognitive and behavioural approaches. These perspectives offer no complete explanation for either the causes of abnormality or its treatment, and for this reason people working in the field of abnormal psychology tend to adopt an overall point of view, selecting from each perspective those aspects that increase understanding.

THE PSYCHOLOGICAL APPROACH TO PSYCHOPATHOLOGY

According to the psychological approach, abnormal thoughts, feelings and behaviour have their origins in our psychology. It does not regard the person with the mental health problem who has difficulty dealing with the world around them as being ill, rather the person's thinking, their feelings or their behaviour are regarded as abnormal. Each psychological approach views and treats the person's mental health problem differently.

In this section we will introduce the psychological approach to abnormality which includes psychodynamic, cognitive and behavioural approaches.

PSYCHODYNAMIC APPROACH TO ABNORMALITY

This approach was developed by Sigmund Freud and others towards the end of the nineteenth century. The word *psychodynamic* is used here because this approach sees the mind (or 'psyche') as being influenced by powerful (dynamic) unconscious forces.

The *unconscious* is an important idea in psychodynamic theory. The unconscious contains thoughts and feelings which, if they became conscious, would be painful and unpleasant and therefore get in the way of normal functioning. Psychodynamic theory stresses that the underlying causes of both normal and abnormal behaviours are psychological rather than physical.

The structure of the psyche

Freud claimed that the psyche has three components. There is the id: present at birth, this part of the psyche is completely unconscious and works on the 'pleasure principle', wanting satisfaction at any cost. At around age of 3, the ego develops and operates on the 'reality principle'. At about the age of 5 the superego develops. This operates on the 'morality principle'; it is a person's conscience and attempts to guide behaviour with feelings of guilt and pride. Unlike the id and superego, the ego is aware of the outside world and, because of this, tries to resolve the conflicting demands of the id on the one hand and the superego on the other. It is important that these forces are in balance, otherwise the id or ego will dominate behaviour leading to problems. For example, if the id is powerful and the superego weak then anti-social behaviour might emerge, or if the id is weak and superego strong then a person might have unrealistic standards of behaviour and as a result feel intolerable guilt and shame. The ego uses 'defence mechanisms' to protect itself from anxiety.

According to this theory, abnormal behaviours are the symptoms caused by the *conflict* between the id, ego and superego in the unconscious mind. An example of how this unconscious conflict can lead to abnormal behaviour can be seen in one of Freud's famous case studies, the case of Anna O.

THE CASE OF ANNA O (FREUD, 1910)

Anna O was a client of Freud's who had difficulty drinking and suffered with nausea and quite significant paralysis. Freud said that these problems had a psychological basis and, through his discussions with her during therapy, it became clear that her drinking phobia arose because a dog she did not like drank from her water glass. Her other problems, Freud said, were a result of her anxieties which came about during time caring for her sick father. Freud treated her with psychoanalysis and her paralysis soon disappeared.

Psychosexual development

Freud likened our mind to an iceberg. The tip is the conscious mind and what is hidden below the water is the unconscious mind. The conscious part of our mind is the part of ourselves that we are aware of, the self that we can describe. The unconscious mind contains our deepest thoughts, fears and desires. Unconscious means that even we are not aware of them. Freud believed that it is the unconscious which drives our behaviour and that traumatic childhood memories and experiences may become part of the

unconscious. Memories of these early events are repressed, but can manifest themselves in later abnormal behaviour, for example depression, phobia and obsession. (see the case study of Ratman).

Sigmund Freud – the father of psychoanalysis.

For Freud, childhood experiences are a crucial element in the way we behave as adults. Especially important are our experiences during *psychosexual development*. He said that we go through stages in our early development, which he called 'psychosexual stages'. At each stage we find pleasure and gratification from a different part of our body (he called these areas 'erogenous'). If our experience results in either too much or too little gratification from these erogenous areas we can develop *fixations*, that is, an unconscious preoccupation with that particular psychosexual stage. These result of these fixations are expressed in our behaviour as adults.

Freud's psychosexual stages are:

1 *ORAL STAGE (0-1 YEAR)*: The focus of pleasure at this stage is the mouth. Satisfaction for the baby is gained from putting things in the mouth so feeding is very important. A child may become fixated if its feeding demands are not met or if it is weaned too early. An oral fixation may result in an adult seeking oral gratification, for example from over eating, smoking and drinking, particularly during times of stress.

DEFENCE MECHANISM	EXAMPLE
Denial: A complete rejection of the feeling	'I AM NOT ANGRY'
Suppression: Awareness of the feeling but attempt to hide it completely	'I HATE maths, but will put on a happy face and show the outside world that I enjoy it'
Reaction formation: A reversal of the real feeling	'I LOVE maths. I really really LOVE maths'
Projection: You think that someone else shares your opinions	'You HATE maths too, I now you do'
Displacement: Feelings are redirected elsewhere	'I HATE my little brother!'
Rationalisation: Arriving at reasons to explain your behaviour	'The reason I hate maths is because the only book in our holiday caravan was a maths book. It spoilt my holiday, and that is why I hate maths'
Undoing: Do something that appears to reverse or undo your feelings	'I shall join the "I Love maths" club at school'
Repression: You experienced a traumatic event as a child but have no recollection of it whatsoever	'I'm told something bad happened, but I can't remember it at all'
Regression: Reverting to childish behaviour to offset your feelings	'Let's all draw silly pictures of the maths teacher!'
Sublimation: Redirection of feelings into a socially acceptable activity	'I shall write a play about maths and what it feels like to be a student in a maths class'

2 *ANAL STAGE (1–3 YEARS)*: The anus is now the erogenous area and the child gains pleasure from going to the toilet. Between 2 and 3 years of age parents are demanding that the child becomes potty trained, this can cause conflict. Freud said that the child could become fixated if potty training is too strict or not strict enough. Strict potty training could lead to adult behaviour such as obsessions with cleanliness and order or difficulty in expressing emotions.

3 *PHALLIC STAGE (3–5 YEARS)*: The genital area becomes more sensitive and Freud says that the child begins to have unconscious sexual desires for the opposite sex parent. This leads to conflict within the child, as it fears punishment by the same sex parent. In boys this is called the Oedipus complex. The boy is torn between desire for his mother and fear that his bigger more powerful father will castrate him. This causes castration anxiety and to deal with this the boy identifies with his father. This means that he tries to become like his father and take on his values, attitudes, behaviour and morals. Freud says that this is how the boy learns to behave according to his gender as a male.

The conflict for a girl is known as the Electra complex. Freud's ideas on this are a lot less clear. According to his theory girls are attracted to the father but believe that they have been found out and castrated for this. This leaves her with a sense of inadequacy and inferiority. As with the boy, the girl is also in a state of conflict about this and to resolve it she identifies with her mother (although this process is much slower). The girl also learns to behave as a female and gains a sense of morality.

4 *LATENCY STAGE (5–12 YEARS)*: This is a period of consolidation and rest. Sexuality lies dormant and the child is busy learning their gender roles, social rules and developing self-confidence.

5 *GENITAL STAGE (12 YEARS ONWARDS)*: The genitals become the erogenous area and the individual becomes more interested in the opposite sex. After a period of quiet during latency, the fixations of the first five years become active and begin to exert their influence on personality. There is also a drive towards independence, making adolescence a time of potential storm and stress.

> **ASK AN EXAMINER**
>
> *"Don't worry, you don't have learn all this stuff on psychosexual stages – you are not expected to write about it in the exam. However, psychosexual development is a really important part of the theory and tells us something about the origin of abnormal behaviour. It's in here because it's important for your understanding of the psychodynamic approach."*

Psychodynamic therapy

The principal psychodynamic therapy is called *psychoanalysis*. This was developed by Sigmund Freud in the 1890s. The therapy aims to bring to consciousness repressed wishes and painful memories, thus making the patient aware of the unconscious conflicts responsible for the symptoms being experienced. This allows the patient to face up to these conflicts rather than bury them away. Such 'burying away' takes a great deal of mental energy and, by not having to do this, a sense of release is felt that mental energy can now be invested in finding better ways of coping. Many different types of psychoanalysis have been developed over the years but they all share basic techniques.

Free association is one of the most important techniques used by analysts, and aims to overcome ego defences which block painful thoughts. This technique involves the patient talking openly without holding anything back. The ego will attempt to censor what is said, but the free thinking and talking allows previously unconscious thoughts to slip through. There are many ways of achieving this but it might involve a patient relaxing on a couch, encouraging them to wander through their thoughts and speak freely about whatever comes to mind. The therapist then interprets the content and feeds this back to the patient so that they might begin to understand their problem.

'RAT MAN' - A CASE STUDY

In 1909, Freud saw a client (a patient) he called 'rat man' to protect his identity. The pseudonym came about because of rat man's references to a torture he had heard about involving rats gnawing at the bodies of prisoners, and his obsession that this may happen to a loved one, particularly his father or a woman he felt attracted to. Rat man was obsessive. When he had a guilty thought, such as the idea of murdering his father so he could inherit all his money, he would punish himself by thinking that his father had died and left him nothing. Freud thought that the route of his problem lay in unresolved conflicts about sexual and aggressive feelings he had for his loved ones. These began in childhood because of harsh punishments for masturbation and guilt because of his sexual curiosity. Rat man died in the first world war, and Freud was never able to follow up on his case. His real name was Ernst Lanzer.

Another important technique is *dream analysis*, where the dreams related by patients during their therapy sessions are interpreted. For Freud, dream content could have meaning since it is through dreams that unconscious thoughts are expressed more freely.

He suggested that the *manifest content* of dreams (that is, the literal dream events as reported) often conceal a *latent content* (which is some form of wish fulfilment in symbolic form). Thus the most important aspects of a dream do not appear literally but in a *symbolic* form. For example, a patient might report a dream where kings and queens appear prominently. This is the manifest content. For Freud, kings and queens in dreams are not to be taken literally, but are parents in symbolic form. This would be the latent content of the dream. It is the latent content of a dream which is interpreted and discussed with the patient. There are many different dream symbols, a small selection of which can be found below. At times during therapy the patient might find certain things difficult to talk about, they can't remember things or they start missing sessions. This behaviour is

called *resistance*, and is used by the patient to avoid pain and anxiety caused by having to think about things that they would rather not. This self-protection can be a good indicator that the therapy is touching on something important.

Psychoanalysis may take years, and therefore a key element of the therapy is the relationship which develops between the analyst and patient. Because the therapist attempts to be neutral and imparts very little about themselves to the patient, any feelings about the relationship felt by the patient are unlikely to be a realistic assessment. The relationship then encourages *transference*. This is where unresolved conflicts and feelings about past relationships, often to do with the patient's mother or father, are projected on to the analyst. This transference offers another opportunity to the therapist for interpretation and the patent will be helped to 'work through' the transference.

Ultimately, psychoanalysis is considered successful when the patient has gained sufficient insight about their unconscious conflicts so as to reduce the symptoms of

DREAM SYMBOLS

Dancing, or any rhythmic motion, symbolises masturbation; any phallic-like item, such as a cigar, symbolises the penis; a cave or tunnel represents the female genitalia. There are other symbols: common dreams such as those about teeth falling out symbolise castration, or a punishment for masturbation.

abnormal behaviour. 'Rat Man' (see page 232) revealed problems of his childhood during psychoanalysis that Freud used in his treatment.

HOW EFFECTIVE ARE PSYCHODYNAMIC THERAPIES?

In classical psychoanalysis, treatment might involve therapy for three or four times a week for two to five years. This is because, rather than a reduction of symptoms, the therapy seeks to find the underlying conflicts causing the problem, and this is a much lengthier process. This means that the effectiveness of psychoanalysis must be judged against the great deal of time, effort and money that it requires.

According to Grünbaum (1993), any apparent benefits of psychoanalysis are the result of an unintended *placebo effect*. In effect, it is the action of being treated itself that results in the 'cure' not actually how the person is being 'treated'. The reason why psychoanalysis might lead to a 'cure' is that the 'patient' is in a powerful relationship with the therapist. Part of the power of the therapist is that they can never be wrong. For example, should the patient challenge the therapist then their challenging behaviour could be interpreted as just another symptom of their disorder. This means that the patient is under strong pressure to conform to the therapist's expectations.

Grünbaum also points out that the very earliest evidence for effectiveness of psychoanalysis is flawed. Freud himself only ever presented 12 case studies of psychoanalysis for public scrutiny, and none of these were fully evaluated in terms of outcomes and benefits for the patient.

Eysenck (1952) claimed that psychoanalysis provides no benefits to a person beyond those that would naturally occur due to *spontaneous remission* (this is when symptoms disappear without treatment). He compared the results of 24 studies in order to see if psychoanalysis was more likely than other forms of therapy to result in positive mental health changes. Eysenck found that whilst patients did recover with psychoanalysis, the rate was comparable to the rate of recovery without treatment and that psychoanalysis was less effective than behavioural therapies.

BEHAVIOURAL APPROACH TO ABNORMALITY

According to this approach, all behaviour, whether it is normal or abnormal, is *learned*.

The behavioural approach emphasises the importance of the environment – internal or biological explanations are rejected. Everything we are is a result of our experience, or more precisely, what we have learned. Whilst most learning is positive and helpful, some learning is maladaptive (i.e. it is not helpful to us and perhaps harmful in some way). Abnormal behaviour is considered as maladaptive learning. The process of learning is explained using the principles of classical and operant conditioning.

Classical conditioning

According to classical conditioning we learn by forming new *associations* between something in the environment (a stimulus) and a physical reaction (a response). Pavlov (1927) demonstrated this form of learning in his experimental animals. He found that the dogs behaved in the same way to the sound of researchers' footsteps as they did when they saw food (i.e. salivation and excitable behaviour). Pavlov suggested that the dogs were demonstrating new learning – they had made a new association between the researchers and food, which he called a 'conditioned response'.

This kind of learning is not restricted to animal learning however – it is readily seen in humans. For example, if we are ill after eating something then we might create an

"It's a good idea to understand operant and classical conditioning and know the differences between the two. This will really help you when you come to describe the behavioural approach, which is just the sort of thing you might have to do in an exam."

association between the illness and whatever it is we've eaten. This could result in us avoiding this food item – whenever we see, taste or smell it, we are reminded of our illness. The aversion to the food is the new learning – the conditioned response.

Classical conditioning can be used to explain abnormal behaviour. For example, a phobia develops because we learn an association between a physical or emotional state and some object. An example might be someone who is not afraid of dogs getting bitten by one. This experience creates an association between dogs and anxiety (we don't want to get bitten again!). It is a relatively short step from anxiety to fear. The case of Little Albert (on page 236) illustrates this nicely.

Operant conditioning

Classical conditioning is a rather *passive* form of learning – an organism doesn't really have to actually do anything for learning to occur because it has little control of the kinds of physical reactions to which environmental events are associated. Even a fairly casual observation of our own learning experiences however tells us that classical conditioning cannot explain all learning. Sometimes we play an active part in our own learning in that we learn as a consequence of something we have already done. For example, we learn early in life that some things we do are likely to result in a reward such as praise, making them more likely to occur again. We also learn that some things are likely to lead to punishment, making it less likely that we engage in this behaviour. This kind of learning is called *operant conditioning*. According to Skinner

(1957) operant conditioning is learning by reward and reinforcement. A reinforcer is anything which increases the likelihood of a behaviour occurring again. So, if a behaviour is reinforced (rewarded) it is more likely to be repeated. Likewise, if a behaviour is not rewarded then it is less likely to be repeated.

Someone on a diet may receive compliments for the way they look after the weight loss. This praise may mean that they have learned that weight loss is rewarding and gives pleasure so they lose more weight leading to obsession with food and anorexia.

Whilst classical and operant conditioning are separate processes, they both work together in developing and maintaining abnormal behaviour. With phobia, the initial learning can be best understood in terms of classical conditioning but operant conditioning helps us understand how the phobia is maintained. For example, a person might develop a fear of dogs because, having been bitten by a dog, they have associated dogs with pain and fear. However, this does not explain many of the other behaviours associated with this fear, such as the lengths someone will go to avoid contact with dogs. In this example, avoiding dogs makes the person feel good because they have avoided the associated emotion and tension. Thus, this avoidance behaviour is reinforced by these feelings of relief.

Another area of psychology that can be related to operant conditioning is social learning. This theory, written about extensively by Albert Bandura, suggests that we learn by watching others behave. If people are rewarded for their behaviour then we are more likely to learn that if we behave in the same way we ourselves will be rewarded. This is called 'vicarious reinforcement'.

Behavioural therapies

Many therapies have been developed from the principles of the behavioural approach, but all have the same basic idea: if behaviour can be learned through classical and operant

LITTLE ALBERT
WATSON AND RAYNOR (1920)

John Watson had the idea that children were afraid of loud noises because they had learned to fear them. To investigate this he conducted an experiment in Harvard (in the United States). Albert had been raised in a hospital and at 9 months old he was chosen for the study. He was a quiet child and showed no fear at all to any of the stimuli (masks, animals, etc.) that Watson and Raynor showed him. Now Watson presented Albert with a rat, an animal that Albert had previously felt no fear of. On presentation, Watson struck a metal bar with a hammer, behind Albert's back. Albert was, understandably upset. After a few of these rat-hammer pairings, Albert became distressed only on the presentation of the rat. Interestingly (and worryingly) Albert transferred his fear to other things. A rabbit, even though a different colour to the rat, presented 17 days after the rat-hammer trials brought the same fear response, as did a mask of Father Christmas, whose beard drew a fear response, whereas masks with just hair did not. The hammer blow had been paired with the rat stimulus, making the rat the conditioned stimulus and the fear response the conditioned response.

conditioning, then through the same processes it can be unlearned.

One of the most successful behavioural therapies is *systematic desensitisation*. This therapy is based on classical conditioning and is designed to reduce distressing levels of anxiety. Therefore, it is most commonly used in the successful treatment of phobias.

The therapy generally begins with the client being taught to relax through progressive relaxation training, where the patient learns breathing exercises and muscle control. After several sessions of this, the patient is usually able to report the experience of deep relaxation and develops some control over how they feel. This process is very important to the success of this therapy because of *reciprocal inhibition* – this is where one response is inhibited or stopped because it is incompatible with another. In this case, anxiety involves tension, and tension is incompatible with relaxation – one cannot be relaxed and anxious at the same time! The client might be given relaxation tasks and tapes to practise at home between therapy sessions.

A key component of desensitisation is the *anxiety hierarchy*. This is a list, developed in discussion with the client, of situations or stimuli ranked from the least to most frightening. The therapist and client then work through this list, maintaining relaxation at each point in the hierarchy. For example, the therapy might start with the client imagining the first item in the hierarchy. If the client remains relaxed then the therapist asks the client to imagine the next level, and so on. If anxiety is experienced at any point then relaxation is reintroduced. Gradually, the therapist moves the client up the hierarchy until the highest point in the hierarchy can be reached in a state of relaxation.

It is thought that the more realistic the situation the more effective the therapy. Therefore, the higher up the hierarchy a client goes the more real-life the situations become. For example, instead of imagining something, a client might be shown a photograph. Following this, a client might be asked to actually face the object or situation in the photograph. For instance, a fear of flying may be treated by carefully introducing the phobic person to the stimulus that they are scared of. They may, for instance, watch films of planes, or look at pictures of them. Later in their therapy they may spend some time at an airport, just socially, drinking coffee perhaps, then eventually progressing to watching aeroplanes take off and land. Later they may spend some time on an aeroplane on the ground, finally taking off and facing their fear. Experiencing these stimuli desensitises them to the object of their phobia.

THE EFFECTIVENESS OF SYSTEMATIC DESENSITISATION

Systematic desensitisation is generally considered to be the most effective treatment for a number of anxiety disorders, particularly phobias. For example, it is estimated that 80–90% of simple phobias (that is, fear of specific things such as snakes or heights) are reduced in severity using this therapy, without a return of the original or new symptoms. Paul (1960) compared the effectiveness of systematic desensitisation, insight therapy and an attention placebo (where participants took a harmless pill and listened to a 'stress tape') in reducing the fear caused by public speaking. He not only found that those participants who received systematic desensitisation showed the greatest improvement, but that this reduction in anxiety to public speaking was still evident two years later.

Systematic desensitisation is also effective because it is a *robust* therapy. For example, the object of fear does not have to be experienced in real life for it to work – imagination can be sufficient. Research has shown that

The phobia of flying is relatively common.

desensitisation using purely imagined fear-arousing stimuli can be at least as effective as the more traditional standard exposure approach (where there is a hierarchy of imaginal to real-life stimuli). Some researchers are even using virtual reality systems to help people experience the objects of their anxiety. Rothbaum et al (2002) compared the effectiveness of a standard exposure treatment to one which used virtual reality in treating people with a fear of flying. They found the techniques to be similar in effectiveness, with eight out of 15 *virtual*

STUDY IN FOCUS

A comparison of the effectiveness of psychological therapies for generalised anxiety disorder (GAD)

Hunot et al (2007)

What were they doing and why? GAD is a common mental health problem where there is excessive worry about everyday events and problems. A wide range of psychological therapies are used to treat it, and all report evidence of success. The aim of this study was to compare the effectiveness of different forms of psychological therapy in the treatment of GAD.

How did they do it? This study was a meta-analysis, that is, it combined the findings from other studies. 25 studies were included, with a total of 1,305 participants. The participants ranged from 18–75 years of age, all having been clinically diagnosed with GAD. All studies used compared CBT to either another psychological therapy or to a treatment as usual/waiting list condition.

STUDY IN FOCUS cntd

Three categories of therapy were compared:

CBT: This included forms of therapy sharing CBT assumptions, such as relaxation therapy/training, desensitisation and anxiety management training.

Psychodynamic therapy: This included various forms of therapy sharing psychoanalytic assumptions.

Supportive therapy: (a) Active support therapy – This included person-centred therapy, gestalt therapy, transactional analysis and counselling.

(b) Inactive support therapy – This was called an attention-placebo control because, whilst receiving therapy, participants were receiving attention for their problem through support groups and informal advice and guidance.

In each condition participants were assessed for reduction in anxiety using a valid scale.

Control comparison: All those undergoing psychological therapy were compared to treatment as usual and waiting list participants, where participants could receive appropriate medical care if necessary.

What did they find? Compared to those on a waiting list or receiving treatment as usual, psychological therapy using a CBT approach is effective for GAD, with over 46% of people undergoing CBT showing improvement in their anxiety symptoms, compared to 14%. More research is needed to find out whether CBT is more helpful than other psychological therapies in treating GAD.

Compared to psychodynamic therapy and active support therapy, CBT showed benefits early in treatment, but after six months this reduced so that there were no significant differences in terms of symptom reduction.

No reliable conclusion could be drawn from this study regarding the effectiveness of the different therapies. This is in broad agreement with other studies which show that no type of psychological therapy is any more efficient than another when compared over a limited span of time.

Take a closer look
- It is not clear that all the studies included by Hunot et al in their analysis obtained consent from their participants. Informed consent is an ethical requirement for psychological research.

- The studies included by Hunot et al originated from a range of countries – nine from the US, three from Canada, ten from the UK and three from other European countries. Even though these countries are similar in that they are Western and industrialised, they still have their differences. It may be that there were cultural differences between the participants from different countries, as well as differences in attitudes to therapy. These differences may have been such that combining them all into one data set was inadvisable, and the large variation between members of the set could have influenced the results in a way not anticipated by the researchers.

- A relatively small number of studies were used, and none of them looked at the long-term effectiveness of therapy so we have to be careful about the conclusions we draw regarding the effectiveness of CBT.

- There was considerable variation in the therapies used. A number of different therapies were classed in the same category because they shared basic assumptions about abnormality and its treatment. Some of the findings in this study were no doubt due to inconsistencies in the therapies used.

reality and ten out of 15 standard exposure clients accepting an invitation to take a post-treatment flight. This is compared to a non-treatment control group where, after a similar period of time, only one out of 15 waiting list clients agreed to take the flight.

COGNITIVE APPROACH TO ABNORMALITY

In this approach, abnormality is not the behaviour itself (as in the behavioural approach), nor is it a reflection of unconscious forces (as the psychodynamic approach would have us believe). Rather, abnormality results from faulty internal mental processes. That is, *faulty cognition*.

"He was a very claustophobic person."

The cognitive approach to abnormality therefore is interested in how people think and how certain kinds of thinking, for example, irrational and distorted thinking, might lead to psychological problems.

Kendall (1993) suggests that there are two important kinds of thinking that can cause psychological problems. These are cognitive *deficiencies* and cognitive *distortions*.

Cognitive deficiency is where a lack of sufficient thinking and planning affects behaviour in negative ways. For example, someone who doesn't properly think through a problem may decide on an inappropriate solution, such as giving up study after failing an exam rather than trying again but this time with a different approach to their learning, or

"Students often have difficulties describing the cognitive approach to abnormality. When you are revising, think about the key elements of the approach. The cognitive approach is about faulty THINKING; for example, thinking that is irrational and distorted. Remember 'cognitive distortion', 'cognitive deficiency' and 'cognitive triad' and a little about each. This will really help you show understanding."

a focus on what opportunities passing the examination might provide them with.

Cognitive distortion occurs when our cognitive system does not accurately process the information it receives. For example, someone with a severe phobia of spiders might believe that the spiders they see are 'huge', or might even conclude from its actions that a spider has something against them personally. This kind of exaggerated thinking will certainly lead to behaviours that hinder everyday functioning and affect quality of life.

The threat presented by an 'object' can sometimes be exaggerated by those with phobias.

The cognitive approach has been used to explain the origins of many psychological problems, but it has been most successfully applied to depression. According to Beck (1967) depression is a result of a tendency in some people to interpret everyday events in negative ways. He points out that depressed people think negatively all the time, and that this tendency is the result of many different kinds of automatic *cognitive error*. For example, a teacher might provide a student with lots of positive feedback on a piece of homework, but a tendency to be overly critical of their own performance causes the student to focus only on the negative things. These cognitive errors lead depressed people to think negatively about themselves, the world and the future, something which Beck called the *cognitive triad*.

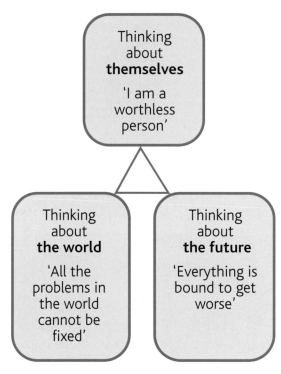

Figure 11: Beck's cognitive triad. According to Beck, a depressed individual typically thinks negatively in each of these three ways.

Cognitive therapies

Although there are a number of different therapies based on the cognitive approach, the most popular and successful one is *cognitive behavioural therapy* (CBT).

CBT assumes that problems in thinking underlie psychological disorders. By identifying these problems and being given help in finding alternative ways of thinking the client will overcome the disorder. There is also an assumption that beliefs, attitudes,

expectations, etc. (i.e. cognitive processes) have an impact on behaviour, therefore changing the way a client thinks will also bring about changes in how they behave.

The goal then of CBT is to focus on the patterns of thought and behaviour that are causing problems. There is an emphasis on current difficulties rather than events from the distant past, such as childhood.

The first task of therapy is to understand the problem. This will involve an analysis of the client's thoughts, behaviours and feelings in order to find out which are unrealistic and therefore unhelpful and how the client is affected by them.

The next step is to work out how to change these unwanted thoughts, feelings and behaviours. There are many strategies available which the therapist can use to help the client. For example, negative and unhelpful thoughts which have been identified might be addressed by techniques which replace them with more positive and realistic ones. A fear of cars and traffic, for instance, brought about by an involvement in an accident of some kind, may be damaging to the person because they have difficulty travelling in cars or even walking beside roads. The negative thoughts associating cars with anxiety may be replaced with more pleasant associations, such as 'cars can be fun, they can take us to fun places'. Travelling in them and driving them can be a leisure activity.

The client will be required to do 'homework' between therapy sessions, for example practising the techniques for changing thought that have been discussed with the therapist, or keeping a diary of thoughts, feelings and behaviours. At each CBT session the therapist will review progress with the client and address any problems experienced with the tasks required by the therapy. Because CBT techniques are practised and are integrated with day-to-day life, the symptoms which brought the client to therapy in the first place are less likely to return when the therapy ends. How long therapy lasts depends on the nature of the problem, but typically a course of CBT lasts between eight and 12 sessions.

THE EFFECTIVENESS OF COGNITIVE BEHAVIOURAL THERAPY

Whilst drugs can be extremely effective at treating symptoms of illness, such as depression and phobia, there is a risk of relapse once the medication stops. For example, it has been estimated that about 50% of people who use medication to treat depression experience the problem again within two years. Since CBT aims to tackle the cause of the problem rather than the symptoms, the need for future drug therapy should reduce. Evans et al (1992) found that CBT was at least as good as drug therapy in preventing relapse over a two year period. They also found that relapse rates were lowest when CBT was combined with medication. This is supported by Keller et al (2001) who looked at the effectiveness of CBT in the treatment of major depression. They found that patients benefited more from a combination of CBT and drug therapy than from either therapy alone.

It seems that the effectiveness of CBT depends to a large extent on the type and severity of the mental health problem. According to Butler et al (2006), when the main problem is depression or anxiety it can be the most effective treatment available, better in the long term than drug therapy because it deals with the root of the problem. However, when the problems are severe, CBT is most effective when used in combination with medication. For example, people with severe depression have difficulty concentrating and they feel very low. This means that a talking therapy like CBT might be very difficult or impossible for them, making the therapy unsuitable. If medication is used to lift the sufferer out of the worst of the symptoms, however, then they will be better able to engage with the therapy and benefit from it. The same issue applies to other mental health problems where the severity of the symptoms makes CBT inappropriate. For example, schizophrenics experience disturbances of thought and it is only when these symptoms are alleviated by medication that CBT can be considered as an effective option.

WANT TO KNOW MORE?

If you'd like to read more about individual differences and abnormality, you should find these books interesting.

Appignanesi, R. (2003) *Freud for Beginners*, Pantheon Books

Barlow, D. H. and Durand, M. V. (1999) *Abnormal Psychology: An Integrative Approach*, Brooks Cole

Ramachandran, V. S. (1999) *Phantoms in the Brain: Human Nature and the Architecture of the Mind*, Fourth Estate

Sachs, O. (1986) *The Man Who Mistook His Wife for a Hat*, Picador

Image credits

Cover: © Janne Ahvo

Page 8: © Volodymyr Vasylkiv, Fotolia.com

Page 10: © LUC, Fotolia.com

Page 11: © Mike Baldwin, CartoonStock

Page 12: © Jupiterimages Corp.

Page 13: © Julian Addington-Baker, Fotolia.com

Page 14: (L) © Sandra Ford, Fotolia.com

Page 14: (R) © Stas Perov, Fotolia.com

Page 15: © Jupiterimages Corp.

Page 16: © GustoImages/Science Photo Library

Page 17: © Ioannis Kounadeas, Fotolia.com

Page 20: © Mikael Damkier, Fotolia.com

Page 22: © Jupiterimages Corp.

Page 25: © Randall McIlwaine

Page 28-29: © Les Evans

Page 30: © Pedro Nogueira, Fotolia.com

Page 31: © caraman, Fotolia.com

Page 33: © Jupiterimages Corp.

Page 36: © Podfoto, Fotolia.com

Page 38: © caraman, Fotolia.com

Page 39: © FotoShoot, Fotolia.com

Page 40: © Lisa F. Young, Fotolia.com

Page 42: © Mary Evans Picture Library

Page 45: © Marlee, Fotolia.com

Page 55: (L) © Eldin Muratovic, Fotolia.com

Page 55: (R) © FotoWorx, Fotolia.com

Page 56: © Jupiterimages Corp.

Page 58: © Fyle, Fotolia.com

Page 60: © Timothy Boomer, Fotolia.com

Page 61: © Jupiterimages Corp.

Page 67: © Crown House Publishing

Page 69: © Photo Ambiance, Fotolia.com

Page 73: © York University

Page 74: © PhotoBristol, Fotolia.com

Page 75: © Mike Baldwin

Page 78: © Jedphoto, Fotolia.com

Page 81: © Les Evans

Page 83: © Crown House Publishing

Page 86: © Rostphoto, Fotolia.com

Page 88: © Douglas Freer, Fotolia.com

Page 90: © Rene Drouyer, Fotolia.com

Page 94: © Jupiterimages Corp.

Page 96: © Jupiterimages Corp.

Page 97: © Marisz Blach, Fotolia.com

Page 98: © Photoshot

Page 99: © Science Photo Library

Page 100: (L) © Harlow Primate Laboratory

Page 100: (R) © Science Source/Science Photo Library

Page 101: © Richard Bowlby

Page 105: (L) © Tinu/Simon Green, Fotolia.com

Page 105: (R) © Jupiterimages Corp.

Page 107: © Mona Makela, Fotolia.com

Page 109: © Karen Struthers, Fotolia.com

Page 112: © Jupiterimages Corp.

Page 114: © T. Boussac, Fotolia.com

Page 115: © Roberta Bianchi

Page 118: © Family Shibuya

Page 120: © Jupiterimages Corp.

Page 122: © Marzanna Syncerz, Fotolia.com

Page 124: © Joseph Nettio/Science Photo Library

Page 127: © Action Press/Rex Features

Page 128: © Action Press/Rex Features

Page 132: © Jupiterimages Corp.

Page 133: © Jaimie Durplas, Fotolia.com

Page 134: © Monika Adamczyk

Page 136: © Jupiterimages Corp.

Page 139: © Cliff Parnell

Page 144: © Millymanz, Fotolia.com

Page 146: © Stephen Coburn, Fotolia.com

Page 147: © Steve Woods

Page 150: © Thomas Mounsey, Fotolia.com

Page 152: © Jupiterimages Corp.

Page 153: © Jupiterimages Corp.

Page 156: © Jupiterimages Corp.

Page 157: © Leah-Anne Thompson, Fotolia.com

Page 158: © Jupiterimages Corp.

Page 159: © Jupiterimages Corp.

Page 160: © Sebastian Kaulitzki, Fotolia.com

Page 163: © Jupiterimages Corp.

Page 164: © Jupiterimages Corp.

Page 166: *(Top)* © Andrey Kiselev, Fotolia.com
Page 166: *(Bottom)* © Jean Cliclac, Fotolia.com
Page 167: © Roger Vorheis, Fotolia.com
Page 169: © Christos Georghiou, Fotolia.com
Page 172: © Jupiterimages Corp.
Page 174: © pst, Fotolia.com
Page 176: © Jupiterimages Corp.
Page 180: © piccaya, Fotolia.com
Page 182: © Gary Cowles
Page 183: © iofoto, Fotolia.com
Page 187: © Bruno Passigatti, Fotolia.com
Page 189: *(Top)* © Jupiterimages Corp.
Page 189: *(Bottom)* © Alexandra Milgram[i]
Page 190: © Alexandra Milgram[i]
Page 192: © Jupiterimages Corp.
Page 194: © RTimages, Fotolia.com
Page 196: © Joselito Briones
Page 197: © Jupiterimages Corp.
Page 202: © UPPA/Photoshot
Page 203: © Philip Zimbardo
Page 205: © Rex Features
Page 206: © Sipa Press/Rex Features
Page 207: *(L)* © JupiterImages Corp.
Page 207: *(R)* © Jupiterimages Corp.
Page 210: © iMAGINE, Fotolia.com
Page 212: © Tom Poletek, Fotolia.com
Page 213: *(Top)* © Eva Serrabassa
Page 213: *(Bottom)* © Jupiterimages Corp.
Page 214: © Jupiterimages Corp.
Page 216: © Jupiterimages Corp.
Page 218: © Jupiterimages Corp.
Page 220: © Amy Walters
Page 221: © Kiyoshi Takahase Segundo
Page 222: *(L)* © John Dee/Rex Features
Page 222: *(R)* © US National Library of Medicine/Science Photo Library
Page 223: © Jupiterimages Corp.
Page 224: © AlienCat, Fotolia.com
Page 225: © Damien Lovegrove/Science Photo Library
Page 226: © Will McIntyre/Science Photo Library

Page 228: © Jupiterimages Corp.
Page 229: © Jupiterimages Corp.
Page 230: © CSU Archives/Everett Collection/Rex Features
Page 233: *(L)* © Arman Zhenikeyev, Fotolia.com
Page 233: *(M)* © Thomas Weitzel, Fotolia.com
Page 233: *(R)* © Cre8tive Studios, Fotolia.com
Page 237: © Jupiterimages Corp.
Page 239: *(L)* © Thomas Bros.
Page 239: *(R)* © Jason Winter, Fotolia.com

[i] *From the film OBEDIENCE © 1968 by Stanley Milgram ©Renewed 1993 by Alexandra Milgram, and distributed by Penn State, Media Sales.*

Index